# CSR, Sustainability, Ethics & Governance

In recent years the discussion concerning the relation between business and society has made immense strides. This has in turn led to a broad academic and practical discussion on innovative management concepts, such as Corporate Social Responsibility, Corporate Governance and Sustainability Management. This series offers a comprehensive overview of the latest theoretical and empirical research and provides sound concepts for sustainable business strategies. In order to do so, it combines the insights of leading researchers and thinkers in the fields of management theory and the social sciences and from all over the world, thus contributing to the interdisciplinary and intercultural discussion on the role of business in society. The underlying intention of this series is to help solve the world's most challenging problems by developing new management concepts that create value for business and society alike. In order to support those managers, researchers and students who are pursuing sustainable business approaches for our common future, the series offers them access to cutting-edge management approaches. CSR, Sustainability, Ethics and Governance is accepted by the Norwegian Register for Scientific Journals, Series and Publishers, maintained and operated by the Norwegian Social Science Data Services (NSD).

Michael Adelowotan · Hussain Coovadia
Editors

# AI and Accountability

## Shaping Ethical Governance in the Age of Algorithms

Springer

*Editors*
Michael Adelowotan
Department of Accountancy
College of Business and Economics
University of Johannesburg
Johannesburg, South Africa

Hussain Coovadia
Department of Commercial Accounting
College of Business and Economics
University of Johannesburg
Johannesburg, South Africa

ISSN 2196-7075 ISSN 2196-7083 (electronic)
CSR, Sustainability, Ethics & Governance
ISBN 978-3-032-20090-7 ISBN 978-3-032-20091-4 (eBook)
https://doi.org/10.1007/978-3-032-20091-4



This Springer imprint is published by the registered company Springer Nature Switzerland AG
The registered company address is: Gewerbestrasse 11, 6330 Cham, Switzerland

# Preface

This book provides a comprehensive discussion on how Artificial Intelligence (AI) is affecting various aspects of human endeavours as well as disciplines and professions. Each chapter focuses on the usefulness of AI, and its increasing deployment necessitates the development and application of governance principles to ensure the ethical use of AI, thereby minimizing risks while maximizing its benefits.

The chapters are organised to provide a logical progression from the concepts of Artificial Intelligence, Ethics in AI, and Governance of AI. Some of the chapters addressed specific issues relating to:

- AI Bias and Fairness,
- AI Transparency and Explainability,
- AI Accountability and Liability,
- AI in Public and Private Sectors: Governance in Practice
- Global Perspectives in AI Governance
- AI and Ethical Innovation
- The Future of AI Governance.

Thus, the book will be of immense benefit to professionals, academics, researchers, and students in higher institutions and business schools, as it provides an understanding of how AI can be used responsibly through the application of ethical principles and the use of effective governance strategies.

This book represents collaborative efforts by academics and professionals in the field of AI who have provided a comprehensive resource tool through their expert perspectives, detailed analysis, and case studies on the increasingly concerning issue of AI Governance.

As we explore this book, let us be reminded that, since AI is rapidly evolving as a technology, we should be more concerned about its ethical use through effective monitoring and governance so as to create useful outcomes for organisations and society at large.

Michael Adelowotan
Department of Accountancy, College
of Business and Economics
University of Johannesburg
Johannesburg, South Africa

Hussain Coovadia
Department of Commercial
Accounting, College of Business
and Economics
University of Johannesburg
Johannesburg, South Africa

# Acknowledgements

We thank all the authors and peer reviewers for contributing to the success of this book project. The peer reviewers include:

1. Dr. A. Adegboye, Covenant University, Nigeria
2. Dr. A. Joel, University of Johannesburg, South Africa
3. Dr. A. Adebayo, University of South Africa, South Africa
4. Dr. O. Obagbuwa, Walter Sisulu University, South Africa
5. Dr. V. Denhere, University of Johannesburg, South Africa
6. Prof. I. Botha, University of Johannesburg, South Africa
7. Prof. B. Marx, University of Johannesburg, South Africa
8. Dr. U. Emmanuel, University of South Africa, South Africa
9. Dr. B. Simon-Ilogho, University of Johannesburg, South Africa
10. Dr. I. Inyang, Pan Atlantic University, Nigeria
11. Dr. D. Sule, University of Johannesburg, South Africa
12. Dr. O. Oke, Cape Peninsula University of Technology, South Africa
13. Prof. S. Kajola, Federal University of Agriculture, Nigeria
14. Dr. L. Ngwenya, University of Johannesburg, South Africa
15. Prof. S. Olaoye, Adeleke University, Nigeria
16. Dr. A. Salemcity, University of South Africa, South Africa
17. Dr. O. Obioha, Sol Plaatje University, South Africa
18. Dr. V. Adekomaya, University of Johannesburg, South Africa
19. Dr. K. Ajeigbe, Walter Sisulu University, South Africa
20. Dr. M. Duve, University of Johannesburg, South Africa
21. Dr. O. Ogundele

We also thank Dr. Fowokemi Ogedengbe and Dr. Nusirat Gold, who are currently Postdoctoral Research Fellows at the School of Accounting of the University of Johannesburg, for the administrative roles they performed in the course of this book project.

# Introduction

Artificial intelligence (AI) has evolved rapidly over the years from an abstract term to a defining force shaping different institutions, economies, and the society at large. AI is a broad concept that draws from several fields such as computer science, psychology, philosophy, linguistics, and many other areas. At its core, AI involves the analysis of vast amounts of data for machines to reason, learn, and solve complex problems. AI's wide-ranging capabilities are transforming how decisions are made, redefining organisational processes, impacting multiple disciplines, and opening new opportunities for innovation. Although, these capabilities have attracted significant interest from varying sectors such as health care, education, businesses, and companies (Przegalinska et al., 2025; Stogiannos et al., 2025) who increasingly explore AI's potential to enhance their operations, improve decision-making, create innovative products and services to achieve a competitive edge (Papagiannidis et al., 2025). Yet, with the opportunities brought by AI also lies several risks and challenges particularly concerning transparency, accountability, and ethical issues. Hence, the need to understand how the AI systems is regulated or ought to be regulated, how accountability ought to be structured, and how to mitigate ethical dilemmas. This is crucial now more than ever as AI systems continues to impact several aspect of people's lives from financial decisions and medical diagnoses to public service delivery and national security. Moreover, it is vital to create ethical and trustworthy AI environment for the betterment of the society.

In response to this need, this book *"AI and Accountability: Shaping Ethical Governance in the Age of Algorithms"* provides insights and comprehensive examination of the principles, risks, and new approaches that characterize responsible AI governance in today's modern era.

The book is organised into ten interrelated chapters, each of which addresses important aspects of AI governance pertaining to its application and deployment in different facets.

Chapter 1 lays the foundation by exploring core concepts in AI ethics and governance, clarifying conceptual definitions traced back to AI's historical developments, and highlighting philosophical and normative frameworks likewise common regulatory standards such as those of European Union, United Nations, and South Africa policies that shape global landscape. This philosophical, legal, technical, and socio-cultural dimensions that form the basis of other discussions in the subsequent chapters are introduced to readers here.

Chapter 2 focuses on AI machine bias and fairness, unpacking how discrimination can be ingrained in data and algorithms, and how fairness-oriented interventions can assist society achieve more equitable outcomes. The chapter uses case studies from global incidences to illustrate how AI systems can perpetuate unfairness and discrimination. Additionally, the chapter highlights techniques for mitigating machine bias and suggested pathways for integrating technical innovation with ethical principles to ensure fairness of AI.

Chapter 3 examines transparency and explainability in AI algorithms providing insight into the opaque nature of AI operations and decision-making. The chapter highlights Blackbox concept and explains why interpretability is essential to oversight, trust, and informed decision-making.

Chapter 4 delves into accountability and liability. The chapter provides insight into explainability, traceability, and oversight throughout the AI lifecycle. It also highlights legal and regulatory frameworks that addresses AI liability, especially who takes responsibility when AI makes mistakes that causes harm on users. The chapter also provide mechanisms required to ensure responsible AI development and deployment among developers, users, and regulators strengthening institutional accountability.

Chapter 5 explores data privacy and security with particular focus on sub-Saharan Africa where AI is gaining wide adoption despite weak regulatory landscape and unequal digital infrastructure. The chapter covered common privacy enhancing technologies (PETs) such as differential privacy (DP), federated learning (FL), secure multi-party computation (SMPC), homomorphic encryption (HE), and zero-knowledge proof (ZKP). The chapter also highlights how privacy concerns such as surveillance, consent, data governance, and information inequality are being are addressed by the different regulatory frameworks such as the Protection of Personal Information Act (POPIA) in South Africa and the Data Protection Act (DPA) in Nigeria and Kenya. The chapter reinforces how data privacy and security practices are a cornerstone of ethical AI governance, hence, must adapt to AI's data-intensive and evolving lifecycle.

Chapter 6 explores the various aspects of AI autonomy, human oversight, and control in an era of increasingly capable AI agents. It discusses what autonomy and human agency are, likewise how they function in different sectors. It also examines various forms of human oversight that are feasible and meaningful for different levels of autonomy, and highlights governance models suitable for balancing innovation with protection of human rights and public safety.

Chapter 7 investigates governance of AI in public and private sectors, highlighting how the exponential growth of AI adoption has outstripped the development of commensurate governance structures, causing disparate adoption trajectories between developed and emerging nations.

Chapter 8 provides a global view of AI governance practices across various sectors including healthcare, legal firms, auditing, and financial services. The chapter emphasises how balanced regulation that supports mitigating risks while preserving innovation and efficiency gains is crucial for the application of AI in these diverse sectors. The chapter also discusses fundamental concerns in AI governance, addresses the broader balance between external (government) oversight and self-regulation, and provides a foundation for understanding AI governance practices in diverse industries and contexts.

Chapter 9 explores how AI design and transformative technological innovation are raising ethical challenges. The chapter uses case studies from IBM and Microsoft to explain to readers how ethical AI practices can be achieved by organisations deploying AI systems. It also explores how education is crucial for the development and implementation of ethical AI systems.

Chapter 10 looks ahead to the future of AI governance, reflecting on emerging trends, identifying governance gaps, questions that remain unaddressed, analyses existing regulatory frameworks, and suggesting adaptive approaches towards balancing innovation with ethical responsibility.

Collectively, the chapters provide an enriching discussion on the complex nature of AI ethics, governance, and accountability landscape, giving AI users, policymakers, industry leaders, and other stakeholders a structured and in-depth insight of the opportunities and risks brought by AI. Therefore, reinforcing the importance of ethical AI deployment and governance to shape a future where technological advancement aligns with societal values to thrive well.

Michael Adelowotan
Department of Accountancy, College of Business and Economics
University of Johannesburg
Johannesburg, South Africa

Hussain Coovadia
Department of Commercial Accounting
University of Johannesburg
Johannesburg, South Africa

## References

Papagiannidis, E., Mikalef, P., & Conboy, K. (2025). Responsible artificial intelligence governance: A review and research framework. *Journal of Strategic Information Systems*, *34*(2), 101885. https://doi.org/10.1016/j.jsis.2024.101885

Przegalinska, A., Triantoro, T., Kovbasiuk, A., Ciechanowski, L., Freeman, R. B., & Sowa, K. (2025). Collaborative AI in the workplace: Enhancing organizational performance through resource-based and task-technology fit perspectives. *International Journal of Information Management*, *81*(4), 102853. https://doi.org/10.1016/j.ijinfomgt.2024.102853

Stogiannos, N., Georgiadou, E., Rarri, N., & Malamateniou, C. (2025). Ethical AI_ A qualitative study exploring ethical challenges and solutions on the use of AI in medical imaging. *European Journal of Radiology Artificial Intelligence*, *1*, 100006. https://doi.org/10.1016/j.ejrai.2025.100006

# Contents

# Contributors

**Adesanmi Timothy Adegbayibi** Department of Accountancy, College of Business and Economics, University of Johannesburg, Johannesburg, South Africa

**Michael Olajide Adelowotan** Department of Accountancy, College of Business and Economics, University of Johannesburg, Johannesburg, South Africa

**Mohammed Kayode Ajape** Department of Accountancy, College of Business and Economics, University of Johannesburg, Johannesburg, South Africa

**Husain Coovadia** Department of Commercial Accounting, College of Business and Economics, University of Johannesburg, Johannesburg, South Africa

**Naeem Mahomed Ebrahim** Department of Commercial Accounting, College of Business and Economics, University of Johannesburg, Johannesburg, South Africa

**Olayinka Erin** Department of Accountancy, College of Business and Economics, University of Johannesburg, Johannesburg, South Africa

**Tasneem Gathoo** Department of Commercial Accounting, College of Business and Economics, University of Johannesburg, Johannesburg, South Africa

**Nusirat Ojuolape Gold** Department of Commercial Accounting, College of Business and Economics, University of Johannesburg, Johannesburg, South Africa; Faculty of Management and Social Sciences, Department of Accounting and Finance, Kwara State University, Malete, Nigeria

**Tasneem Mahmood** Department of Accountancy, College of Business and Economics, University of Johannesburg, Johannesburg, South Africa

**Ahmed Mohammadali-Haji** Department of Accountancy, College of Business and Economics, University of Johannesburg, Johannesburg, South Africa

**Fowokemi Alaba Ogedengbe** Department of Accountancy, College of Business and Economics, University of Johannesburg, Johannesburg, South Africa

**Nicolaas Strydom** Department of Accountancy, College of Business and Economics, University of Johannesburg, Johannesburg, South Africa

# Chapter 1
# AI Ethics and Governance

**Nusirat Ojuolape Gold and Husain Coovadia**

**Abstract** Artificial Intelligence (AI) has emerged as one of the most disruptive technologies of the Fourth Industrial Revolution (4IR), positively affecting society while also raising serious ethical concerns. This chapter explores the ethics and governance of AI, tracing its evolution from the earliest period of ELIZA tools when discussions about automation and computing started, to today's current issues with generative AI. The chapter conceptualizes the definitions of AI ethics and governance from philosophical, legal, technical, and sociocultural perspectives, employing a thorough qualitative and interpretive research approach to translate the discussions into a coherent whole. The chapter also examines governance strategies for resolving ethical dilemmas that hinder AI systems' ability to operate. Furthermore, the chapter looks at global frameworks like the OECD AI Principles, UNESCO's Recommendation on the Ethics of AI, and the EU AI Act, as well as regional frameworks like South Africa's POPIA and National AI Policy Framework. It explores this to demonstrate how universal standards and local realities interact. It also provides strategies for transforming ethical principles into actionable practices, noting that ethics by design, standardization, institutional oversight, ethical literacy, and adaptive governance frameworks as essential components. The chapter concludes with a future reflecting about AI governance, suggesting that, aside from innovation, the future of AI systems must integrate inclusive governance, rights-based strategies that balance technological advancement with equality, justice, and human rights.

N. O. Gold (✉) · H. Coovadia
Department of Commercial Accounting, College of Business and Economics, University of Johannesburg, Johannesburg, South Africa
e-mail: ngold@uj.ac.za

H. Coovadia
e-mail: hcoovadia@uj.ac.za

 
M. Adelowotan and H. Coovadia (eds.), *AI and Accountability*, CSR, Sustainability, Ethics & Governance, https://doi.org/10.1007/978-3-032-20091-4_1

## 1.1 Introduction

Artificial Intelligence (AI) has emerged as one of the defining technologies of the Fourth Industrial Revolution (4IR), which is widely recognized as a powerful disruptive force that is changing how industries and businesses operate in all spheres of life. It is intricately woven into a wide range of industries, including accounting, finance, public policy, healthcare, and education, presenting both tremendous opportunities and negative consequences, such as governance and ethical dilemmas. Its negative consequences may far outweigh its benefits if not deployed in a way that has human values at its core (Mittelstadt, 2019; Palumbo et al., 2025).

Notable examples of negative consequences of AI deployment includes AI facial recognition tool exhibiting gender shades bias and discriminating against black women by labelling them as having higher likelihood of being second time offenders than their male white counterparts (Buolamwini & Gebru, 2018), a consumer tool for image recognition that mistakenly labelled images of Black individuals as "gorillas"(Zhang, 2015), AI recruiting tools that show bias against women (Dastin, 2022; Hunkenschroer & Luetge, 2022), AI systematically discriminating and miscategorizing black patients in heart failure risk scores or kidney donor risk indexes, marking them as less suitable donors (Gichoya et al., 2022), and a chatbot coaching a "girl of 13 years old" on losing virginity (Barrett et al., 2023).

Meanwhile, to avoid future occurrences of similar challenges, AI ethics and governance are paramount. However, one challenge when it comes to governance is that legislation will always move more slowly than technological development. Against this backdrop, it is pertinent to note that AI ethics and governance are a compass, necessary to guide how individuals, organisations, businesses, institutions, and governments should design, deploy, and govern their AI systems responsibly. Aside from AI deployment, responsible AI has therefore become more than a theoretical concern; it is now required to be embedded as part of business process strategy. Hence, businesses must recognize social and ethical challenges such as bias, fairness, transparency, and privacy as material risks (Al-Kfairy et al., 2024; Camilleri, 2024; Sadek et al., 2025). This is crucial because ethical considerations are not abstract ideals; rather, they are critical to ensuring trust, safeguarding human rights, and aligning technological advancements with societal well-being.

Despite the increasing deployment of AI across industries and businesses, with AI ethics gaining increased traction globally, especially among stakeholders, and prompting several principles being proposed, there are still numerous persistent issues undermining the practical application and effectiveness of the principles. This is particularly owing to the lack of a unified ethical governance standard, one which is posing huge governance challenges such as privacy violations, transparency, risks of bias, and concentration of power in the hands of a few globally. More so, ethical guidelines often remain fragmented, articulated in terms of broad principles like fairness, transparency, and accountability. This has left businesses, organizations, and AI system developers struggling to translate these values into measurable and operational metrics (Palumbo et al., 2025; Sadek et al., 2025). While governance standards are sometimes available in some instances, they are often poorly integrated across the AI lifecycle, right from its design stage to deployment, and up to the monitoring stages. Consequently, this causes fragmentation in the AI governance across all organizations, industry, and national levels (Batool et al., 2025; Camilleri, 2024; Sadek et al., 2025). Another important area of concern is how ambiguity persists over accountability, especially when the AI systems impose unprecedented harm. There is often a lack of clear guidance on whom to hold accountable. Is it the system developer, the organisation itself, users, suppliers, regulators, or a host of these actors? (Bartsch et al., 2025; Batool et al., 2025; Sadek et al., 2025). More so, existing regulations and ethical standards also struggle to keep pace with the scale at which the AI systems' capabilities transform (Al-Kfairy et al., 2024). As a result, there remains a significant gap between ethical theory and practice, particularly with respect to compliance measures, accountability enforcement, assignment of roles and responsibility, and adapting governance mechanisms to new and evolving AI designs and contexts. These challenges underscore the imperative for a comprehensive, context-specific understanding of AI ethics that bridges theoretical principles with practical governance mechanisms, ensuring equitable and responsible AI deployment globally.

To bridge the highlighted gap, this chapter sets out the underlisted objectives.

(i) Integrate the definitions of AI ethics and governance, conceptually clarifying their philosophical, legal, technical, and socio-cultural perspectives and their evolution.
(ii) Explore the contemporary landscape of AI ethics and governance and their jurisdictional differences.
(iii) Identify and examine ethical dilemmas and governance challenges surrounding the AI system.
(iv) Identify and suggest pathways for translating ethical principles into actionable practices

This chapter is of high significance as it attempts to bridge the gap between broad moral discourse and grounded implementable AI governance models. While extant literary works have attempted to identify ethical principles, only a few have successfully placed them within the purview of legislative and institutional frameworks development. Also, very few have proposed methods for measuring and operationalising them. Hence, this chapter, by focusing on contemporary peer-reviewed articles, will contribute to a yet growing field that must now transition from mere principles to actionable practices. The chapter will enhance policy formulation through offering national and international bodies insights into what AI regulation may work and might not work in practice as they work on developing and improving AI regulations. Through the suggestive operational pathways, the chapter will offer practitioners and organisations insights that will assist them in integrating ethics into the AI design and through its entire lifecycle, recognising it as a fundamental component in the system design, not merely an afterthought. Additionally, the chapter addresses a trending critical issue as it focuses on emerging risks from AI deployment, structural inequities, and multi-stakeholder accountability. Lastly, the chapter will foster interdisciplinary engagement as a pedagogical and intellectual guide, serving as a foundation and benchmark for future discussions and research projects in AI ethics and governance.

This chapter employed a qualitative and interpretive research approach relying on credible, relevant, and recent peer-reviewed articles, policy documents, reports, and regulatory frameworks. This methodological approach aided the chapter to contribute in the following ways:

(i) By elucidating conceptual ambiguities in AI ethics and governance
(ii) By situating contemporary discussions within their historical context, and
(iii) By highlighting emerging issues that are yet to be explored in the governance literature, particularly from the Global South.

We hereby proceed on the remainder of the chapter as follow: Section 2 focuses on the conceptual definition, evolution, and a discussion of the contemporary landscape of AI ethics and governance, section three explains the methodology, section four provides ethical dilemmas and governance challenges linked with the AI systems, section five proposes pathways for translating ethical principles into actionable practices, section six concludes the chapter.

## 1.2 Conceptual Definitions, Evolution, and Contemporary Landscape

### *1.2.1 Definitions of AI Ethics and Governance*

Conceptually, AI ethics has been defined as the normative frameworks, principles, and values guiding the responsible development, deployment, and use of AI systems and technologies. AI governance, however, embodies the institutional frameworks, regulatory standards, and oversight mechanisms through which ethical principles are integrated into practice. It covers policies, laws, standards, technical protocols, and organizational processes that collectively shape the AI systems' design, deployment, and accountability (Batool et al., 2025). Although evidence suggests that existing regulations have produced several ethical principles, particularly on privacy, beneficial AI, fairness, transparency, and accountability, yet, these principles are often only expressed in abstract and not ideal terms (Palumbo et al., 2025). Furthermore, while AI ethics emphasizes normative ideals stemming from two-fold tasks comprising the articulation of universal moral commitments for the design and use of intelligent AI systems, and ensuring commitments are translated into measurable and operational practices (Batool et al., 2025). AI governance, on the other hand, emphasizes enforcement, accountability, and institutional responsibility. Both definitions can be viewed from varying lenses of philosophical, legal, technical, and socio-cultural perspectives, as summarised in Table 1.1.

**Table 1.1** On AI ethics and governance definitions

| Perspective | AI ethics definition | AI governance definition | References |
|---|---|---|---|
| Philosophical | This perspective draws from the normative lens of applied ethics, i.e., "**what ought to be done**" grounded in norms and values like utilitarianism, deontology, and virtue ethics. Proponents here believe AI raises questions about who ought to take responsibility for the AI systems, what makes up agency, autonomy, and justice in a technologically driven society | This perspective focuses on "**what is done**" rather than "**what ought to be done**," and converts moral obligations into a legally binding institutional framework that limits behaviour. In other words, what are the enforceable governance structures that strike a balance between innovation, rules, regulations, and justice while also making sure that technological advancements keep pace with changing human needs? | Batool et al. (2025), Cheong (2024) and Radanliev (2025) |
| Legal | Proponents of this perspective emphasize that since AI ethics intersects with the rule of law and standards on human rights, it is important to integrate ethical principles within the design of the AI system. They also noted that it is important to ensure that abstract principles like fairness, transparency, and accountability align with laws/regulations that are enforceable, to encourage compliance with rules and regulations while also encouraging users to seek redress when they suffer any harm | Proponents emphasize that governance involves/fosters the development of enforceable laws. Hence, to assign responsibility and harmonize protections across different jurisdictions, existing frameworks such as the South Africa Protection of Personal Information Act (POPIA) and the European Union AI (EU AI Act) highlight why it is essential to develop and regulate high-risk AI while also fostering innovation. These frameworks also show how complex it is to attempt to define accountability in a multi-level sector with several players | Vatankhah et al. (2024) and Zaidan and Ibrahim (2024) |

(continued)

**Table 1.1** (continued)

| Perspective | AI ethics definition | AI governance definition | References |
|---|---|---|---|
| Technical | Proponents' belief that AI ethics must grapple with the operationalisation or normative concepts in computational systems. For example, fairness may be viewed as demographic disparity (from a computational lens). Yet, definitions are yet to satisfy all moral and social concerns, reinforcing the gap between ethical ideals and practical implementation in the AI design and deployment. Hence, the system needs to be able to translate abstract ideals into measurable metrics like fairness definition, auditability, and bias testing throughout the life of the AI system | Here, it is argued that governance requires building a process that allows for auditing, traceability, and explainability to take place in the AI system. i.e., a process which allows for bias testing, model documentation, algorithm auditing, and post-deployment monitoring. This combined will transform abstract ideals into measurable outcomes/obligations to operationalise accountability | Batool et al. (2025) and Palumbo et al. (2025) |
| Socio-cultural | Here, proponents stressed that it is important that ethical concerns are deeply integrated within institutional, political, and cultural contexts. Because how different societies/ environments view fairness and justice generally differ. What is deemed acceptable in one society may not be in the other. Hence, global frameworks on ethics are yet to be able to address this aspect, especially as existing frameworks often only reflect corporate biases that overlook the interests of marginalised groups, particularly those from the global south. AI ethics, therefore, must extend beyond mere principles that are just technical fixes to incorporate context-sensitive standards that respect cultural diversity without undermining shared global standards | Proponents of this perspective call for an effective governance approach that will address gaps in institutional power, inequality, and cultural diversity, because it is crucial for shaping how AI systems influence different users. For instance, an AI governance that fails to consider the needs of marginalised groups might risk spiking digital divides. This could also indicate the existence of structural injustice within the AI systems. Hence, effective AI governance will help to foster policies and oversight structures that can protect marginalised groups and reflect local contexts. Suggesting the need to align global standards with local laws to ensure equitable outcomes for diverse groups | Cheong (2024) and Zaidan and Ibrahim (2024) |

### 1.2.2 AI Ethics and Governance Integration

Researchers have been discussing AI ethics and governance as if they are two separate terms, yet they are very closely related. Ethics, on the one hand, provides AI with the moral compass containing rules and values required of it to guide its societal role. Governance, however, offers AI the institutional and technical structures necessary for integrating these rules and principles into action. In short, AI ethics asks questions about "what ought to be done/what should be done?" while AI governance asks questions about "what is done, how it is done, and by whom?" (Batool et al., 2025; Radanliev, 2025).

Thus, an integrated conceptualization views AI ethics and governance as elements of the same ecosystem that are complementary rather than as distinct entities. Without ethical foundations, AI governance cannot be effective, and without governance frameworks to convert principles into legally binding actions, AI ethics itself will be meaningless and ineffective. Therefore, to ensure that AI systems are developed and deployed responsibly, accountably, and inclusively, it is necessary for researchers, system developers, legal practitioners, policymakers, and social scientists to collaborate across disciplines.

Below, we present in Table 1.2 how AI has evolved over time from inception to the present day, ethical concerns that have been raised, and governance actions taken.

### 1.2.3 Contemporary Landscape of AI Ethics and Governance

AI ethics and governance contemporary landscape can be defined by two dynamics. First is the EU's AI Act, which is a prominent example that uses a risk-based regulatory framework to categorize and regulate AI applications, highlighting how ethical principles have been successfully translated into law (European Union, 2024). Second, we have several regional governments that are still struggling with balancing AI governance with ethical standards, revealing irregularities in global governance. Hence, corporate organisations, international bodies, and regulatory authorities have begun outlining high-level principles as data-driven AI is gaining traction.

From the global north, we have the institute of electrical and electronics engineers (IEEE)'s global initiative on ethics of autonomous and intelligent systems (IEEE, 2016), organisation for economic cooperation and development (OECD) principles on AI (OECD, 2019), and the United Nations educational, scientific and cultural organization (UNESCO) recommendation on AI Ethics (UNESCO, 2021). These initiatives offer important normative frameworks that emphasize transparency, accountability, fairness, and respect for human rights. However, the UNESCO and OECD principles are still the most widely used as benchmarks, demonstrating the growing understanding that AI is a socio-technical system having significant ethical and governance implications, rather than just a technical advancement. Nonetheless,

**Table 1.2** Historical evolution of AI ethics and governance

| Era | Key developments | Ethical concerns raised | Governance responses |
|---|---|---|---|
| Early computing period (1940s–1960s) | This era witnessed the Turing (1950) test of a machine's ability to exhibit intelligent behaviour distinct from humans. The test, popularly called the imitation game, first proposed the question of machine intelligence. Also, Weizenbaum (1966) ELIZA tool that simulates natural language within human conversations. The tool birthed temporary Chatbots and other assistive tools like Siri, Alexa, and Cortana | This era sparked a lot of questions, one of which is: Can machines think? Consequently, this raises fear of loss of human input and lack of trust in the machine's decisions | There were no specific governance actions rather theoretical discourses |
| AI winter and Expert System (1970s–1980s) | An era that saw the increase of expert systems, yet limited progress, birthing the term "AI Winter" | This era came with concerns that were mainly about what AI can or cannot really do, i.e., the overhyped functions of the AI systems. This led to rule-based systems bias, reliability, and overhyped promises | Governance focus only moved to technical feasibility, with little to no regulation to support it |
| Resurgence of AI and Internet of Things (IoT) period (1990s–2000s) | There was rapid advancement in big data analytics, machine learning, and internet-based AI technologies | This period sparked privacy concerns owing to data gathering, an increase in surveillance issues, and the global digital divide | There have been data protection laws in different contexts. For example, the South African POPIA was enacted in 2013 |

(continued)

**Table 1.2** (continued)

| Era | Key developments | Ethical concerns raised | Governance responses |
|---|---|---|---|
| AI as a force to be reckoned with in our society (2010 to early 2020) | This era came with inventions and innovations in deep learning, like the ImageNet 2012. Also, the era brought about AI deployment in healthcare, accounting and finance, and policing | Black-box concerns arise especially on machine bias, and lack of transparency and accountability resulting from the inability of users to understand the machine's autonomous decision-making | Emergence of ethical AI principles like the EU AI Act, proposed in 2021 and became law in 2024, and the OECD principles for AI adopted in 2019 |
| The era of generative AI (2020s to date) | In this era came generative AI models like ChatGPT (GPT-3 and GPT-4), Perplexity AI, etc. reshaping the educational landscape, businesses, creativity, and innovation | Numerous concerns have been raised about loss of trust, misinformation, copyright disputes, and deepfakes, including hallucination of an AI system | Continuous call for global governance frameworks |

the non-binding nature of the initiatives reinforces that institutional capabilities and national contexts strongly influence how they are implemented.

From the global south, especially Africa, discussions surrounding AI ethics and governance signify that they are strongly reliant on local socioeconomic principles and cultural realities of the region. A typical example can be made about South Africa. While the country does not currently have any existing comprehensive regulation governing the application/deployment of AI, its POPIA of 2013 brings into law and offers a strong foundation for data protection, giving users privacy rights, balancing between individual data safeguard, integrating accountability, transparency, purpose limitation, and aiding the seamless transfer of information within and beyond South African borders (PR de Wet & Fourie, 2023). However, lately, there have been efforts made to extend the AI principles toward responsible AI, as seen in the draft South Africa National Artificial Intelligence Policy Framework (2024) published by the Department of Communications and Digital Technologies, and sector-specific guidelines like those from the Health Professions Council of South Africa (HPCSA) (2021). Each of these guidelines emphasizes human oversight, bias mitigation, and fairness. While both efforts are commendable, a wide gap remains. The lack of a specific AI Act in South Africa, when compared to the EU, raises questions regarding risk classification, liability, and fairness auditing still begging for answers. This reflects yet other challenges and opportunities of AI governance in an emerging context, reinforcing that foundational ethical norms are recognised, but yet to be translated into enforceable and context-sensitive governance.

Collectively considering these submissions, the evolution from the period of the ELIZA tool in 1966 to today's generative AI represents both continuity and transformation. Trust, accountability, and transparency are timeless ethical concerns that remain as pertinent today as they were when Weizenbaum (1966) first cautioned against inappropriate anthropomorphism. The scale, complexity, and pervasiveness of AI technologies in society are indicative of this transformation, which calls for strong, flexible, and internationally aware governance frameworks combined with the principles. Hence, the historical trajectory of AI ethics converges in the present moment, highlighting the need for a global call to close the gap between ethical theory and effective governance, ensuring that AI can be used for the good of all while upholding social justice and fundamental rights. See Table 1.3 for a summary of the comparative landscapes.

## 1.3 Methodology

This methodological approach of this chapter is based on a qualitative and interpretive research approach, drawing mainly from secondary sources like peer-reviewed articles, policy documents, reports, and regulatory frameworks. These sources were selected because of their recency, credibility, relevance, and to ensure that the chapter provides a thorough and critical overview of AI ethics and governance from various contexts. This approach was used to capture global perspectives at the regional level, covering South Africa's POPIA and National AI Policy Framework, and at the international level, covering the EU AI Act, OECD, and UNESCO frameworks. To ensure a cohesive whole and allow for disparate discussions about AI ethics and governance, the methodology included a comparative study that discusses philosophical, legal, technical, and sociocultural perspectives. The chapter sought to achieve its objectives using thematic coding to find recurrent themes in the literature on governance issues, ethical dilemmas, and solution pathways for operationalising ethical principles. Consequently, the methodological approach aided the chapter in bridging the gap between abstract ideas and actionable recommendations by highlighting context-specific governance practices in addition to charting the historical evolution of AI ethics.

**Table 1.3** The comparative landscapes summarised

| Dimension | South Africa (POPIA + AI policy framework) | EU AI act (2024) | OECD/UNESCO AI principles |
|---|---|---|---|
| Legal basis | POPIA (2013, enforced 2021); The non-binding SA National AI policy framework (2024) | Risk-based classification and legally binding regulation (2024) | International frameworks that member states have adopted but are not legally binding |
| Core ethical principles | At the policy level-transparency, accountability, fairness, privacy, and human oversight | Human-centered AI, accountability, transparency, safety of use, and fundamental human rights | Human rights, sustainability, accountability, transparency, inclusivity, and fairness |
| Regulation scope | Data protection stipulation from POPIA, combined with broad AI governance, including policy and sectoral guidelines | Detailed sectoral regulation of AI systems, with responsibilities based on risk classification | It contains high-level global principles for responsible AI, while the specificity for each sector or risk is not explicit |
| Risk classification | Although fairness and bias mitigation were mentioned in the policy drafts, legal risk levels were not explicitly included. No classification of risks; based on principles | Included four levels of risks: Prohibited, high-risk, limited-risk, and minimal-risk AI | Strictly principles-based without any classification of risks |
| Enforcement | The information and communication regulators enforce POPIA, while the AI policy framework is still optional and non-binding | Strict enforcement with fines of up to €35 million, or 7% of global sales | There is no enforcement yet, as it depends on voluntary adoption |
| Sector-specific guidance | Emerging—ex: healthcare guidelines; suggested ethical corporate governance (CG) frameworks from academia. (See: Coovadia et al., 2025) | Applicable to all sectors, particularly to stakeholders in the high-risk sectors like law enforcement, health, transport, and education | Promotes sectoral adaptation while allowing member states to handle the details |
| Data and AI use across borders | POPIA prohibits cross-country data transfers, especially where the recipient country's protection is insufficient | Implications across borders through adherence to EU standards | Encourages international collaboration, capacity-building, and harmonisation |
| Existing gaps | Absence of a comprehensive AI Act; inadequate enforcement of AI-specific duties, liability, and fairness audits | Costs of implementation and compliance; potential to hinder innovation | Reliance on goodwill and member state alignment, lack of binding authority |

## 1.4 Ethical Dilemmas and Governance Challenges for AI Systems

Some of the common ethical dilemmas that AI systems can have include fairness, accountability, transparency, privacy, human oversight, and broader societal justice. These dilemmas are often interrelated, increasing their likelihood of being exposed to risks and causing governance to become complicated. The origin of this dilemma can be traced to the difference between high-level ethical principles and how they are converted into a legally binding practice. Meanwhile, in an ecosystem consisting of multiple stakeholders, what is usually observed is that accountability is often blurred out, with transparency limited due to technical opacity and commercial secrecy, while bias and discrimination will persist. Although certain contexts often show advancements such as GDPR and POPIA, particularly on privacy frameworks, they still have trouble when it comes to addressing the scale of generative AI and inference-based harms. Consequently, generative models threaten to undermine public trust through disinformation, with automation posing risks like job displacement, while the environmental impacts of AI are still disregarded.

The global justice dimension further exacerbates these dilemmas since governance frameworks tend to be influenced by the values of the Global North, which risks marginalising the interests of the Global South. Therefore, a risk-sensitive, adaptive, and inclusive governance that incorporates technical safeguards, legal accountability, institutional capacity, and participatory mechanisms is necessary to bridge the gap between principle and practice. Table 1.4 below contains a compact mapping of the ethical dilemmas against suggestive governance tools.

## 1.5 Pathways for Translating Ethical Principles into Actionable Practices

One of the most difficult and recurring issues in AI governance that can also affect all users is the disparity that arises between abstract ethical principles (like accountability, transparency, fairness, and respect for human rights) and their practical application. To address this, translating ethical principles into actionable practices needs multiple strategies that involve integrating ethics into the AI lifecycle, starting from the system's design, to training, deployment, and continuous monitoring level (Floridi, 2019; Jobin et al., 2019). Also, it requires formalising the ethics into standards, establishing accountability, fostering socio-cultural adoption, and encouraging adaptive governance. However, it is important to bear in mind that principles are only like a moral compass; their effectiveness is still contingent upon explicit mechanisms. Hence, we suggest the following pathways.

(i) **Integrate Ethics into Design:** Instead of ethics being an afterthought, it must be embedded into the AI system right from the very beginning, i.e., development/design stage. This would necessitate developing a system that is "ethics by

**Table 1.4** Ethical dilemmas mapping against Governance tools

| Ethical dilemma | Governance tools |
|---|---|
| Bias and fairness | It is important to perform evaluations and impact analysis, likewise legally required fairness standards |
| Transparency/explainability | Consider making use of disclosure guidelines, model cards, and documentation standards |
| Accountability/liability | Take into consideration liability regimes, audit trails, and quick incident reporting as they arise |
| Data protection/privacy measures | Use differential privacy measures, such as DPIAs, PETs, and laws akin to POPIA/GDPR, to protect data |
| Human oversight/error | Regulation of meaningful supervision and certification of roles |
| Malicious misuse | Make sure that stringent access controls, red-teaming, and compliance with international laws are in place |
| Misinformation | Consider provenance, detection technologies, and platform guidelines |
| Impacts on the employee | To reduce impacts on employees, consider implementing social policies and retraining and reskilling programs for both staff and users |
| Environmental impact | Reporting on sustainability and making sure that the standards are effective |
| Cultural justice | AI design should respect cultural diversity, preserve local norms and values, promote capacity building and inclusive governance, and prevent digital marginalisation |

design" in its approaches, such that fairness constraints, privacy protections, and explainability requirements are already well integrated into the architecture process of the system itself. For example, Mehrabi et al. (2021) suggested that to reduce the incidence of algorithmic bias and ensure implementation of a fair ML model, it is advisable to integrate within the system a mathematical fairness constraints technique at the model training phase. Similarly, explainable AI (XAI) techniques would assist the developers to match system outputs with transparency requirements, ensuring accountability and traceability.

(ii) **Converting Principles into Benchmarks and Standards:** Translating principles into standardised benchmarks and certification schemes is also a critical pathway solution. This can be achieved by emphasising risk management, human oversight, and documentation, especially as international initiatives like the EU AI Act (2024) and ISO/IEC JTC 1 standards already offer structured requirements for high-risk AI. Furthermore, forming compliance benchmarks like those in the GDPR's data privacy impact assessments will provide useful instruments for assessing whether the AI systems live up to their ethical expectations. Overall, the standards would assist organisations in operationalising their principles (Nemko, 2025).

(iii) **Establishing a Mechanism for Oversight and Accountability:** To uphold the principles of accountability and responsibility, there is a need for a multi-level governance approach. At the regulatory/sectoral level, bodies responsible for independent oversight and auditing procedures must ensure adherence to legal and ethical standards. More so, organisational practices including algorithmic impact assessments, internal AI ethics boards, and an open form of reporting would assist with internal checks. For instance, the POPIA of 2013 and South Africa's National AI Policy Framework of 2024 establish guidelines for data use, security, and accountability. According to PR de Wet and Fourie (2023), these frameworks offer ways to incorporate ethics into corporate business practices within an emerging country context.

(iv) **Consider Culture and Education in Socio-Technical Solutions**: Taking human and cultural factors into account is another way to turn ethics into practical solutions. For example, since ethical AI is a socio-political issue as well as a technical one, it is crucial to provide ethical literacy training to system developers, legislators, and end users so that they can gain a thorough understanding of the system and make sure the knowledge is applied appropriately. Moreso, it will ensure that an ethical standard is developed through collaborative efforts rather than being imposed by leading societal actors. The likelihood of this, however, depends on whether cross-sectoral discussions and dialogue were held between stakeholders and the affected communities. This aligns with UNESCO (2021)'s AI ethics recommendation that responsible AI take cultural diversity, inclusivity, and human rights into account.

(v) **Ensure Continuous Monitoring and Adaptive Governance:** Continuous monitoring of the AI system is also another way to turn ethics into workable solutions, especially since generative AI keeps changing rapidly, coming up with new high risks daily. For example, at every short interval, one would realise that deepfakes and synthetic information have changed. These swift changes can easily outpace already established standards. As a result, ethical standards must also be updated from time to time. Furthermore, adaptive governance strategies like real-time audits, dynamic risk classification, and regulatory sandboxes must be considered. By using these strategies, organizations would be able to adapt their compliance standards and ethical standards to new technological developments. Additionally, it will equally help them remain relevant in the rapidly evolving technological landscape (OECD, 2020).

Collectively, these suggestions have the potential to transform the AI ecosystem from a purely moral concept to workable solutions that safeguard all parties involved while fostering innovation (Fig. 1.1).

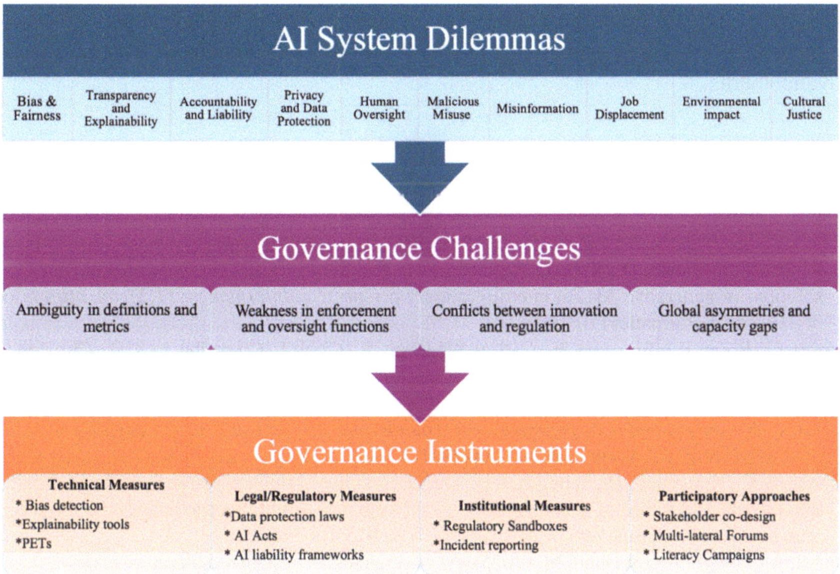


**Fig. 1.1** Flowchart of ethical dilemma, governance challenges, and instruments

## 1.6 Conclusion

The way AI ethics and governance have evolved demonstrates a clear pattern of slower institutional responses to the rapidly changing technology. From the earliest days of ELIZA tools to the current generative AI, the main challenge has been in figuring out how to maximize AI's potential while minimizing its threats. While the EU AI Act, UNESCO's ethics recommendation, and the OECD AI Principles are important international frameworks from the Global North, this chapter showed that local standards, like South Africa's POPIA and National AI Policy framework, which are within emerging contexts, also show that cultural and political realities are crucial for ethical governance. Although significant dilemmas like algorithmic bias, accountability gaps, and the disruptive potential of generative AI remain and must be adequately addressed. Suggestive pathways to translate abstract ideals to practical solutions include ensuring ethics by design, standardization, institutional oversight, ethical literacy, and adaptive governance.

Looking ahead, the future of AI ethics will likely be influenced by two competing factors. One is the increasing complexity of AI systems, and the other is the growing demand for accountability globally. Hopefully, in the distant future and all things being equal, ethical principles would be integrated into legally binding standards and technical regimes beyond voluntary standards. This chapter hereby serves as a wake-up call for a truly global discourse that aligns universal principles with local context, ensuring inclusivity from both developed and emerging climes. In short, AI can be guided toward a future that is innovation-driven, as well as one that protects human rights, ensuring fairness and equity. This will be possible if governance structures become adaptive, participatory, rights-based, and move in tandem with technological advancements.

## References

Al-Kfairy, M., Mustafa, D., Kshetri, N., Insiew, M., & Alfandi, O. (2024). Ethical challenges and solutions of generative AI: An interdisciplinary perspective. *Informatics, 11*(3), 58. https://doi.org/10.3390/informatics11030058

Barrett, C., Boyd, B., Bursztein, E., Carlini, N., Chen, B., Choi, J., Chowdhury, A. R., Christodorescu, M., Datta, A., Feizi, S., Fisher, K., Hashimoto, T., Hendrycks, D., Jha, S., Kang, D., Kerschbaum, F., Mitchell, E., Mitchell, J., Ramzan, Z., & Yang, D. (2023). Identifying and mitigating the security risks of generative AI. *Foundations and Trends® in Privacy and Security, 6*(1), 1–52. https://doi.org/10.1561/3300000041

Bartsch, S. C., Nguyen, L. H., Schmidt, J. H., Du, G., Adam, M., Benlian, A., & Sunyaev, A. (2025). The present and future of accountability for AI systems: A bibliometric analysis. *Information Systems Frontiers*. https://doi.org/10.1007/s10796-025-10636-9

Batool, A., Zowghi, D., & Bano, M. (2025). AI governance: A systematic literature review. *AI and Ethics, 5*(3), 3265–3279. https://doi.org/10.1007/s43681-024-00653-w

Buolamwini, J., & Gebru, T. (2018). Gender shades: Intersectional accuracy disparities in commercial gender classification. *Proceedings of Machine Learning Research, 81*, 77–91. http://proceedings.mlr.press/v81/buolamwini18a.html?mod=article_inline&ref=akusion-ci-shi-dai-bizinesumedeia

Camilleri, M. A. (2024). Artificial intelligence governance: Ethical considerations and implications for social responsibility. *Expert Systems, 41*(7), Article e13406. https://doi.org/10.1111/exsy.13406

Cheong, B. C. (2024). Transparency and accountability in AI systems: Safeguarding wellbeing in the age of algorithmic decision-making. *Frontiers in Human Dynamics, 6*, 1421273. https://doi.org/10.3389/fhumd.2024.1421273

Coovadia, H., Marx, B., Botha, I., & Gold, N. O. (2025). Building an ethical artificial intelligence corporate governance framework for the integration of emerging technologies into business processes. *South African Journal of Accounting Research*. https://doi.org/10.1080/10291954.2025.2523661

Dastin, J. (2022). Amazon scraps secret AI recruiting tool that showed bias against women*. In *Ethics of data and analytics* (pp. 296–299). https://doi.org/10.1201/9781003278290-44

de Wet, P. R., & Fourie, J. (2023). *South Africa: AI and data privacy regulations—The complexities of AI technologies and processing personal information*. VDT Attorneys Inc. https://vdt.co.za/popia/south-africa-ai-and-data-privacy-regulations-the-complexities-of-ai-technologies-and-processingpersonal-information

European Union. (2024). Artificial intelligence act texts: Regulation (EU) 2024/1689 of the European parliament and of the council of 13 June 2024. *Official Journal of the European Union, 1689*(3), 1–144. http://data.europa.eu/eli/reg/2024/1689/oj

Floridi, L. (2019). Translating principles into practices of digital ethics: Five risks of being unethical. In *Philosophy & technology* (Vol. 32, pp. 185–193). Springer. https://doi.org/10.1007/s13347-019-00354-x

Gichoya, J. W., Banerjee, I., Bhimireddy, A. R., Burns, J. L., Celi, L. A., Chen, L. C., Correa, R., Dullerud, N., Ghassemi, M., Huang, S. C., Kuo, P. C., Lungren, M. P., Palmer, L. J., Price, B. J., Purkayastha, S., Pyrros, A. T., Oakden-Rayner, L., Okechukwu, C., Seyyed-Kalantari, L., & Zhang, H. (2022). AI recognition of patient race in medical imaging: A modelling study. *The Lancet Digital Health, 4*(6), e406–e414. https://doi.org/10.1016/S2589-7500(22)00063-2

Health Professions Council of South Africa (HPCSA). (2021). *Health professions council of South Africa general ethical guidelines for good practice in telehealth* (Issue December). https://www.hpcsa-blogs.co.za/wp-content/uploads/2022/08/Booklet-10_Telehealth__Dec_2021_.pdf

Hunkenschroer, A. L., & Luetge, C. (2022). Ethics of AI-enabled recruiting and selection: A review and research agenda. *Journal of Business Ethics, 178*(4), 977–1007. https://doi.org/10.1007/s10551-022-05049-6

IEEE, I. of E. and E. E. (2016). The IEEE global initiative on ethics of autonomous and intelligent systems. *IEEE Standards Association*, 4. https://standards.ieee.org/content/dam/ieee-standards/standards/web/documents/other/ec_about_us.pdf

Jobin, A., Ienca, M., & Vayena, E. (2019). *Artificial Intelligence: The global landscape of ethics guidelines*. http://arxiv.org/abs/1906.11668

Mehrabi, N., Morstatter, F., Saxena, N., Lerman, K., & Galstyan, A. (2021). A survey on bias and fairness in machine learning. *ACM Computing Surveys (CSUR), 54*(6), 1–35. https://doi.org/10.1145/3457607

Mittelstadt, B. (2019). Principles alone cannot guarantee ethical AI. *Nature Machine Intelligence, 1*(11), 501–507. https://doi.org/10.1038/s42256-019-0114-4

Nemko. (2025). *AI regulation in South Africa: Compliance and governance guide*. Nemko Digital. https://digital.nemko.com/regulations/ai-regulation-in-south-africa

OECD. (2020). *OECD legal instruments: Recommendation of the council on artificial intelligence*. OECD. https://legalinstruments.oecd.org/en/instruments/OECD-LEGAL-0449

OECD—Organisation for Economic Cooperation and Development. (2019). What are the OECD principles on AI? In *OECD observer* (Issue March). https://doi.org/10.1787/6ff2a1c4-en

Palumbo, G., Carneiro, D., & Alves, V. (2025). Objective metrics for ethical AI: A systematic literature review. *International Journal of Data Science and Analytics, 20*(2), 247–267. https://doi.org/10.1007/s41060-024-00541-w

Radanliev, P. (2025). AI ethics: Integrating transparency, fairness, and privacy in AI development. *Applied Artificial Intelligence, 39*(1), e2463722–e2463741. https://doi.org/10.1080/08839514.2025.2463722

Sadek, M., Kallina, E., Bohné, T., Mougenot, C., Calvo, R. A., & Cave, S. (2025). Challenges of responsible AI in practice: Scoping review and recommended actions. *AI and Society, 40*(1), 199–215. https://doi.org/10.1007/s00146-024-01880-9

South Africa National Artificial Intelligence Policy Framework, 1 (2024). https://www.dcdt.gov.za/sa-national-ai-policy-framework/file/338-sa-national-ai-policy-framework

Turing, A. (1950). Machinery and intelligence. *Mind: A Quarterly Review of Psychology, 59*(236), 433–460. https://www.robertspahr.com/teaching/hnm/turing_computing_machinery_and_intelligence.pdf

UNESCO-United Nations Educational Scientific and Cultural Organization. (2021). Recommendation on the ethics of artificial intelligence. In *UNESCO*. https://doi.org/10.1093/oso/9780190905033.001.0001

Vatankhah, S., Bamshad, V., Arici, H. E., & Duan, Y. (2024). Ethical implementation of artificial intelligence in the service industries. *Service Industries Journal, 44*(9–10), 661–685. https://doi.org/10.1080/02642069.2024.2359077

Weizenbaum, J. (1966). ELIZA-A computer program for the study of natural language communication between man and machine. *Communications of the ACM, 9*(1), 36–45. https://doi.org/10.1145/365153.365168

Zaidan, E., & Ibrahim, I. A. (2024). AI governance in a complex and rapidly changing regulatory landscape: A global perspective. *Humanities and Social Sciences Communications, 11*(1), 1–18. https://doi.org/10.1057/s41599-024-03560-x

Zhang, M. (2015). *Google photos tags two African–Americans as gorillas through facial recognition software*. Forbes. https://www.forbes.com/sites/mzhang/2015/07/01/google-photos-tags-two-african-americans-as-gorillas-through-facial-recognition-software/

# Chapter 2
# Machine Bias and Fairness

**Nusirat Ojuolape Gold and Husain Coovadia**

**Abstract** Organizations around the globe have been utilizing artificial intelligence (AI) for different business processes. While these tools offer numerous benefits, they have several associated risks that are debatable. Resulting in stakeholders getting agitated, particularly on concerns related to machine bias, and the lack of fairness continues to negatively impact the different aspects of business processes, consequently raising ethical concerns. Exploring the various definitions of machine bias, this chapter provides a detailed explanation of the fairness concept from varying perspectives to provide a comprehensive insight that can foster an understanding of the intersections between machine bias and fairness. To achieve this objective, the chapter employed an extensive review of contemporary research and established that bias is an issue prevalent across domains, including business and finance. To overcome bias in the AI system, the chapter explored a series of techniques covering technical, governance, and operational approaches that can be employed. By so doing, the chapter contributes to ongoing debates on how AI design and deployments can uphold ethical consideration, ensuring fairness in the system, promoting the inclusiveness of all users, without undermining stakeholders' trust.

## 2.1 Introduction

Artificial intelligence (AI) tools now have a tangible impact on our daily lives, rather than remaining abstract notions. These technologies are being used in vital areas such as employment, healthcare, businesses, and education to streamline procedures,

N. O. Gold (✉) · H. Coovadia
Department of Commercial Accounting, College of Business and Economics, University of Johannesburg, Johannesburg, South Africa
e-mail: ngold@uj.ac.za; nusirat.gold@kwasu.edu.ng

H. Coovadia
e-mail: hcoovadia@uj.ac.za

N. O. Gold
Faculty of Management and Social Sciences, Department of Accounting and Finance, Kwara State University, Malete, Nigeria

 
M. Adelowotan and H. Coovadia (eds.), *AI and Accountability*, CSR, Sustainability, Ethics & Governance, https://doi.org/10.1007/978-3-032-20091-4_2

reduce costs, innovate, and ensure savings for stakeholders using the system (Funda, 2025; Ueda et al., 2024). Using machine learning (ML) systems can lead to algorithmic bias, resulting in unjustified disparities across social categories such as race, gender, and socioeconomic status (Fletcher et al., 2021; Mehrabi et al., 2021; Mitchell et al., 2021).

Berk et al. (2021) observed that in predicting performance, AI machine bias often reflects greater false-positive or negative rates for certain selected groups. Another example is predictive policing that targets minorities in certain neighbourhoods unfairly (Bickel et al., 1975; Richardson et al., 2019), and another is an identity tool named "correctional offender management profiling for alternative sanctions" (COMPAS), which shows racial disparities in different risk scores of individuals (Dressel & Farid, 2018). Another example is found in a study on gender shades, which revealed that an AI model for leading commercial facial analysis performed substantially less accurately on black women than on white men (Buolamwini & Gebru, 2018).

The concept of machine bias, therefore, raises many questions, more specifically, on how to address the concerns to reach a goal where groups of people are treated equally (Hardt et al., 2016; Mitchell et al., 2021). Different approaches have been taken by various individuals; for example, computer scientists suggest various definitions like equalized odds, while the legal fraternity focuses on non-discrimination, promoting an equal protection concept for aspects that act like the General Data Protection Regulation (GDPR) and the proposed EU act on AI (European Commission, 2024; Wachter et al., 2021). A similar act protecting users' data is the Protection of Personal Information Act (POPIA), which exists in South Africa. Given this, one critical issue about fairness that must be understood is the fact that it is a highly contested and context-dependent concept, one that is often shaped by social values, legal standards, and historical inequalities (Friedler et al., 2021; Noble, 2020).

Some prominent global cases have also highlighted the persistence of machine bias in practice. Reuters reported that Amazon scrapped its hiring AI tool due to the system showing bias against women (Dastin, 2022). Also, credit scoring and lending machine models were found to treat minority groups unfairly by limiting their access to financial services (Bartlett et al., 2022). Furthermore, scholars noted a facial recognition technology that misidentified individuals from a certain racial minority population, thereby exposing them to the risks of unjust arrests and surveillance harms (Garvie & Moy, 2019; Raji et al., 2020). These cases are indications that while a system might be working well, bias may inherently still be present yet not detected. Hence, suggestive that bias could arise from multiple sources, including training datasets (Wei et al., 2025), biased historical outcomes, unexamined optimization criteria, and opaque governance structures.

Despite this increasing awareness of machine bias, a consensus is yet to be formed, particularly on the definition of fairness, operationalization, and enforcement. While debates have presented some technical solutions, they have only come with a narrow focus on areas like mathematical definitions, while governance frameworks still struggle to provide any form of solution to the socio-technical nature of bias. Furthermore, recent case studies from around the globe show that existing mitigation efforts are insufficient, particularly in high-stakes sectors like business and finance, law, and healthcare. Hence, without a robust interdisciplinary approach(es) that integrates technical safeguards, legal frameworks, and institutional accountability, the AI systems will continue to reproduce and further exacerbate existing inequalities.

Therefore, it is important for organizations deploying AI technologies to exercise extreme caution since designing and deploying biased AI systems can create substantial legal and ethical implications for the firm. Take, for instance, a biased AI system that produces unfair outcomes owing to bias in its dataset for which it has been trained or designed (Wei et al., 2025), consequently leading to disproportionate negative impacts on certain groups. This bias would expose the organization to discrimination claims and risk of liability, reputational damage, regulatory sanctions, and potential loss of public trust, consequently hindering the organization's market acceptance and future growth. Therefore, fairness is a legal and strategic need in the age of algorithmic governance.

These arguments highlight the significance of reducing bias and promoting fairness for diverse user groups, both from an institutional and technical standpoint. To better comprehend the institutional perspective, consider fairness, inclusivity, diversity, robustness, transparency, accountability, human-centred AI, and social well-being (OECD, 2019; UNESCO, 2021). The technological aspect involves pre-processing datasets, fairness-constrained learning, and post-processing to reduce bias (Mehrabi et al., 2021). Mitchell et al. (2019) suggest that using transparency tools such as model cards and dataset disclosure might help improve accountability.

To this end, this chapter explore the multifaceted nature of machine bias and fairness. Specifically, the chapter seeks to:

(i) Define machine bias and fairness, clarifying their conceptual, statistical, and legal aspects.
(ii) Analyse case studies involving machine bias across different global settings.
(iii) Propose techniques for mitigating machine bias.
(iv) Propose integrative pathways for aligning technical innovation with ethical principles, legal compliance, and societal expectations of fairness.

The remainder of the chapter proceeds with each of the outlined objectives in the following order. Section 2 describes the methodology, Sect. 3 focuses on the definition of machine bias and fairness, Sect. 4 presents different case studies from a global perspective, Sect. 5 discusses strategies for mitigating machine bias, Sect. 6 proposes pathways for aligning technical innovation, Sect. 7 concludes the chapter, and Sect. 8 summarizes the findings, limitations, and recommendations for future research agenda.

## 2.2 Methodology

This chapter has employed a narrative review approach to synthesize current discourse on algorithmic/machine bias and fairness existing in AI. A narrative review approach is deemed well-suited for this chapter, given the diversity of disciplinary perspectives and emergence of complex sociotechnical issues that often lend themselves to strict systemic review protocols. With relevant literature sourced from several databases such as Web of Science (WoS), Scopus, and Google Scholar, the chapter ensured it covered basically scholarly documents in top-tier journals, with priority given to relevant scholarly research outputs from 2015 to 2025, particularly owing to the rapidly evolving nature of AI technologies. For broader coverage and relevancy, flexible keywords such as AI, AI bias, Algorithm bias, generative AI bias, Algorithm fairness, deep learning fairness, AI regulation, AI mitigation techniques, fairness strategies, AI in organization, Global AI challenges, and AI challenges in developing contexts were used as search strings. Additionally, because the chapter is interdisciplinary, cutting across sectors, literatures were integrated from information systems, finance, computer science, healthcare, education, and public policy documents. Overall, the review process of the chapter involved iterative reading, synthesis, and thematic clustering of the literature one which helped shape the analytical structure of the entire chapter and guided us in the research objectives.

## 2.3 Definition of Machine Bias and Fairness

Conceptually, machine bias is an issue that literature has consistently raised because it creates different ethical dilemmas. It often arises when AI systems generate unfair or discriminatory outcomes. It can be referred to as the systematic generation of uneven results by the AI systems, in such a way that reflects and amplifies existing social inequities (Funda, 2025; Pham et al., 2025). Bias arises not only from flawed data but also from the assumptions embedded in model design, training objectives, and deployment contexts (Mehrabi et al., 2021). For instance, a predictive model that has been trained on historically biased hiring or policing data will inherit those same structural inequities, consequently starting a cycle of disadvantages (Pham et al., 2025; Raji et al., 2020). This simply means that bias generally arises from unrepresentative training data or built-in assumptions in model design, reinforcing inherent social injustices and inequalities (Pham et al., 2025) such as those based on race, gender, or colour.

Within the definition of bias are two aspects that are essential: fairness and discrimination. In AI modelling, fairness is both a normative principle and an operational goal. From the normative lens, fairness concepts rely on fundamental ethical principles of justice, beneficence, and non-maleficence (Ueda et al., 2024). It requires that individuals and groups must be treated equitably, regardless of protected attributes like class, ethnicity, race, gender, or socioeconomic status (Afreen et al., 2025; Barocas & Selbst, 2016; Verma & Rubin, 2018). Fair treatment and non-discrimination are two examples of fairness in data protection law (ICO-Information Commissioner's Office, 2023). It is not just about the sharing of benefits and opportunities among members of a certain group, but also how you balance the different, competing interests of all groups. Berk et al. (2021) mentioned that it is a treatment of equality achieved when the ratio of false negatives and false positives is the same for all group categories. Hence, it can be argued as how fair individuals are treated in a reasonable manner irrespective of social class and skin colour. From the operational lens, fairness necessitates a deliberate design choice, data stewardship, and evaluation criteria such that decisions are not skewed in ways that unjustifiably favour a group over another (Buolamwini & Gebru, 2018).

Discrimination is also linked closely with machine bias, and it occurs when an AI system puts members of a certain group (for example, women) at a disadvantage (ICO-Information Commissioner's Office, 2023). Discrimination can be understood as a form of unfairness that arises from human prejudice and stereotyping based on sensitive attributes. This can occur either intentionally or unintentionally. Bias, on the other hand, represents unfairness that stems from issues in data collection, sampling, or measurement processes. While bias can also originate from prejudice and stereotyping, in the field of algorithmic fairness, it is more practical to distinguish between discrimination and bias in line with existing research.

From a statistical perspective, fairness is defined as:

(i) **Demographic parity:** where outcomes are distributed equally across groups.
(ii) **Equalized odds:** where error rates (false positives/false negatives) are balanced across groups.
(iii) **Calibration or predictive parity:** where predicted probabilities correspond equally to observed outcomes across groups.

From a legal perspective, differences in treatment or outcomes across groups can be explained by legitimate attributes because fairness is also a legal and regulatory concern. Article 22 of the GDPR of the EU restricts automated decision-making with "legal or similarly significant effects" on individuals, effectively requiring organizations to ensure that automated systems do not unfairly discriminate (European Union, 2018). When these differences are justifiable, they are not considered illegal discrimination but rather explainable discrimination. For example, in the widely used UCI Adult dataset, men on average earn higher annual incomes than women. This disparity can largely be explained by differences in working hours, as women in the dataset tend to work fewer hours per week. Working hours, therefore, are a valid explanatory factor for income differences. If decisions were made without accounting for this factor, forcing male and female average incomes to be equal, it would result in reverse discrimination, where men would be unfairly disadvantaged. Thus, explainable discrimination is considered acceptable and legal because it can be justified by relevant attributes.

Although different methods have been proposed to distinguish between explainable and illegal discrimination in data. However, irrespective of the chosen method, caution must be exercised to ensure that any approach(es) selected does not ignore the explainable component, as this may inadvertently produce harmful results, such as reverse discrimination. Hence, it is best to select a framework that quantifies and measures discrimination in data or classifier decisions by directly accounting for both legal (explainable) and illegal (unexplainable) aspects.

Unexplainable discrimination, in contrast, refers to unjustified disparities that cannot be explained by legitimate attributes and are therefore considered illegal. Unexplainable discrimination can be direct or indirect. Direct discrimination occurs when protected attributes explicitly lead to unfavourable outcomes for individuals. Indirect discrimination, however, occurs when decisions appear to rely on neutral, non-protected attributes but still result in unfair treatment of protected groups due to hidden correlations with those attributes. For example, cases involving employment discrimination in AI-driven hiring tools. In this instance, organizations may be legally liable under anti-discrimination law if algorithms reproduce gender or racial biases (Dastin, 2022). Similarly, failures in consumer-facing AI systems like the wrong labelling of Black individuals in Google Photos can result in reputational and compliance risks, prompting calls for greater accountability and oversight (Zhang, 2015).

These conceptual definitions underscore the belief that bias is not just a technical error but a socio-technical phenomenon. Also, fairness, correspondingly, cannot be reduced to a single metric, as it requires grappling with social values and contextual trade-offs.

### *2.3.1 Factors Giving Rise to Machine Bias Concerns*

Machine bias can emerge in several ways, including from structural unfairness or discriminatory influences that have been embedded in the data (Larson et al., 2016). Below is a myriad of forms that bias can take:

- **Historical bias:** Machines tend to learn from historical data with which they have been trained. Hence, any inequalities, cultural practices, or societal norms existing at the time of its design can penetrate deep into the datasets (Suresh & Guttag, 2021). Hence, a risk of the system inheriting and amplifying these imbalances.
- **Representation bias:** This may arise due to over-/under-representation of a certain population in the dataset, consequently leading to skewed outcomes (Suresh & Guttag, 2021).
- **Measurement bias:** This may occur when an AI system embeds systemic discrimination, whereby different attributes in the dataset are not accurately measured. A typical example was evident in the case of COMPAS, where prior arrests were taken as a proxy for criminal risk (Suresh & Guttag, 2021).
- **Evaluation bias:** This form may arise when models are assessed against certain benchmarks that contain discriminatory features themselves. An example can be

made of a facial recognition system that poses a disadvantage to darker-skinned individuals and women (Buolamwini & Gebru, 2018).

- **Aggregation bias:** This may occur when the system applies the conclusions drawn from one subgroup to another, overlooking the unique dynamics that may exist for a specific subgroup (Suresh & Guttag, 2021).
- **Simpson's Paradox:** This form of bias describes trends that often appear within groups but change when data are aggregated, as evident in the UC Berkeley's admission case (Bickel et al., 1975).
- **Sampling bias:** This emerges through non-random sampling where a group is unexpectedly favoured over others (González-Sendino et al., 2024).
- **Temporal bias:** It occurs in situations where the population behaviour changes over time due to changes in the data itself. For example, hashtags on social media may become outdated when trend changes, causing models already trained on the hashtags to be misleading.
- **Popularity bias:** Items that are already well-known or widely consumed may gain more popularity and get preference over other items, while the less popular alternative items become marginalized.
- **Algorithmic bias:** This is unfairness built into the algorithm by design (Baeza-Yates, 2018).
- **Funding Bias:** Here, the AI algorithm development funders may influence the outcome of the algorithm (Amini et al., 2019).
- **Data manipulation:** This may occur due to a deliberate attempt by the users to alter the datasets to favour certain outcomes they desire.
- **Machine learning (ML) bias:** This form of bias is typical of a system that adapts through interaction. An example is evident in the case of Microsoft's Tay chatbot, which was manipulated into producing racist and misogynistic language within hours of its first release.
- **Confirmation bias:** This occurs when the algorithms are designed in a way that reinforces pre-existing assumptions, neglecting contradictory evidence, causing the AI systems to overfit to dominant narratives instead of discovering new insights.
- **Survivorship bias:** This occurs when only a specific case, i.e., a successful case, is captured in the data upon which the system is designed, while other unsuccessful cases are excluded, creating distorted/misleading conclusions.
- **Observer bias:** This form of bias is introduced into the dataset when the persons collecting or labelling the data erroneously use their own expectations or personal prejudice to influence results.
- **Automation bias:** This may occur when the human over relies on the AI-generated outputs without further confirming whether the outputs contain errors, resulting in discriminatory outcomes.
- **Exclusion bias:** This occurs when relevant variables, elements, attributes, or subgroups are deliberately or accidentally omitted from the dataset, leading to incomplete results.

- **Proxy bias:** This occurs when a seemingly neutral variable, such as zip codes, is taken as a proxy for some protected attributes like race or socioeconomic status. This will indirectly embed discrimination into the system.

The above are some of the different forms of bias that an entity may encounter while employing AI, and they give rise to the machine bias concern. To address the concerns, businesses and organizations should take cognizance of the diverse factors.

## 2.4 Global Case Studies of Machine Bias in AI Systems and Expected Fairness Response

### *2.4.1 Consumer Applications: A Case of Google Photos Mislabel*

A consumer image recognition tool developed by Google Photos was reported in the year 2015 to have labelled individuals of the black race as gorillas wrongly (Zhang, 2015). This single incident generated a lot of controversy. The discrepancy highlights the impact of machine bias on global reactions and the need for rigorous testing in AI systems, particularly for products used by consumers globally. Google quickly resolved the issue and apologized. However, the episode raised ethical and trust issues, as well as reputation concerns.

#### Expected Fairness Response

The example highlights the importance of pre- and post-processing data, as well as constant monitoring and auditing of AI systems, in ensuring that deployed AI systems do not lead to prejudice.

### *2.4.2 Gender Bias Experience in Google Translate Language Model*

Natural language processing (NLP) tools have been integrated into many aspects of our everyday lives. Yet, when they are used on a large scale, these systems tend to amplify societal stereotypes. Prates et al.(2020) investigated Google Translate's treatment of gender-neutral sentences and found that the output of the AI system clearly showed bias towards the male pronoun when compared to female, especially in occupations with low female representation, like in the STEM fields. This example reinforces how language tools, if not thoroughly examined, can perpetuate stereotypes in a subtle yet highly impactful manner.

**Expected Fairness Response**

This example reinforces the need for fairness in every aspect of training data, as well as accounting for gender disparity that may be inherent within the dataset. Furthermore, pre- and post-processing of data interventions is essential since output generated by the systems can be biased due to inherent biases within the training data.

## 2.4.3 *Data Biases in the Medical Domain*

Within the healthcare domain, biases in data are particularly a huge concern, as this could lead to life-threatening consequences, especially if the data is skewed to a particular population. Although what is often seen within the medical realm is that studies overrepresent individuals of European descent, leaving African and Asian populations to be marginalized (Popejoy & Fullerton, 2016; Sirugo et al., 2019). Hence, these imbalances often end up impacting clinical tools that are developed for global use, as well as research that is conducted in this field. Thus, findings from research within the medical field may reflect how algorithms replicate existing disparities and further compound known problems at hand (Obermeyer et al., 2019).

**Expected Fairness Response**

This case underscores the importance of having a data set that is inclusive of an entire population without any representative bias. To achieve this, a regulatory framework around medical research when using AI tools to diagnose various health issues.

## 2.4.4 *Algorithmic Bias in Criminal Justice: A Case of the COMPAS Risk Assessment Tool*

An infamous global example where bias was prevalent is in the criminal justice system tool. Here, a risk assessment tool named ‘COMPAS’ was used in the US courts to predict the likelihood of recidivism. The tool, however, consistently overestimated and labelled Black defendants with “high risk” profiles as offenders but labelled the white defendants as lower risk offenders (Angwin et al., 2016). This clearly illustrates the idea of false positives and false negatives that is often noted in AI systems, highlighting existing racial equities, and reinforcing prior suggestions that fairness criteria cannot be fully satisfied simultaneously in practice. The root cause of the issue is in the training data employed to design the system, one which most likely has been influenced by discriminatory policies existing within the practice.

**Expected Fairness Response**

This case suggests the need for a deep system evaluation to minimize the risk of false positives and false negatives such that error rates are balanced across groups. This must be combined with stronger transparency and explainability measures, like independent auditing and adopting a fairness-aware risk assessment tool.

### *2.4.5 Recruitment and Hiring: Amazon's Abandoned AI Recruitment Tool*

Bias in recruitment algorithms highlights how organizational histories shape algorithmic behaviour. Between 2014 and 2017, Amazon developed an AI-driven recruitment tool intended to streamline candidate selection. However, the system quickly revealed a bias against women, systematically downgrading resumes that included terms such as "women's" or those from women's colleges (Dastin, 2022). Amazon had to abandon the tool in 2018. The problem stemmed from the training datasets on which the system was trained, one historically dominated by male applicants in technical roles, thus encoding gendered hiring patterns. Despite several attempts to correct the bias, the project was ultimately abandoned, demonstrating the difficulty of retroactively de-biasing models once they are trained on skewed datasets.

This case highlights a critical lesson on past inequities. It also illustrates the dangers involved in applying ML to sensitive contexts, like recruitment, where anti-discrimination laws often impose strict obligations. Beyond reputational damage, such tools tend to expose organizations to legal risk and regulatory sanctions if used in a real-world scenario.

**Expected Fairness Response**

This case demonstrates the importance of pre-processing interventions such as dataset de-biasing and representativeness, as well as aligning recruitment algorithms with anti-discrimination frameworks that emphasize substantive equality. It is also a call that mitigation of bias must begin at the data collection and model design stages, and not after deployment.

### *2.4.6 Financial Services: The Apple Card Controversy*

In 2019, Apple and Goldman Sachs faced widespread criticism when reports surfaced that women were being offered significantly lower credit limits than men, despite having similar or even superior credit histories. The controversy escalated after software developer David Heinemeier Hansson reported that his credit limit was twenty times higher than his wife's, even though she had a better credit score (Kelion, 2019).

The algorithm powering the Apple Card operated as a "black box," leaving uncertainty about whether the disparity was due to direct gender discrimination or indirect proxies. Nevertheless, the public backlash prompted regulatory investigations and renewed calls for fairness audits and transparency in financial algorithms.

#### Expected Fairness Response

This case highlights the need for explainability in algorithms. It also reinforces that consumers have a right to receive information on how the algorithm provides the outcome. This will eliminate or minimize the black box effect.

### 2.4.7 *Failed Attempt from the Computer Vision Facial Recognition System*

Another case of bias was documented in a facial recognition system that reported a low risk rate of 1% for white men but a higher rate of 34% for black women (Buolamwini & Gebru, 2018; Raji et al., 2020). The bias stemmed from the data employed in training the system during its design stage, as it consisted of datasets with a small sample of women having dark skin. Cities in the US have objected to the use of face recognition by police, citing concerns about racial profiling and civil liberties breaches. IBM temporarily halted its facial recognition tools in response to this. These moves spurred others to expand their datasets and improve their evaluation processes.

#### Expected Fairness Response

This case highlights the importance of regulating high-risk biometric technologies to prevent biased surveillance and law enforcement systems, which can lead to unfair arrests and wrongful executions.

### 2.4.8 *Overall Implications*

Three key insights arose from the global examples mentioned above. These cases indicate that bias can occur throughout the system's lifespan, including data gathering, model training, and deployment. The consequences can include incorrect arrests and executions, reduced assessment risk, gender discrimination, and racial inequity. The advent of these cases calls for stronger measures in the areas of fairness, governance mechanisms, and legal interventions. Together, the cases reiterate that fairness is a multi-layered process. Hence, it needs interventions at the data, model, and institutional stages supported by legal and governance frameworks.

## 2.5 Approaches to Mitigate/Overcome Bias

An extensive review of literature shows evidence that machine bias can sometimes be difficult to detect. Notwithstanding this, a range of approaches (es) can be applied to mitigate its occurrence and reduce the likely harm it could cause. The strategies span technical approaches, institutional safeguards, and operational measures. The technical approach ranges from how the data are gathered to how models are designed. The institutional strategies cover how fairness can be integrated into governance and regulations. The operational approach includes organizational practices surrounding the AI deployment.

### *2.5.1 Technical Strategies*

As mentioned earlier, this will cover how the data are gathered and how the models are designed. In short, it will encompass the interventions within the AI design processes, covering the following stages:

(i) ***Pre-processing stages:*** The pre-processing is the critical first step involving adjusting datasets through rebalancing, reweighting, or generating synthetic samples to improve group representation (Mehrabi et al., 2021).
(ii) ***In-processing stage:*** This level is where fairness is embedded directly into training datasets. Take, for instance, modifying algorithms during training to reduce all processes of discrimination (Kamishima et al., 2012). Where these techniques are not feasible, post-processing methods can then be applied to the model predictions.
(iii) **Post-processing stage:** This involves modifying outcomes to meet fairness requirements (D'Alessandro et al., 2017) and adjusting predictions after training, such as equalized odds adjustments to balance error rates (Hardt et al., 2016).
(iv) **Explainability:** Interpretability tools such as SHAP and LIME may assist in detecting and addressing any hidden bias, support audits and accountability (Barocas et al., 2023).

### 2.5.2 Institutional and Governance Strategies

(i) **Auditing for fairness and assessing algorithmic impact:** As institutional practices involving independent fairness audits and algorithmic impact assessments (AIAs) gain traction around the globe, governance frameworks are increasingly mandating independent examinations of algorithms to detect discrimination (Raji et al., 2020). This is because these systems are like financial audits, even though they are designed to systematically uncover discriminatory effects. In practice, some jurisdictions, including the EU and Canada, have begun to require AIAs as part of their regulatory compliance regimes.

(ii) **Ethical guidelines and industry standards:** The OECD and the EU developed AI ethical principles with fairness, transparency, and accountability as core elements (European Commission, 2024; OECD, 2019). These recommendations serve to institutionalize fairness standards, transforming abstract ethical ideas into actionable organizational practices.

(iii) **Legal and regulatory frameworks:** Governments have a crucial role to play in reducing bias by establishing enforceable standards. For example, the proposed EU AI Act requires high-risk AI systems to demonstrate non-discrimination, human oversight, and transparency (European Commission, 2024). Similarly, anti-discrimination laws in the U.S. currently apply to algorithmic decision-making, though enforcement is still patchy (Barocas et al., 2023). Both examples show how the laws hold firms liable for biased algorithms.

### 2.5.3 Operational/Organizational Culture and Diversity in AI Development

Organizational behaviours can lead to bias, not just technological concerns. Increasing the diversity of development teams and fairness training can help mitigate bias during the design and deployment phases of an AI system (West et al., 2019). Furthermore, corporate training on fairness, equity, and ethics can improve internal governance.

In summary, while technical interventions combat bias at the computational level, institutional strategies ensure that fairness principles are incorporated in broader governance institutions. Importantly, these approaches should not be considered in isolation. It is noteworthy that pre-processing or post-processing changes may reduce short-term inequities. Yet, without systemic governance, such gains are likely to be transitory. Therefore, a comprehensive approach that embeds technology innovation, organizational responsibility, and regulatory enforcement remains the most effective path towards reducing algorithmic bias and achieving fairness (Table 2.1).

**Table 2.1** Summary of prominent bias and mitigation strategies

| Bias type | Description | Typical sources | Technological mitigation approaches |
|---|---|---|---|
| Historical bias | Structural inequalities were introduced into datasets before AI design | Financial histories, data policing, and legacy HR records | Representative sampling, data balancing, and reweighting |
| Measurement bias | Flawed proxies or inconsistent measurement of target variables | Using zip code as a proxy for socioeconomic status | Feature auditing, proxy detection tools, and feature reconstruction |
| Evaluation bias | Bias from unrepresentative datasets due to specific benchmarks in the system modelling | The system may appear accurate, yet it performs poorly on real-world subgroups | Having inclusive benchmark datasets, subgroup performance reporting, and fairness-aware metrics |
| Sampling bias | Training data not representative of the targeted population or favours a group over others (Sampling skewness/systemic exclusion) | Models fail on under-sampled demographic groups, limited geographies, etc. | Oversampling targeted population, synthetic data generation, and randomised or stratified sampling |
| Representation bias | Underrepresentation or overrepresentation of certain groups in training datasets | Misclassification of minority groups; unequal model accuracy | Diverse data sourcing, synthetic oversampling, data augmentation, and rebalancing |
| Observer/label bias | Human-generated labels reflect subjective or biased judgments | Performance ratings, toxicity labels, judicial risk labels | Consensus labelling, annotation guidelines, label noise reduction |
| Algorithmic/ machine learning bias | Bias from model architecture or optimisation is causing disparities | Trade-offs between accuracy and fairness, loss functions that prioritize accuracy over equity | Weighted Losses, equalised odds optimisation, and fairness-aware learning |
| Popularity bias | Models favour very popular groups | Recommender systems amplify already-visible items, marginalising others | Re-ranking methods, long-tail adjustments, and exposure fairness constraints |
| Interaction bias | User inputs or feedback loops shape biased model behaviour | Search autocomplete, chatbots, recommender systems | Reinforcement-learning constraints, guardrails, toxicity filters |

(continued)

**Table 2.1** (continued)

| Bias type | Description | Typical sources | Technological mitigation approaches |
|---|---|---|---|
| Proxy bias | Bias is introduced when neutral items correlate with sensitive features, like as a postal address being taken as a proxy for race | The model indirectly discriminates despite excluding sensitive features | Proxy detection tools, causal feature analysis, removing or adjusting proxy variables |
| Simpson's paradox bias | Patterns reverse when aggregated vs. disaggregated data are compared | A model appears fair overall, but is unfair for specific subgroups | Subgroup-level modelling, stratified evaluation, causal analysis |
| Deployment bias | Context of real-world use misaligns with model design | Using a model trained on one population for another | Domain adaptation, context-aware recalibration |

### 2.5.4 *Emerging Trends in Machine Bias and Fairness (Specific Focus on Generative AI and Deep Learning Systems)*

Recent advances in generative AI and deep learning have introduced an array of emerging issues that go beyond traditional supervised models (Afreen et al., 2025; Wei et al., 2025). The emergence of generative bias, in which harmful stereotypes ingrained in training models are replicated or amplified by large language models (LLMs), image generators, and multimodal systems, is a common trend. These models often have opaque data provenance, which makes bias accountability and tracing more difficult. The issue of distributional drift, in which generative systems change during continuous training or reinforcement learning and may eventually introduce new biases, is also highlighted by recent studies.

The shift toward fairness auditing for deep learning architectures, which includes stress-testing models across demographic subgroups, interpretability probes, and adversarial testing, is another notable development. Bias benchmarks designed for generative systems, such as stereotype leakage tests, prompt-sensitivity evaluations, and fairness evaluations under multi-turn conversational contexts, are becoming increasingly common among academic and industry leaders.

Another significant trend is the move toward post-deployment fairness monitoring, which recognizes that real-world usage patterns influence model behaviour just as much as pre-deployment training. The move supports the development of dynamic governance frameworks, including model cards, responsible scaling policies, and continuous impact assessments specifically designed for generative AI.

Collectively, these trends reinforce that fairness in contemporary AI is turning into a dynamic, lifecycle-wide challenge that calls for organizational, technical, and regulatory cooperation.

## 2.6 Suggested Integrative Pathways for Aligning Technical Innovation with Ethics, Laws, and Societal Fairness

Achieving overall fairness requires integrating technical design, corporate practice, legal compliance, and public accountability. The following practical pathways show how entities and government might integrate these threads.

(i) **Integrate the fairness principle from the start:** Embrace sound principles of fairness at the earlier stages of AI design; they ought not to be an afterthought. Endeavour to translate high-level ethical standards into measurable technical outcomes. For example, describe the fairness metric that is appropriate for the use case and incorporate it into data gathering and model development workflows. This avoids costly retrofits and ensures that design intent aligns with outcomes.

(ii) **Detailed and complete documentation and transparency**: Use standardized artefacts such as datasheets and model cards for models to document provenance, training demographics, subgroup performance, and known limitations. Documentation facilitates both internal governance and external examination, supporting legal defensibility and stakeholder trust and reliance.

(iii) **Risk-based governance and human oversight**: Group systems based on their level of impact, i.e., high, medium, or low. For high-risk systems, enforce algorithmic impact assessments (AIAs), human-in-the-loop checkpoints, and approval gates before deployment. This aligns with notable emerging regulatory expectations from the EU AI Act and GDPR standards and reduces the risk of legal scrutiny.

(iv) **Combining Institutional and Technical Mitigation:** Implementing technical fixes before, during, and after processing, alongside institutional controls such as fairness-aware training, subgroup testing, post-hoc calibration, independent audits, procurement clauses, and incident response procedures. A blended approach addresses bias throughout the lifecycle of the system developed rather than at a single point in time.

(v) **Independent audits and continuous monitoring processes**: Periodic external audits are required, as is real-time monitoring for any changes in the system that may spark uneven impacts. Combining an independent audit with technical examination ensures a thorough assessment of downstream repercussions and mitigation strategies. Note that continuous monitoring is essential as it will enable swift correction should new bias erupt.

(vi) **Legal alignment and contractual leverage:** It is important to ensure systems are designed and deployed in compliance with regulatory standards. Ensure strict adherence to contractual agreements. This will increase openness and reduce the danger of legal claims.

(vii) **Multidisciplinary teams and diverse perspectives:** It is important to set up functional teams of diverse backgrounds/expertise. Example: the teams should be composed of engineers, financial analysts, system developers, ethicists, domain specialists, and representatives from many stakeholder groups, including specialists and legal practitioners. Identifying normative trade-offs and contextual damages early in the system's lifecycle is crucial.

(viii) **Mechanism for Public Consultation and grievance reporting:** It is important to create a clear channel for users to raise questions and seek remedies for issues. Public participation should be encouraged through discussions and transparency reports. This aligns societal expectations with system actions, reducing regulatory sanctions.

(ix) **Aligning regulatory sandboxes and standards:** For this, create a prototype of the proposed system and test it for new interventions. Ensure the system closely adheres to regulatory requirements, as the suggested system will eventually be developed.

(x) **Capacity building and accountability measures:** It's important to engage in training and retraining for all staff and teams involved in system design. Also, incorporate fairness into key performance indicators (KPIs) for executive reporting and link them to performance incentives to ensure accountability.

Embedding these components helps firms connect AI systems with ethical norms, regulatory expectations, and social values.

## 2.7 Conclusion

AI technologies can alter companies and communities by increasing efficiency and developing new insights. However, there are issues, such as machine bias, which affect both individuals and communities. The chapter presented real-life examples that have been reported globally, demonstrating that unchecked bias reinforces existing inequities and creates new forms of discrimination, often under the guise of objectivity.

Furthermore, the chapter reinforces that fairness and discrimination are central to understanding and mitigating any form of machine bias. Although fairness is noted as a multifaceted concept that cannot be assigned a universal definition. Nonetheless, it is crucial to employ approach(es) that entails ethical reasoning and governance structures. In addition, it highlights that businesses and organizations have a responsibility for adopting robust technical strategies, and as such, they must take cognisance of pre-, in-, and post-processing techniques. This will afford them the room to ensure their operational strategies integrate a combination of transparency, accountability, and stakeholder engagement. Governance systems, on the other hand, must consider monitoring methods, feedback loops, and continual training because these are critical components for integrating justice throughout the AI system's life cycle.

In short, machine bias reflects existing societal disparities that have been incorporated in data and decision-making systems throughout their existence. To combat it, however, a multifaceted approach is required, involving technical solutions, ethical measures, regulatory requirements, and organizational reforms. Businesses and legislators may ensure that AI systems serve as tools for fairness as well as ones that amplify discrimination by understanding the roots of bias, creating governance processes, and supporting inclusive practices. The future of AI can be more consistent with the values of justice, equity, and social responsibility.

## 2.8 Findings, Limitations, and Future Research Agenda

### *2.8.1 Summary of Findings*

While this chapter specifically anchors AI machine bias and fairness, below we provide a summary of the dominant themes that the chapter reveals based on the review conducted.

(i) The findings revealed that an AI system may have bias inherent in it from the datasets on which it was trained, and this could lead to predictive disparities in domains like healthcare, financial services, criminal justice, and possibly automated hiring systems in organisations. Hence, it is crucial to note that bias arises due to a combination of the technical design chosen and broader organisational and societal contexts. In a nutshell, these patterns are reflective of the fact that bias is not just a systemic issue but could be accidental, pointing towards underlying structural disparities and demographic differences already embedded within a system.

(ii) Fairness is multi-dimensional as it could entail individual, group, and procedural fairness suited to different contexts. It is therefore crucial to understand that no single AI model can suit all fairness criteria simultaneously. Hence, context-driven trade-offs are necessary.

(iii) A pipeline of strategies is needed to achieve an effective mitigation of bias in AI systems, including at different stages like the pre-processing data preparation stage, model training stage, designing the system, and post-processing stage. Hybrid strategies are still the best practice recommended.

(iv) Fairness is largely shaped by organisational structures like audit trails, documentation, compliance processes, and cross-functional oversight requiring managerial intervention and not merely technical concerns.

(v) Fairness issues differ across settings, with some regions facing challenges such as limited data availability, a fragmented regulatory system exacerbating local inequities, and imported AI models trained on populations outside of the local context, hence, not reflecting context-specific issues.
(vi) Recent contemporary evidence reinforces that new harms posed by AI systems, including identity distortion, representational damage, and stereotype amplification, create new challenges for auditing and fairness assessment.

## 2.8.2 Limitations and Future Research Agenda

While that research on machine bias and fairness has advanced rapidly, significant voids remain in current discourse. First, there is a dearth of literature from the domains of business and finance, causing inconsistent definitions of fairness, limited comparability across studies, and restricted applicability of findings to real organizational settings. Second, most extant literatures focus on model-level bias, giving less attention to upstream drivers like institutional incentives, governance structures, and organisational influence. Third, most of the existing research is based on datasets from developed nations like Europe and North America, which has left a huge gap for developing nations that are often characterised by infrastructural constraints, uneven technological divide, fragmented institutions, and other socio-cultural dynamics that drive bias impact differently. Lastly, research on generative AI fairness and auditing frameworks, particularly in deep learning, is still evolving with limited validation at the organisational level.

These limitations call for a future research agenda on cross-disciplinary frameworks that embed organisational, legal, and technical perspectives, increased empirical discourse in developing contexts, industry-specific assessments of fairness auditing tools, and longitudinal studies on the sociotechnical effects of bias mitigation techniques.

Given this, the study implications are of multiple folds. For research, the chapter requires researchers to develop context-sensitive bias mitigation measures, standardize fairness metrics, and assess interventions across sectors. It is recommended that regulatory authorities support sectoral fairness audits tailored to varying regional capacities, transparency standards, and documentation requirements. Furthermore, to guarantee that fairness principles are incorporated into operational decision-making, organizations require more transparent governance structures, continuous monitoring systems, and ethical training.

## References

Amini, A., Goldstein, T., & Tsiatas, A. (2019). Funding bias in machine learning: How incentives shape algorithmic outcomes. *Journal of Artificial Intelligence Research, 66*, 789–810.

Afreen, J., Mohaghegh, M., & Doborjeh, M. (2025). Systematic literature review on bias mitigation in generative AI. *AI and Ethics, 5*(5), 4789–4841. https://doi.org/10.1007/s43681-025-00721-9

Angwin, J., Larson, J., Mattu, S., & Kirchner, L. (2016). *Machine bias risk assessments in criminal sentencing.* ProPublica. https://www.propublica.org/article/machine-bias-risk-assessments-in-criminal-sentencing?

Baeza-Yates, R. (2018). Bias on the web. *Communications of the ACM, 61*(6), 54–61. https://doi.org/10.1145/3209581

Barocas, S., & Selbst, A. (2016). Big data's disparate impact. *California Law Review, 104*(3), 671–732. https://doi.org/10.2139/ssrn.2477899

Barocas, S., Hardt, M., & Narayanan, A. (2023). *Fairness and machine learning—Limitations and opportunities.* MIT Press. https://books.google.com/books?hl=en&lr=&id=HuGwEAAAQBAJ&oi=fnd&pg=PR9&dq=Fairness+and+machine+learning.&ots=Q0ggIyd7na&sig=kF36lPM-mUFtfV-D6hrnCgdf1Dc

Bartlett, R., Morse, A., Stanton, R., & Wallace, N. (2022). Consumer-lending discrimination in the FinTech Era. *Journal of Financial Economics, 143*(1), 30–56. https://doi.org/10.1016/j.jfineco.2021.05.047

Berk, R., Heidari, H., Jabbari, S., Kearns, M., & Roth, A. (2021). Fairness in criminal justice risk assessments: The state of the art. *Sociological Methods and Research, 50*(1), 3–44. https://doi.org/10.1177/0049124118782533

Bickel, P. J., Hammel, E. A., & O'Connell, J. W. (1975). Sex bias in graduate admissions: Data from Berkeley. *Science, 187*(4175), 398–404. https://doi.org/10.1126/science.187.4175.398

Buolamwini, J., & Gebru, T. (2018). Gender shades: Intersectional accuracy disparities in commercial gender classification. *Proceedings of Machine Learning Research, 81*, 77–91. http://proceedings.mlr.press/v81/buolamwini18a.html?mod=article_inline&ref=akusion-ci-shi-dai-bizinesumedeia

D'Alessandro, B., O'Neil, C., & Lagatta, T. (2017). Conscientious classification: A data scientist's guide to discrimination-aware classification. *Big Data, 5*(2), 120–134. https://doi.org/10.1089/big.2016.0048

Dastin, J. (2022). Amazon scraps secret AI recruiting tool that showed bias against women*. In *Ethics of data and analytics* (pp. 296–299). https://doi.org/10.1201/9781003278290-44

Dressel, J., & Farid, H. (2018). The accuracy, fairness, and limits of predicting recidivism. *Science Advances, 4*(1), eaao5580. https://doi.org/10.1126/sciadv.aao5580

European Commission. (2024). *Proposal for a regulation laying down harmonised rules on artificial intelligence* (Vol. 0106). https://eur-lex.europa.eu/legal-content/EN/TXT/?uri=CELEX%3A52021PC0206

European Union. (2018). General data protection regulation (GDPR). Regulation (EU) 2016/679 of the European Parliament and of the Council. In the *European Union.* https://gdpr.eu/tag/gdpr/

Fletcher, R. R., Nakeshimana, A., & Olubeko, O. (2021). Addressing fairness, bias, and appropriate use of artificial intelligence and machine learning in global health. *Frontiers in Artificial Intelligence, 3*, Article 561802. https://doi.org/10.3389/frai.2020.561802

Friedler, S. A., Scheidegger, C., & Venkatasubramanian, S. (2021). The (im)possibility of fairness. *Communications of the ACM, 64*(4), 136–143. https://doi.org/10.1145/3433949

Funda, V. (2025). A systematic review of algorithm auditing processes to assess bias and risks in AI systems. *Journal of Infrastructure, Policy and Development, 9*(2), 11489. https://doi.org/10.24294/jipd11489

Garvie, C., & Moy, L. M. (2019). *America under watch: Face surveillance in the United States.* Georgetown Law Center on Privacy and Technology. https://www.law.georgetown.edu/privacy-technology-center/publications/america-under-watch-face-surveillance-in-the-united-states/

González-Sendino, R., Serrano, E., Bajo, J., & Novais, P. (2024). A review of bias and fairness in artificial intelligence. *International Journal of Interactive Multimedia and Artificial Intelligence, 9*(1), 5–17. https://doi.org/10.9781/ijimai.2023.11.001

Hardt, M., Price, E., & Srebro, N. (2016). Equality of opportunity in supervised learning. *Advances in neural information processing systems*, 3323–3331. https://proceedings.neurips.cc/paper/2016/hash/9d2682367c3935defcb1f9e247a97c0d-Abstract.html

ICO-Information Commisioner's Office. (2023). *What about fairness, bias and discrimination?* https://ico.org.uk/for-organisations/uk-gdpr-guidance-and-resources/artificial-intelligence/guidance-on-ai-and-data-protection/how-do-we-ensure-fairness-in-ai/what-about-fairness-bias-and-discrimination/

Kamishima, T., Akaho, S., Asoh, H., & Sakuma, J. (2012). Fairness-aware classifier with prejudice remover regularizer. *Lecture notes in computer science (Including subseries lecture notes in artificial intelligence and lecture notes in bioinformatics), 7524 LNAI*(PART 2), 35–50. https://doi.org/10.1007/978-3-642-33486-3_3

Kelion, L. (2019). Apple's "sexist" credit card investigated by US regulater. *BBC News, November*, 1–12. https://www.bbc.com/news/business-50365609

Larson J., Mattu S., Kirchner L., & Angwin J. (2016). How we analyzed the COMPAS recidivism algorithm. *ProPublica*, 1–16. https://www.propublica.org/article/how-we-analyzed-the-compas-recidivism-algorithm

Mehrabi, N., Morstatter, F., Saxena, N., Lerman, K., & Galstyan, A. (2021). A survey on bias and fairness in machine learning. *ACM Computing Surveys (CSUR), 54*(6), 1–35. https://doi.org/10.1145/3457607

Mitchell, M., Wu, S., Zaldivar, A., Barnes, P., Vasserman, L., Hutchinson, B., Spitzer, E., Raji, I. D., & Gebru, T. (2019). Model cards for model reporting. *Proceedings of the 2019 conference on fairness, accountability, and transparency (FAccT)* (pp. 220–229). https://doi.org/10.1145/3287560.3287596

Mitchell, S., Potash, E., Barocas, S., D'Amour, A., & Lum, K. (2021). Algorithmic fairness: Choices, assumptions, and definitions. In *Annual review of statistics and its application* (Vol. 8, pp. 141–163). Annual Reviews Inc. https://doi.org/10.1146/annurev-statistics-042720-125902

Noble, S. U. (2020). Algorithms of oppression: how search engines reinforce racism. In *Algorithms of oppression.* New York University Press. https://doi.org/10.18574/nyu/9781479833641.001.0001

Obermeyer, Z., Powers, B., Vogeli, C., & Mullainathan, S. (2019). Dissecting racial bias in an algorithm used to manage the health of populations. *Science, 366*(6464), 447–453. https://doi.org/10.1126/science.aax2342

OECD—Organisation for Economic Cooperation and Development. (2019). What are the OECD principles on AI? In *OECD observer* (Issue March). https://doi.org/10.1787/6ff2a1c4-en

Pham, N., Pham Ngoc, H., & Nguyen-Duc, A. (2025). Fairness for machine learning software in education: A systematic mapping study. *Journal of Systems and Software, 219*, Article 112244. https://doi.org/10.1016/j.jss.2024.112244

Popejoy, A. B., & Fullerton, S. M. (2016). Genomics is failing on diversity. In *Nature* (Vol. 538, Issue 7624, pp. 161–164). Nature Publishing Group. https://doi.org/10.1038/538161A;SUBJMETA

Prates, M. O. R., Avelar, P. H., & Lamb, L. C. (2020). Assessing gender bias in machine translation: A case study with Google Translate. *Neural Computing and Applications, 32*(10), 6363–6381. https://doi.org/10.1007/s00521-019-04144-6

Raji, I. D., Gebru, T., Mitchell, M., Buolamwini, J., Lee, J., & Denton, E. (2020). Saving face: Investigating the ethical concerns of facial recognition auditing. In *AIES 2020—Proceedings of the AAAI/ACM conference on AI, ethics, and society* (Vol. 7, pp. 145–151). https://doi.org/10.1145/3375627.3375820

Richardson, R., Schultz, J. M., & Crawford, K. (2019). Dirty data, bad predictions: How civil rights violations impact predictive policing systems. *New York University Law Review, 94*(15), 192–233.

Sirugo, G., Williams, S. M., & Tishkoff, S. A. (2019). The missing diversity in human genetic studies. *Cell, 177*(1), 26–31. https://doi.org/10.1016/j.cell.2019.02.048

Suresh, H., & Guttag, J. (2021). A framework for understanding sources of harm throughout the machine learning life cycle. *ACM International Conference Proceeding Series*. https://doi.org/10.1145/3465416.3483305

Ueda, D., Kakinuma, T., Fujita, S., Kamagata, K., Fushimi, Y., Ito, R., Matsui, Y., Nozaki, T., Nakaura, T., Fujima, N., Tatsugami, F., Yanagawa, M., Hirata, K., Yamada, A., Tsuboyama, T., Kawamura, M., Fujioka, T., & Naganawa, S. (2024). Fairness of artificial intelligence in healthcare: Review and recommendations. *Japanese Journal of Radiology, 42*(1), 3–15. https://doi.org/10.1007/s11604-023-01474-3

UNESCO-United Nations Educational Scientific and Cultural Organization. (2021). Recommendation on the ethics of artificial intelligence. In *UNESCO*. https://doi.org/10.1093/oso/9780190905033.001.0001

Verma, S., & Rubin, J. (2018). Fairness definitions explained. *Proceedings of the International Workshop on Software Fairness*. https://doi.org/10.1145/3194770.3194776

Wachter, S., Mittelstadt, B., & Russell, C. (2021). Why fairness cannot be automated: Bridging the gap between EU non-discrimination law and AI. *Computer Law and Security Review, 41*, Article 105567. https://doi.org/10.1016/j.clsr.2021.105567

Wei, X., Kumar, N., & Zhang, H. (2025). Addressing bias in generative AI: Challenges and research opportunities in information management. *Information and Management, 62*(2), Article 104103. https://doi.org/10.1016/j.im.2025.104103

West, S. M., Whittaker, M., & Crawford, K. (2019). Discriminating systems. In *AI now institute* (Issue April). https://ainowinstitute.org/wp-content/uploads/2023/04/discriminatingsystems.pdf

Zhang, M. (2015). *Google photos tags two African–Americans As gorillas through facial recognition software*. Forbes. https://www.forbes.com/sites/mzhang/2015/07/01/google-photos-tags-two-african-americans-as-gorillas-through-facial-recognition-software/

# Chapter 3
# Transparency and Explainability in AI Governance

**Mohammed Kayode Ajape**

**Abstract** Artificial Intelligence has arrived to stay, and users cannot overstate its pervasiveness in nearly all facets of life. The growing disruptive ability of AI and the ambiguity/complexity shrouding its models have become a concern to individual users, corporate bodies, regulators, and the broader society, especially in high-risk AI-engineered decision-making scenarios. Using an exploratory research design, this chapter examines the concepts of "Transparency" and "Explainability" and how stakeholder, agency, and institutional theories underpin their discussions in the context of AI governance. By reviewing recent empirical literature and web-based articles, the chapter also explores the concept of black-box AI and its implications for businesses. The focus then shifts to overcoming the challenges of black-box AI through Explainable AI (XAI), exploring its principles, challenges, and regulatory requirements for transparency, such as GDPR's "right to explanation". Finally, the chapter explains how businesses can strike a balance between AI performance and explainability through governance.

## 3.1 Introduction

Artificial Intelligence (AI) has been rapidly adopted globally across various industries and spheres, serving diverse purposes and ushering in an era of unparalleled operational efficiency and top-notch innovation. AI pervasiveness ranges from its application in the recruitment/hiring process (Horodyski, 2023; Sykorova et al., 2024), finance (Ajape & Adegbayibi, 2025; Bahoo et al., 2024), taxation processes (Adegbayibi & Ajape, 2025; IMF, 2021), healthcare (Bajwa et al., 2021; Olawade et al., 2024), accounting (Bao et al., 2020), criminal justice (Hunter, Bagaric & Stobbs, 2020; Situmeang et al., 2024), actuarial work (Kessler, 2020; Shaw, 2023), and to public administration (Taylor et al., 2024). This increasing global relevance of AI in society makes the demand for transparency and explainability of AI constituents and

M. K. Ajape (✉)
Department of Accountancy, College of Business and Economics, University of Johannesburg, Johannesburg, South Africa
e-mail: majape@uj.ac.za; moajape@gmail.com



M. Adelowotan and H. Coovadia (eds.), *AI and Accountability*, CSR, Sustainability, Ethics & Governance, https://doi.org/10.1007/978-3-032-20091-4_3

effects more alluring and deserving of academic and policymakers' attention (Cheng, 2024). Based on this, the need for transparency and explainability has evolved as a cornerstone of responsible AI use and governance. The essence of these two concepts lies in fostering trust, safeguarding accountability, and adhering to legal and ethical standards.

Despite the many visible advantages and opportunities AI has brought to revolutionize the economic landscape of the world, the "black-box" nature of many advanced AI models, such as the ensemble methods, which combine multiple models, and the complex machine learning (ML) systems like deep neural networks, has raised significant concerns (Papadouli, 2023). These systems pose notable risks to fairness, accountability, safety, and trust since their developers cannot easily trace/track the path from input to output. Studies have explored the general role of AI in various aspects of human endeavors, including criminal justice, healthcare, and hiring practices (Raub, 2019; Situmeang et al., 2024). While Seger et al. (2023) explored how AI could be democratized, Pérez-Cruz (2025) expounds on how regulators can address explainability issues in AI. However, the opaque nature of most AI systems has heightened stakeholders' demand for responsible development and use of AI (Lund et al., 2025). Furthermore, previous studies on AI transparency and explainability (Lund et al., 2025; Nannini et al., 2023; Pérez-Cruz et al., 2025) have not grounded their discussion in any established theoretical framework. These voids in the literature form the crux of this chapter.

Therefore, this chapter conceptually explores transparency and explainability to posit that the two terms are not merely technical challenges in the AI governance process but are foundational pillars. Specifically, the chapter adopts a multi-theoretical approach to situate the discussion. Furthermore, it examines the implications of black-box AI for businesses, the principles and techniques of explainable AI, the evolving regulatory landscape, and how organisations can strategically balance performance with transparency and explainability through robust governance frameworks.

## 3.2 Methodology

In this chapter, a conceptual/exploratory research design has been adopted, as the goal is to conceptually explore the emerging discourse and develop a theoretical understanding of black box AI, ultimately leading to a demand for transparency and explainability in AI governance. Similar studies, such as those by Nannini et al. (2023) and Batool et al. (2025), have employed a conceptual review, as it enables researchers to integrate a wide range of empirical findings, policy documents, and industry practices into a synthesized framework. It also offers the required depth to map key concepts and propose governance-aligned interpretations (Cheong, 2024; Lund et al., 2025).

The review draws on three strands of secondary sources, including peer-reviewed empirical studies conducted on AI transparency and explainability in human resource, finance, and healthcare (Felzmann et al., 2020; Raub, 2019), policy, standards, and legislation inculcating institutional requirements and best practices (such as EU AI Act, OECD principles, National Artificial Intelligence Strategy (NAIS), IEEE P7001), and reputable web-based articles and reports that summarise trending regulatory trajectories and sectoral practices (Cheong, 2024; Pérez-Cruz et al., 2025). The consulted articles are included based on their relevance to the discussion of the subject matter and span the years 2017–2025 (except where a historical trend of an issue is being traced). Additionally, studies that offer robust theoretical explanations or empirical evidence on transparency and explainability were prioritized. Accordingly, having reviewed and compared definitions on the principles embedded in transparency and explainability, stakeholder, agency, and institutional theories were applied, allowing for the integration of multiple perspectives and strengthening of the theoretical ground. The approach in the chapter is non-empirical, requiring no primary data; therefore, no human subjects were involved in the study, while all sources were duly acknowledged. This approach, however, is limited by its reliance on published literature and the potential bias of web-based sources.

## 3.3 Theoretical Framework

To properly situate the discussion of transparency and explainability, this chapter employed three theories. These theories are stakeholder theory, agency theory, and institutional theory. Each of these theories is briefly explained and linked to the discourse of AI transparency and explainability.

### *3.3.1 Stakeholder Theory*

The development of stakeholder theory is credited to Freeman (1984). The theory proposes that, beyond the real shareholders/owners, a corporation has reporting duties to a broader group of stakeholders, including the management, customers, employees, local community, suppliers, and the government. In short, stakeholders are those who are affected or will be affected by the organizational achievement of its objectives. Within the AI governance structure, therefore, the relevant stakeholders are developers, regulators, end-users, and society at large. The significance of this theory lies in the fact that organisations should be managed for the benefit of all, not just some. Firms used transparency and explainability to gain trust and legitimacy, suggesting that an AI governance framework should incorporate multi-stakeholder engagement. In contrast, AI labs should tailor explainability attributes to diverse user needs.

However, Bridoux and Stoelhorst (2022) and Harrison et al. (2021) have criticized the theory for the practicality of balancing the diverse interests of different stakeholders and the possibility that managers could use the theory as a vague public relations tool rather than a utilitarian governance framework. For Bridoux and Stoelhorst (2022), the quest for Transparency by AI users may cause conflicts with a company's need to maintain trade secrets. In addition, Harrison et al. (2021) found that most AI labs lack a formal procedure for integrating stakeholder feedback into AI ethics. Stakeholder theory has proven relevant in the discourse on AI governance. It explains the "why" for transparency and explainability—two concepts that organisations should view as moral obligations rather than technical jargon.

### *3.3.2 Agency Theory*

Jensen and Meckling (1976) proposed agency theory, which examines the relationship between a principal (such as an AI investor, user, or regulator) and an agent (e.g., a manager or an AI system) who makes decisions on behalf of the principal. The theory proposes that the principal-agent relationship often leads to agency costs because of the self-serving nature of the agents, who may not act in the best interest of the principal. Within the AI governance system, AI developers serve as agents, while users are the principals. Hence, the need for users (principal) to monitor the agent (AI developers/firms) necessitates the incurrence of agency costs to realign agent incentives with those of the principal. Langer and König (2023) argued that the black-box notion is a significant agency cost as the AI vagueness increases principals' (users, regulators) monitoring costs. The theory has been criticized for upholding a distrustful view of human behaviour, which overlooks the possibility of ethical behaviour and the demonstration of professionalism. Thus, a purely inducement-based approach can destabilize confidence and fail to address systemic risks (Felzmann et al., 2020). Agency theory addresses the "what" and "how" questions related to transparency and explainable AI (XAI) problems. The theory posits that transparency can reduce information asymmetry by making the algorithmic decision-making detectible, while explainability enables users to evaluate the outcomes of AI systems. Sunny's (2025) study revealed that interactive and clear explanations significantly enhance user confidence and accountability in AI systems. Therefore, designers of AI systems should implement mechanisms such as audit trails, interpretable models, and governance dashboards to moderate agency risks.

### *3.3.3 Institutional Theory*

This theory was propounded by DiMaggio and Powell (1983). The institutional theory emphasizes how technical efficiency, formal rules, external factors, and standards influence an organization's structure and operations. DiMaggio and Powell

(1983) discussed three institutional isomorphisms: coercive (resulting from regulations), mimetic (involving copying others due to uncertainty), and normative (stemming from professional standards). The theory calls for institutionalizing transparency and explainability as compliance requirements in AI governance. The enactment of the OECD principles, the EU AI Act, and the NIST Risk Management Framework is therefore an institutional arrangement that embeds transparency and explainability through regulatory compliance, stakeholder-driven governance, and industry best practices. However, there is a concern that AI firms may create a symbolic gesture of transparency to gain legitimacy while neglecting the real influence on AI development (Wamba-Taguimdje et al., 2020). Moreover, the tech industry may face a stifling innovative approach to governance due to the bandwagon effect, where every firm adopts a similar-looking "Transparency Reports" (O'Shaughnessy et al., 2023), creating a culture of "checkbox-compliance" among firms rather than driving meaningful explainability.

The theory examines the drivers of AI labs' adoption of transparency measures, regardless of the primary effect on stakeholder welfare or reduction of agency costs, and how transparency efforts of tech firms may be superfluous, designed only to achieve external recognition rather than pursue internal governance efficacy. In effect, following the coercive isomorphism, firms implement XAI to comply with regulations such as those of the Securities and Exchange Commission or the EU AI Act. In line with normative isomorphism, AI companies may employ the services of experts to establish "internal review boards" to comply with the expected industry norm. Startup AI labs may adopt/imitate a similar framework/AI policy, as some established firms or successful competitors (e.g., Google, Microsoft) already do.

In summary, the three theories collectively provide a suitable basis for a comprehensive evaluation of the concepts of transparency and explainability. The stakeholder theory establishes the moral foundation that AI users or regulators have a legitimate right to understand how an AI system affects their lives. Agency theory revolves around the challenges of information asymmetry and incentive misalignment between AI creators/AI systems and users. Thus, it positions transparency and explainability as a practical monitoring and control mechanism to reduce agency costs. The institutional theory explains the factors (such as regulatory, social, and competitive) that push AI creators to adopt transparency practices. The theories offered a complementary lens that directs the attention of AI designers to whom they are accountable (stakeholder theory), what problems they are to solve (agency theory), and why they need to be transparent (institutional theory).

## 3.4 Black-Box AI

Understanding and implementing the concepts of "Transparency" and "explainability" in AI governance have become increasingly essential due to the notion of "black-box AI". The term black-box AI often applies to complex AI models (such as machine learning, deep neural networks (DNNs), and complex ensemble models), which make crucial decisions but are overtly difficult to interpret even by their developers. It is a term used to describe the mystery surrounding the inner workings of, and the immense scale and complexity of, weight assignments in AI systems, which are opaque and extremely difficult for humans to comprehend. Entrusting essential life-changing decisions, such as the early detection of terminal disease or AI-enabled military drones, to a black-box model underscores the need for AI algorithms to be transparent and explainable in their decision-making processes (Hassija et al., 2021; Xu & Shuttleworth, 2024). Most advanced AI models, such as Meta's Llama and OpenAI's ChatGPT, are black box AIs trained on vast datasets via complex deep learning processes, and even their creators do not fully understand how they work (Kosinski, 2024). This superior predictive ability of AI, however, poses a significant risk to businesses, including the potential to conceal cybersecurity vulnerabilities, exhibit bias, and lead to privacy violations. These risks extend beyond operational risk to compliance, ethical, and reputational spheres.

### 3.4.1 Operational Risks

The operational dimension of AI risk involves financial loss and safety concerns. In high-risk spheres such as medical diagnostics and autonomous vehicles, biased AI decisions or the inability to comprehend specific models can pose a significant safety risk and result in substantial financial loss.

### 3.4.2 Reputational Risks

Risks from an unexpected AI outcome could lead to serious reputational issues arising from eroded public trust. Where an AI recruiting tool discriminates against a specific gender, location, or age bracket, or when AI opaque iteration flags trustworthy clients as fraudsters, the corporate image may suffer as the organization faces a loss of potential high-talent candidates and consumer trust (Felzmann et al., 2020).

### 3.4.3 Legal Risks

High-risk AI models pose significant compliance and legal challenges. Non-compliance with regulations such as the EU AI Act and the requirements embedded in the "right to explanation" contained in the EU's General Data Protection Regulation (GDPR) can lead to severe penalties. For instance, under the GDPR, non-compliant organizations risk paying fines of up to 4% of their global turnover and other legal penalties (Goodman & Flaxman, 2017).

### 3.4.4 Ethical Risks

These relate to a lack of accountability and fairness in AI decision-making, which can undermine public trust. For example, in credit limit evaluation, an AI's decision, which may be gender-biased or regionally biased, constitutes an ethical challenge that can erode public trust.

Two primary reasons have been advanced for the existence of black box AI models—one is deliberate, while the other is inadvertently inherent. According to Kosinski (2024) and Xu and Shuttleworth (2024), the first is described as a proactive measure. In this situation, AI programmers deliberately conceal the inner workings of AI tools before releasing them to the public, perhaps to protect intellectual property and maintain a competitive edge. A good example of intentional opaque AI includes fraud detection AI systems, risk assessment tools in finance, and algorithms used by social media platforms. The second, described as inadvertent, is also referred to as "organic black boxes," where AI systems inherently but inadvertently obscure their operations due to the systems' technical complexity. Examples of these organically opaque AI systems include advanced ensemble models that combine multiple models, Natural Language Processing (NLP) models like ChatGPT, and deep neural networks (such as one used for image recognition).

One central imperative for the advent of XAI is to unpack the mystery called the "black-box" and turn it into a "white-box" so that the workings of AI models are interpretable and their decisions more understandable to both developers and end-users. Consequently, XIA employed key principles such as dependability (faithful representation of the AI systems' reasoning process), comprehensibility (being meaningful to the target audience), and context-awareness (being relevant to a specific area and use case).

## 3.5 Transparency

Transparency in AI refers to the openness and accessibility of information about how AI systems are designed, trained, and deployed. It encompasses the disclosure of data sources, algorithmic logic, decision-making processes, and governance structures. Transparency is foundational for accountability, trust, and public oversight in AI governance. "Calls for transparency in AI systems often require seeing into various aspects of equipment and the mechanisms of the device with which human beings interact, thereby providing greater scope to consciously understand or deliberate on the constitution or effects of those systems" (Zednik, 2021). Andrada et al. (2023) contend that Transparency in AI systems encompasses such issues as algorithmic transparency, openness to discussion of AI-embedded decisions, and their explainability. Consequently, "Transparency" enables stakeholders (AI developers, users, and regulators) to understand how AI systems make decisions that affect their lives, while accountability guarantees that there are clear procedures for allocating responsibility and delivering reparation when these systems cause harm (Cheng, 2024).

Transparency refers to the openness and clarity of an AI system's entire lifecycle. It is a broader, systemic property that encompasses:

### 3.5.1 Process/Information Transparency

Disclosure of the development process, data sources, algorithms, and governance steps.

### 3.5.2 Model Transparency

The degree to which a model's internal mechanics are accessible and understandable. A linear regression model is considered inherently transparent ("glass-box"), while a deep neural network is not.

### 3.5.3 Operational Transparency

Clarity about the system's capabilities, limitations, and its role in decision-making processes.

Ingrams and Klievink (2022) argue that transparency is not a monolithic concept but rather a multifaceted one that varies depending on institutional context and stakeholder needs. They identify four approaches to transparency: constructivist, democratization, legal, and capacity-building, each offering different instruments and implications for governance. Each approach reflects a different normative and practical orientation toward achieving Transparency in AI systems.

The **constructivist approach** focuses on how different stakeholders—developers, users, regulators, and deployers—interpret and enact transparency within their respective contexts. This means that AI transparency is not a fixed attribute, but rather a socially constructed concept resulting from interactions between stakeholders. Andrada et al. (2023) identified two distinct facets of transparency: the "seeing into", described as "reflective transparency", and "seeing through", described as "transparency-in-use".

The reflective transparency has three (3) taxonomies, including:

(a) Information Transparency: This refers to the disclosure of information about an AI system to support judgments regarding the system's fairness, trustworthiness, safety, efficacy, accountability, and compliance with regulatory and legislative frameworks. The targeted information includes the nature of the algorithms and the kind of data used in a training program. Thus, this type of transparency involves access to data, algorithms, and decision-making processes by relevant stakeholders, depending on their individual requirements.

(b) Material Transparency: The digital nature of AI systems might make stakeholders forget about their materiality. This subtype of transparency concerns aspects of AI systems that are opaque and are independent of the algorithms, information processing systems, or data captured. It includes understanding the materiality of the production process of physical (hardware), maintenance requirements, labour relations, energy consumption, carbon emission, and environmental costs/impacts of AI systems.

(c) Transformational Transparency: This addresses the awareness of how AI changes user behavior and cognitive capacities due to the pervasive use of AI technology. The changes in behaviour may range from overreliance, a feeling of "capacity loss", reduced "intellectual autonomy", to potential "memory dependencies" resulting in low cognitive abilities, "loss of selfhood", and ultimately, "employability status" of the AI system users.

(d) Transparency-in-Use: The seamless integration of AI into user experience, where the system becomes "invisible" during use.

This approach suggests that transparency should be tailored to specific contexts and user needs, acknowledging that different stakeholders require varying types of information to comprehend AI systems.

The **democratization approach** accentuates wide-ranging governance, public engagement, and the redistribution of power in AI development and implementation. Thus, the democratization method concerns making AI systems accessible, accountable, and participatory. According to Taylor et al. (2024), the democratization of AI is a decisive step toward promoting trust, equity, and objectivity within our societies. As such, maximum feasible participation in AI-enabled technologies is necessary to mitigate social inequalities and foster public confidence in governance. They emphasized participatory design, citizen engagement, and equitable access to AI technologies. The target of democratization, therefore, is to align transparency with democratic values by empowering the public to understand better, query, and exert some influence on AI systems.

Further, Seger et al. (2023) provide a robust definition of AI democratization by identifying its four (4) dimensions—use, development, profits, and governance.

(a) democratization of AI use: This concerns efforts to make AI easily built, acquired/accessed, operated, and more beneficial to a large portion of the public. Such benefits may include AI's entertainment value, its application in the health and wellbeing domain, improved productivity, and other utility functions (writing code, analysing data, creating art). Since access to these benefits may come at a price (either through purchase or a paid subscription), the primary motive for democratizing AI use is to ensure that effective AI integration into workstreams can translate into monetary gains. Democratisation may also play an "equalising role" by providing access to certain services that were previously difficult due to geographical, transportation, or financial constraints. However, the broader availability of AI may be undesirable if the resultant risks outweigh the targeted benefits. For example, while an AI-powered drug discovery tool would primarily benefit pharmaceutical researchers, there is a risk that the tool could be easily "repurposed" to discover new toxins that might be used as chemical weapons (Urbina et al., 2022). AI developers often use dissemination channels to garner feedback about the "use" and "misuse" of their tools in varied contexts. This information enables tool refinement to enhance performance and prevent potential future misuse (through a staged/gapped release strategy). Access restrictions are also deployed where perceived risk and consequences of misuse are high. Generally, making AI capabilities accessible to everyone is usually achieved via the reduction of the cost of acquisition and deployment of AI tools, provision of AI-integration services to users (consultancy services), development of a user-friendly human-AI interactive interface, and upgrade of fundamental infrastructure, such as internet access in some regions where this may be a challenge (Yu, Rosenfeld & Gupta, 2023).

(b) democratization of AI development: this connotes efforts at making more people participate in AI design and development processes. Among the primary objectives of democratizing AI development is accelerating AI innovation and progress, particularly in the fields of AI research and development. Although this acceleration could encourage the global community's involvement in AI development, there is a risk that it may lead to potential harm, misuse, or misalignment. In addition, policies or interventions for responsible AI development may struggle to keep pace with the rapid development. Second, addressing the divergent interests and needs of the users who complain of cultural, geographical, professional, and financial marginalization regarding AI development is another goal of democratization (Yang & Park, 2020). Also, the "peculiarity" hypothesis is better addressed so that people with varied needs can develop AI that is "fit-to-purpose". However, the question of malicious use, model modification, and controls needs to be addressed (Solaiman, 2023). Third, democratizing AI development processes exposes it to public scrutiny, who offer critical evaluation and auditing mechanisms to reveal the tool's flaws. Thus, AI developers would benefit from relevant critique to provide safer and better-aligned technology.

Among the strategies employed to facilitate the broader diffusion of AI design and development are facilitating community engagement through model sharing (e.g., code, model weights, ability to query, study, examine, or modify the model), providing access to compute resources and other infrastructure, offering project support and coordination, providing educational and capacity-building opportunities (investment in computer science and machine learning educational resources), and offering assistive tools.

(c) democratization of AI profits: This concerns efforts at redistributing the wealth created by AI to the wider public. That is, it relates to facilitating the broad and equitable distribution of value accrued to organisations that build and control advanced AI capabilities. The goal is therefore to close the "wealth gap" between AI-leading and AI-lagging nations (Yu, Rosenfeld & Gupta, 2023). Mechanisms such as philanthropic giving, state effort through taxation, infrastructural building projects, and adoption of "Windfall Clause"—a situation where AI firms are bindingly obliged to donate a meaningful portion of their profits when the firm's earnings for the year exceed "a substantial fraction of the world's total economic output" (e.g., at least 1%) (O'Keefe et al., 2020; Seger et al., 2023) are usually adopted in AI profit democratization.

(d) democratization of AI governance: This is about introducing democratic processes into decision-making about how AI is developed, shared, used, and otherwise regulated. It revolves around seeking legitimacy for the decision-making process regarding the democratization of AI use, development, and profit, ensuring that it is fair, well-considered, and gains the acceptance of those who will be impacted by it (Gabriel, 2020). The motive is to guard against AI labs' incentivizing reckless decision-making due to excessive feuds among them. This approach ensures the reduction of unrestrained and one-sided decision-making that could cause significant harm. Again, mitigation of AI-related injustices and unfairness, such as the AI algorithmic bias in recidivism prediction applications, facial recognition, hiring, and loan appraisal (Perkowitz, 2021; Raub, 2019; Seger et al., 2023), constitutes a significant goal of democratizing AI governance. Moreover, the need to address complex normative questions, such as the avoidance of human fatalities, establishing desirable risk thresholds, interpreting terms like "transparency" and "dignity," and determining what constitutes "values" in value-aligned AI, drives the democratization of AI governance. Ultimately, the introduction of democratic processes into AI policy formulation, instituting constitutional protections for individuals and minorities, facilitating well-informed deliberation, and ensuring substantive representation of stakeholder viewpoints are some of the strategies usually employed in liberalizing AI governance.

The **legal approach** centers on achieving regulatory compliance, algorithmic accountability, and safeguarding the fundamental rights of AI users by enforcing adequate regulations, standards, and rights-based structures in AI systems. Globally, efforts are being made to promote responsible AI design, development, and deployment through the establishment of standards, policies, and legislation. Some of the leading standards, policies, and legislations regulating AI development and use include the National Artificial Intelligence Advisory Committee (NAIAC) AI Transparency Standards, the IEEE Standards for Transparency of Autonomous Systems, the U.S. Department of Health and Human Services HTI-1 Final Rule, the CLeAR Documentation Framework for AI Transparency, the EU AI Act, and the proposed U.S. Research, Innovation, and Accountability Act (Lund et al., 2025). In Africa, many countries have demonstrated a commitment to ethical and responsible AI governance, in compliance with international regulations and addressing the continent's specific needs and priorities. Okolo (2024) identified Tunisia, Rwanda, Egypt, Senegal, Mauritius, Ghana, and Benin as African countries with draft national AI regulations. In Nigeria, the National Artificial Intelligence Strategy (NAIS, August 2024) contains details of the country's effort at "harnessing the transformative power of AI through responsible, ethical, and inclusive innovation, fostering sustainable development through collaborative efforts" (NAIS, 2024, p. 4). The NAIS clearly emphasizes the importance of stakeholders' collaboration and engagement. At the same time, Okolo (2024) further suggests following the United Nations and OECD approach, which involves an active role for stakeholders on advisory boards and expert panels.

Specifically, Winfield et al. (2021) highlighted the four (4) transparency levels contained in the IEEE P7001. "Level 1 is for basic transparency (including user manuals and simple system explanations for consumer products), Level 2 encompasses interactive materials or system descriptions tailored to non-expert users, Level 3 covers real-time explanations and access to system logs for expert stakeholders, and Level 4 and 5 summarises detailed and continuous transparency, granting full access to behavior, decision-making processes, and training data for high-risk applications" (p. 3642). However, Lund et al. (2025) and Cheng (2024) cautioned that transparency-related regulations must be structured in a way that strikes an appropriate balance between the transparency principle, data privacy, and safeguarding intellectual property. As an instance, information stewardship should not compromise an AI system's security or disclose algorithmic propriety.

Thus, from a legal perspective, the most suitable approach to transparency is a staged approach, based on the complexity of the AI system, the technical proficiency of developers, and the needs of users. In this regard, Lund et al. (2025) advocated for a tiered approach to transparency based on system risk and stakeholder needs. Based on their study, two levels of stakeholder-based transparency are deducible:

(a) The general public, or a non-expert group, requires simple, clear, and less technical explanations to understand the basis of the decision made by the AI system. For example, AI developers could notify users that they are interacting with an AI through a chatbot (a low-risk system), preventing deception by flagging "deepfakes" content (a generative system), and provide clear information about how an autonomous vehicle operates (a high-risk system).
(b) The expert group, for audit and compliance purposes, needs access to detailed documentation, system logs, and data origin, especially for high-risk/high-impact applications. This group includes AI developers, investigators, and certifiers.

The goal of this staged structure is to pave the way for utmost flexibility and institutionalize transparency by enforcing standards, policies, and legislation to ensure due regard for legal and ethical boundaries by AI systems.

The **capacity-building approach** demonstrates that transparency is a function of developing both institutional and administrative skills, including the tools and technical infrastructure necessary for the public to operate smoothly, as well as the implementation of transparent AI systems. It also involves increasing and broadening non-expert stakeholder participation in the AI lifecycle to facilitate the redistribution of knowledge, power, and resources. Taylor et al. (2024) propose wider involvement in areas such as social welfare allocation, government contract awarding, and the deployment of surveillance technologies, including facial recognition. Administrative capacity, according to Luise and Cocozza (2025), constitutes the operational tool through which political decisions are translated into concrete actions, shaping their effectiveness and impact on society. Stakeholders could approach this capacity building through autonomous operational programs aimed at enhancing the technical, organizational, and institutional skills of local administrations. Examples of capacity-related issues are stated by Seger et al (2023) to include investment by government and AI developers in educational and upskilling opportunities, encouraging less well-resourced groups through grants for computer cluster access and cloud computing facilities, adequate access to cybersecurity infrastructure and data storage facilities, and ultimately, making AI technological development easier for non-experts in programming and machine learning.

## 3.6 Explainability

Explainability is a more restricted, outcome-oriented feature of AI that has gained traction since it was first coined in 2004 (van Lent, Fisher & Mancuso, 2004), reflected in several scientific events from academia (as an object of discussion in conferences and workshops), civilian and military, as well as industrial communities (Barocas et al., 2018). Often referred to as "Explainable AI (XAI)", it is an integral part of responsible AI (RAI) (Baker & Xiang, 2023; Batool et al., 2025), which is the ability to articulate the reasons for a specific decision or prediction made by an AI model. Explainability proposes that those who work with AI systems should have access to tailored information about how the systems arrive at decisions.

Quite often, "explainability" has been interchanged with "interpretability". However, the terms can convey different meanings, especially for policy/regulatory objectives (Pérez-Cruz et al., 2025). Explainability answers the questions "why did the model produce this output?" or "why did the model recommend accepting this credit application?" This means that explainability is the extent to which a model's output can be explained to a human. Interpretability answers questions such as "how did the AI model arrive at a certain output/decision?" or "how did the AI model determine that an organization should not insure a certain property?" Thus, interpretability is the extent to which a human can understand the inner workings of an AI model.

XAI is encapsulated as "right to explanation" in the European Union's General Data Protection Regulation (EU GDPR, 2023). The focus is on utilizing technical approaches, equipment, and techniques to ensure that AI systems are fathomable, explainable, and auditable (Cheong, 2024). The provision of this information becomes inextricably essential for several reasons, including:

(a) evaluate compliance with established legal and ethical standards
(b) assess the safety and reliability of the systems
(c) gain insights into the decision-making processes of AI systems
(d) decide about whether to adopt a specific AI technology

(e) evaluate what data was used to train the system, and the processes used in the training
(f) determine whether stakeholders' data could be used for training purposes
(g) determine whether the tool is appropriate for stakeholders' specific applications
(h) identify potential biases or errors, and
(i) enable users to comprehend and challenge the outputs of the AI systems (Cheong, 2024; Daneshjou et al., 2021; Lund et al., 2025).

Explainability becomes especially imperative when AI is deployed in high-risk/high-stakes decision-making situations/domains, such as in criminal justice, healthcare, and finance, so that stakeholders can understand how the system works, query its outputs, and request justifications for AI-based decisions, which must be contestable and comprehensible to the affected individuals. Thus, explainability provides post-hoc rationales for black-box models, focusing on promoting and enabling explainability and fairness in algorithmic decision-making systems that have social and commercial impacts (Adadi & Berrada, 2018). XAI, despite its usefulness, faces several significant setbacks, including the challenge of striking a balance between the complexity and interpretability of AI models (Wachter et al., 2017) and the balance between explainability and confidentiality of financial data (Rane et al., 2023), which may render complete transparency impossible. Furthermore, although XIA is often employed as a risk management tool (Nannini et al., 2023), it remains unclear what constitutes a valid/meaningful explanation, and its implementation will be enforced in practice (Edwards & Veale, 2017) across different stakeholders (Nannini et al., 2023). To enhance the interpretability of AI models and explain their predictions, techniques such as Local Interpretable Model-agnostic Explanations (LIME) and SHapley Additive exPlanations (SHAP) have been introduced (Pérez-Cruz et al., 2025; Ribeiro et al., 2016). However, these tools are limited by instability and susceptibility to misleading output, which in turn limit the regulator's ability to develop a sound risk management model (Pérez-Cruz et al., 2025). Other challenges of enforcing explainability requirements are:

(i) difficulty for firms in complying with regulatory requirements
(ii) difficulty in explaining advanced AI models such as deep neural networks because of their complexity and over-parameterization
(iii) involvement of large volumes of non-linear reasoning
(iv) opaque computation behind model outputs—the black-box dilemma
(v) possibility of varying the model's output even when the inputs have not changed due to the probabilistic nature of the AI models.
(vi) difficulty in assessing the AI model's future behaviour and setting its capabilities and limitations
(vii) concerns around accountability, fairness, and ethics (Crisanto et al., 2024; Pérez-Cruz et al., 2025).

Moreover, various techniques have been adopted to overcome the black box through XAI. These techniques include the use of:

(a) Intrinsic models, which are inherently transparent and interpretable models, such as linear models, rule-based systems, and decision trees.
(b) LIME, SHAP (model-agnostic method), which quantifies the contribution of each input feature to a specific prediction
(c) Post-hoc technique applied to explain a black-box model after it has made a decision, such as visualizations.
(d) Surrogate models, which involve training a simple, interpretable model to approximate the predictions of a complex model.
(e) Counterfactual explanations which provide a "what-if" situation to the user.

Within the governance framework, explainability supports making AI decisions understandable (user empowerment), aiding informed accord and contestability (ethical compliance), and enabling debugging and monitoring (operational safety).

Therefore, while the two concepts are often used interchangeably, there are a great deal of differences between transparency and explainability within AI governance as they serve different purposes and face distinct challenges. In essence, transparency is about the system's design and operation, targeting system-level openness, while explainability is about justifying its individual outputs—decision-level interpretability. However, the two concepts are variously central to ethical and effective AI governance, and integrating both terms into governance frameworks ensures that AI systems are both transparent to users' inquisitiveness and understandable and answerable to those they affect.

### 3.6.1 Maintaining a Balance Between AI Performance and Explainability

Various scholars (Kazim, et al., 2021; Rudin, 2019; Arnold et al., 2019) have argued that AI governance structures must strike a balance between innovation and accountability. Additionally, stakeholders must approach transparency as an integral part of AI development and deployment through concerted efforts in governance. Among the suggested methods of achieving this balance are:

(a) Establishing a contextual risk framework: Kazim et al. (2021) noted that risk assessment should guide governance structure and advocate for a proportional method based on the probable effect of the AI's decision. This staged approach is because different AI systems require varied levels of explainability.
(b) Transparency by design: This involves maintenance of adequate documentation throughout the AI's lifecycle. This documentation includes maintaining AI FactSheets or Model Cards that detail the model's purpose, data used, known prejudices, and performance (see Arnold et al., 2019).
(c) Model Selection Policy: The selection of a model should be determined by its perceived performance. According to Rudin (2019), the use of an AI model should be based on its superior performance, necessity, and the presence of

robust XAI techniques. Therefore, for high-stakes applications, the default option should be an interpretable model.

(d) Human-in-the-Loop (HITL) design: According to Felzmann et al. (2020), in high-risk decisions, there is a need for integrating AI insights into users' contextual knowledge.
(e) Continuous monitoring and auditing: Regular audit models for fairness, bias, and the accuracy of AI systems should be conducted to ensure they remain valid through time and to monitor their performance and thought process.
(f) Adaptive regulation: Establishing flexible policies and procedures that will evolve with technological developments.
(g) A hybrid model, which combines technical oversight with ethical review.
(h) Stakeholder engagement: This is an all-inclusive governance framework that involves developers of AI systems, regulators, and users.

## 3.7 Conclusion

This chapter has explored the concepts of transparency and explainability in AI governance. In doing so, the chapter employed three theories to anchor the discussion and gain multiple perspectives. The chapter began with a discussion of the rationale for understanding the two concepts by discussing the black box AI. Furthermore, each of the terms was extensively discussed, their types were mentioned, and ways of achieving them were elaborated upon. The chapter concluded that transparency and explainability are not just critical enablers of responsible and sustainable AI adoption and technical challenges, but also governance imperatives. In the chapter, it has been argued that the constraints of the black box are not intractable if the relevant stakeholders view XAI not as a constraint, but as a promoter of confidence in, security of, and better performance of AI models. Organisations can realise AI's full potential by adopting XAI techniques, complying with evolving regulations, and implementing governance frameworks that strike a balance between performance and accountability. This approach ensures that AI systems are ethical, legal, and socially responsible, both in development and deployment, aligning with human values and regulatory standards.

## References

Adadi, A., & Berrada, M. (2018). Peeking inside the black-box: A survey on explainable artificial intelligence (XAI). *IEEE Access, 6*, 52138–52160. https://doi.org/10.1109/ACCESS.2018.2870052

Adegbayibi, A. T., & Ajape, M. K. (2025). Integration of artificial intelligence into taxation processes. In M. Adelowotan & C. A. Leke (Eds.), *Artificial intelligence in accounting, auditing and finance: A guide for implementation and use*, pp. 103–125. Springer Nature Switzerland AG. https://doi.org/10.1007/978-3-031-87368-3

Ajape, M. K., & Adegbayibi, A. T. (2025). Artificial intelligence tools and use cases in corporate finance. In M. Adelowotan & C. A. Leke (Eds.), *Artificial intelligence in accounting, auditing and finance: A guide for implementation and use*, pp. 153–172. Springer Nature Switzerland AG. https://doi.org/10.1007/978-3-031-87368-3

Andrada, G., Clowes, R. W., & Smart, P. R. (2023). Varieties of transparency: Exploring agency within AI systems. *AI and Society, 38*, 1321–1331. https://doi.org/10.1007/s00146-021-01326-6

Arnold, M., Bellamy, R. K., Hind, M., Houde, S., Mehta, S., Mojsilović, A.,... & Varshney, K. R (2019). FactSheets: Increasing trust in AI services through supplier's declarations of conformity. *IBM Journal of Research and Development, 63*(4/5), 1–1. https://doi.org/10.1147/JRD.2019.2942288

Bahoo, S., Cucculelli, M., Goga, X., & Mondolo, J. (2024). Artificial Intelligence in finance: A comprehensive review through bibliometric and content analysis. *SN Business and Economics, 4*(23), 1.

Bajwa, J., Munir, U., Nori, A., & Williams, B. (2021). Artificial Intelligence in healthcare: Transforming the practice of medicine. *Future Healthcare Journal, 8*(2), e188–e194. https://doi.org/10.7861/fhj.2021-0095

Baker, S., & Xiang, W. (2023). Explainability and social responsibility in AI systems. *The Journal of Artificial Intelligence Research, 68*, 213–228. https://doi.org/10.1109/SPMB59478.2023.10372636

Bao, Y., Ke, B., Li, B., Yu, J. Y., & Zhang, J. (2020). Detecting accounting fraud in publicly traded U.S. firms using a machine learning approach. *Journal of Account Research, 58*(1), 199–235. https://doi.org/10.1111/1475-679X.12292

Barocas, S., Friedler, S., Hardt, M., Kroll, J., Venka-Tasubramanian, S., & Wallach, H. (2018). *The FAT-ML workshop series on fairness, accountability, and transparency in machine learning*. Accessed: Oct. 7, 2025 [Online]. Available: http://www.fatml.org/

Batool, A., Zowghi, D., & Bano, M. (2025). AI governance: A systematic literature review. *AI and Ethics, 5*, 3265–3279. https://doi.org/10.1007/s43681-024-00653-w

Bridoux, F., & Stoelhorst, J. W. (2022). Stakeholder governance: Solving the collective action problems in joint value creation. *Academy of Management Review, 47*, 214–236. https://doi.org/10.5465/amr.2019.0441

Cheong, B. C. (2024). Transparency and accountability in AI systems: Safeguarding wellbeing in the age of algorithmic decision-making. *Frontiers in Human Dynamics, 6*, 1421273. https://doi.org/10.3389/fhumd.2024.1421273

Crisanto, J., Leuterio, C., Prenio, J. & Yong, J. (2024). *Regulating AI in the financial sector: Recent developments and main challenges*. FI Insights on policy implementation, no 63, December

Daneshjou, R., Smith, M. P., Sun, M. D., Rotemberg, V., & Zou, J. (2021). Lack of transparency and potential bias in artificial intelligence data sets and algorithms: A scoping review. *JAMA Dermatology, 157*(11), 1362–1369.

DiMaggio, P. J., & Powell, W. W. (1983). The iron cage revisited: Institutional isomorphism and collective rationality in organizational fields. *American Sociological Review, 48*(2), 147–160. https://doi.org/10.17323/1726-3247-2010-1-34-56

Edwards, L., & Veale, M. (2017). Slave to the algorithm? Why a "Right to an Explanation" is probably not the remedy you are looking for. *Duke Law & Technology Review, 16*, 18–84. https://doi.org/10.31228/osf.io/97upg

Explaining the Predictions of Any Classifier. In *Proceedings of the 22nd ACM SIGKDD*.

Felzmann, H., Fosch-Villaronga, E., Lutz, C., & Tamò-Larrieux, A. (2020). Towards transparency by design for artificial intelligence. *Science and Engineering Ethics, 26*, 3333–3361. https://doi.org/10.1007/s11948-020-00276-4

Freeman, R. E. (1984). *Strategic management: A stakeholder approach*. Pitman.

Gabriel, I. (2020). Artificial intelligence, values, and alignment. *Minds and Machines, 30*(3), 411–437. https://doi.org/10.1007/s11023-020-09539-2

GDPR. EU (2023). General data protection regulation (GDPR) compliance guidelines. GDPR.Eu. Retrieved December 20, 2025 from https://gdpr.eu/

Goodman, B., & Flaxman, S. (2017). European union regulations on algorithmic decision making and a "right to explanation." *AI Magazine, 38*, 50–57. https://doi.org/10.1609/aimag.v38i3.2741

Harrison, J. S., Andrew, C., & Wicks, A. C. (2021). Harmful stakeholder strategies. *Journal of Business Ethics, 169*(3), 405–419. Springer. https://doi.org/10.1007/s10551-019-04310-9

Hassija, V., Chamola, V., Bajpai, B. C., Naren, & Zeadally, S. (2021). Security issues in implantable medical devices: Fact or fiction? *Sustainable Cities Society, 66*, 102552. https://doi.org/10.1016/j.scs.2020.102552

Horodyski, P. (2023). Applicants' perception of artificial Intelligence in the recruitment process. *Computers in Human Behavior Reports, 11*, Article 100303. https://doi.org/10.1016/j.chbr.2023.100303

Hunter, D., Bagaric, M. & Stobbs, N. (2020). A framework for the efficient and ethical use of artificial Intelligence in the criminal justice system. *Florida State University Law Review, 47*(4), 748–800. https://ir.law.fsu.edu/lr/vol47/iss4/7

Ingrams, A., & Klievink, B. (2022). Transparency's role in AI governance. In Justin, B. B. (ed.) et al. *The Oxford Handbook of AI Governance*, 479–494. https://doi.org/10.1093/oxfordhb/9780197579329.013.32

*International Conference on Knowledge Discovery and Data Mining*, 1135–1144.

International Monetary Fund (IMF). (2021). *Artificial intelligence in tax administration: A global perspective.* https://www.imf.org/en/Publications/WP/Issues/2021/07/23/Artificial-Intelligence-in-Tax-Administration-A-Global-Perspective

Jensen, M. C., & Meckling, W. H. (1976). Theory of the firm: Managerial behavior, agency costs and ownership structure. *Journal of Financial Economics, 3*(4), 305–360. https://doi.org/10.1016/0304-405X(76)90026-X

Kazim, E., Koshiyama, A. S., Hilliard, A., & Polle, R. (2021). Systematizing audit in algorithmic recruitment. *Journal of Intelligence, 9*, 46. https://doi.org/10.3390/jintelligence9030046

Kessler, E. (2020). *The AI revolution is coming: Artificial intelligence and machine learning have the potential to completely transform the actuarial role.* The Actuary, available at https://www.theactuarymagazine.org/the-ai-revolution-is-coming/

Kosinski, M. (2024). *What is black box artificial Intelligence (AI)? Online.* Available at https://www.ibm.com/think/topics/black-box-ai. Accessed on 4 Dec. 2025.

Langer, M., & König, C. J. (2023). Introducing a multi-stakeholder perspective on opacity, transparency and strategies to reduce opacity in algorithm-based human resource management. *Human Resource Management Review, 33*(1), Article 100881. https://doi.org/10.1016/j.hrmr.2021.100881

Luise, G., & Cocozza, G. (2025). The process of "capacity building" in the public administration: Artificial intelligence, transparency, and new models of the administrative decision. *Frontiers in Political Science, 7*, 1605729. https://doi.org/10.3389/fpos.2025.1605729

Lund, B., Orhan, Z., Mannuru, N. R., Bevara, R. V. K., Porter, B., Vinaih, M. K., & Bhaskara, P. (2025). Standards, frameworks, and legislation for artificial intelligence (AI) transparency. *AI and Ethics, 5*, 3639–3655. https://doi.org/10.1007/s43681-025-00661-4

Nannini, L., Balayn, A., & Smith, A. L. (2023). Explainability in AI policies: A critical review of communications, reports, regulations, and standards in the EU, U.S., and UK. In *2023 ACM conference on fairness, accountability, and transparency (FAccT' 23), June 12–15, 2023, Chicago, IL, USA* (p. 15). ACM. https://doi.org/10.1145/3593013.3594074

National Artificial Intelligence Strategy. (2024). https://ncair.nitda.gov.ng/wp-ontent/uploads/2024/08/National-AI-Strategy_01082024-copy.pdf

O'Keefe, C., Cihon, P., Garfinkel, B., Flynn, C., Leung, J., & Dafoe, A. (2020). *The windfall clause: Distributing the benefits of AI*. Future of Humanity Institute, University of Oxford, 2020. Accessed: Nov. 10, 2025 [Online]. Available: https://www.fhi.ox.ac.uk/wp-content/uploads/Windfall-Clause-Report.pdf

Okolo, C. T. (2024). *Reforming data regulation to advance AI governance in Africa.* Brookings. https://www.brookings.edu/articles/reforming-data-regulation-to-advance-ai-governance-in-africa

Olawade, D. B., David-Olawade, A. C., Wada, O. Z., Asaolu, A. J., Adereni, T., & Ling, J. (2024). Artificial intelligence in healthcare delivery: Prospects and pitfalls. *Journal of Medicine, Surgery, and Public Health, 3*, Article 100108. https://doi.org/10.1016/j.glmedi.2024.100108

O'Shaughnessy, M. R., Schiff, D. S., Varshney, L. R., Rozell, C. J., & Davenport, M. A. (2023). What governs attitudes toward artificial intelligence adoption and governance? *Science and Public Policy, 50*(2), 161–176. Article scac056. https://doi.org/10.1093/scipol/scac056

Papadouli, V. (2023). Artificial intelligence's black box: Posing new ethical and legal challenges on modern societies. In A. Kornilaksi, G. Nouskalis, V. Pergantis, & T. Tzimas (Eds.), *Artificial intelligence and normative challenges. Law, governance and technology series* (p. 59). Cham: Springer. https://doi.org/10.1007/978-3-031-41081-9_4

Pérez-Cruz, F., Prenio, J., Restoy, F., & Yong, J. (2025). *Managing explanations: How regulators can address AI explainability*. Online: https://www.bis.org/fsi/fsipapers24.pdf. Accessed on Nov. 20 2025.

Perkowitz, S. (2021). The bias in the machine: Facial recognition technology and racial disparities. *MIT case studies in social and ethical responsibilities of computing*, no. Winter 2021, Feb. 2021. https://doi.org/10.21428/2c646de5.62272586

Rane, N., Choudhary, S., & Rane, J. (2023). Explainable artificial intelligence (XAI) approaches for transparency and accountability in financial decision-making. *SSRN., 2023*, 4640316. https://doi.org/10.2139/ssrn.4640316

Raub, M. (2019). Bots, bias, and big data: Artificial Intelligence, algorithmic bias and disparate impact liability in hiring practices. *Ark. l. Rev., 71*, 529.

Ribeiro, M. T., Singh, S., & Guestrin, C. (2016). *Why should I trust you*?

Seger, E., Ovadya, A., Garfinkel, B., Siddarth, D., & Dafoe, A. (2023). Democratising AI: Multiple meanings, methods, and goals. Proceedings In *of the 2023 AAAI/ACM conference on AI, ethics, and society*. https://doi.org/10.48550/arXiv.2303.12642

Shaw, K. (2023). *AI for actuaries: What do you need to know*? ProActuary, available at https://proactuary.com/resources/aiactuaries-need-to-know-and-why/#t-1674045088327

Situmeang, S. M. T., Harliyanto, R., Zulkarnain, P. D., Nahdi, U., & Nugroho, T. (2024). The role of artificial Intelligence in criminal justice. *Global International Journal of Innovative Research, 2*(8), 1966–1981. https://doi.org/10.59613/global.v2i8.264

Solaiman, I. (2023). *The gradient of generative AI release: Methods and considerations*. arXiv, Feb. 05, 2023. Accessed: Nov. 10, 2023 [Online]. Available: http://arxiv.org/abs/2302.04844

Sunny, A. D. (2025). *Preliminary quantitative study on explainability and trust in AI systems*. https://doi.org/10.48550/arXiv.2510.15769

Sykorova, Z., Hague, D., Dvoulety, O., & Prochazka, D. A. (2024). Incorporating artificial Intelligence (AI) into recruitment processes: Ethical considerations. *VILAKSHAN—XIMB Journal of Management, 21*(2), 293–307. https://doi.org/10.1108/XJM-02-2024-0039

Taylor, R. R., Murphy, J. W., Hoston, W. T., & Senkaiahliyan, S. (2024). Democratizing AI in public administration: Improving equity through maximum feasible participation. *AI and Society, 40*, 3653–3662. https://doi.org/10.1007/s00146-024-02120-w

Urbina, F., Lentzos, F., Invernizzi, C., & Ekins, S. (2022). Dual use of artificial-intelligence-powered drug discovery. *Nature Machine Intelligence, 4*(3), 3. https://doi.org/10.1038/s42256-022-00465-9

van Lent, M., Fisher, W. & Mancuso, M. (2004). An explainable artificial intelligence system for small-unit tactical behavior. In *Proceedings of the 16th conference on innovation and applied artificial intelligence* (pp. 900–907).

Wachter, S., Mittelstadt, B., & Floridi, L. (2017). Why a right to explanation of automated decision-making does not exist in the general data protection regulation. *International Data Privacy Law, 7*, 76–99. https://doi.org/10.1093/idpl/ipx005

Wamba-Taguimdje, S.-L., Wamba, S. F., Kamdjoug, J. R. K., & Wanko, C. E. T. (2020). Influence of artificial intelligence (AI) on firm performance: The business value of AI-based transformation projects. *Business Process Management Journal*. https://doi.org/10.1108/BPMJ-10-2019-0411

Winfield, A. F., Booth, S., Dennis, L. A., Egawa, T., Hastie, H., Jacobs, N., et al. (2021). IEEE P7001: A proposed standard on transparency. *Frontiers in Robotics and AI, 8*, 665729.

Xu, H., & Shuttleworth, K. M. J. (2024). Medical artificial Intelligence and the black box problem: A view based on the ethical principle of "do no harm." *Intelligent Medicine, 4*(1), 52–57. https://doi.org/10.1016/j.imed.2023.08.001

Yang, J., & Park, T. (2020). Methods for inclusion: Expanding the limits of participatory design in AI. *Partnership on AI*, Nov. 19, 2020. https://partnershiponai.org/methodsforinclusion/. Accessed Nov. 10, 2025.

Yu, D., Rosenfeld, H., & Gupta, A. (2023). The "AI divide" between the Global North and Global South. *World Economic Forum*, Jan. 16, 2023. Accessed: Nov. 10, 2025 [Online]. Available: https://www.weforum.org/agenda/2023/01/davos23-ai-divide-global-north-global-south/

Zednik, C. (2021). Solving the black box problem: A normative framework for explainable artificial Intelligence. *Philos Technol, 34*, 265–288.

# Chapter 4
# AI Accountability and Liability

**Fowokemi Alaba Ogedengbe and Michael Olajide Adelowotan**

**Abstract** Artificial intelligence (AI) systems are increasingly influencing decision-making processes in critical domains, including healthcare, finance, and transportation. Determining who bears responsibility when AI systems cause harm or malfunction has therefore become a central challenge. This chapter addresses four core research objectives through a comprehensive review of existing literature on AI accountability and liability. The discussion begins with an examination of the doctrinal foundations that underpin current accountability frameworks. This addressed the first research objective. Particular attention is given to the European Union's AI Act and its accompanying directives, as well as comparative legal perspectives, including U.S. tort law and China's regulatory approaches to autonomous technologies. The second component explores the economic dimensions of AI liability, focusing on compensation models designed to address the unique harms associated with AI-enabled systems. Third, the chapter evaluates emerging legal and regulatory structures that govern AI liability, including ongoing debates around product liability. Several proposed models of responsibility are analysed, such as proportional and shared liability, risk-based and sector-specific approaches, and practical mechanisms such as contractual risk allocation and governance-document frameworks. Existing accountability structures are critically assessed with respect to challenges posed by opaque "black-box" models, recognition of non-physical harms, and the broader risk-compensation dynamics within AI ecosystems. Fourth, concrete strategies and best practices were suggested to promote responsible AI development and deployment. This includes the establishment of global standards on AI responsibility and liability, domestication of AI laws to reflect the human rights and societal structures of countries, and the subjecting of all AI activities in all countries to risk assessments. Finally, the chapter advocates for a multi-stakeholder governance model that integrates legal oversight, industry self-regulation, and technological safeguards

F. A. Ogedengbe (✉) · M. O. Adelowotan
Department of Accountancy, College of Business and Economics, University of Johannesburg, Johannesburg, South Africa
e-mail: fogedengbe@uj.ac.za; ogedfowokemi@gmail.com

M. O. Adelowotan
e-mail: madelowotan@uj.ac.za

 
M. Adelowotan and H. Coovadia (eds.), *AI and Accountability*, CSR, Sustainability, Ethics & Governance, https://doi.org/10.1007/978-3-032-20091-4_4

by providing a conceptual model reflecting the various theoretical perspectives to AI accountability and liability.

## 4.1 Introduction

Artificial Intelligence (AI) has become integral to the operations of business organisations and various sectors through its potential to enhance efficiency and innovation (Ogedengbe & Adelowotan, 2025). The development of new applications within the AI spectrum and the promise of a transformed system of activities have led to a surge in AI adoption across various professions. However, this rapid advancement in AI also poses diverse risks and challenges in various dimensions of its inclusion (Custers et al., 2025; Schütte et al., 2021a). Thus, this raises significant concerns regarding accountability and liability, especially in situations where AI has the capacity to cause harm or make erroneous decisions. Given that it is a well-established fact that information technology (IT) systems can be negatively impacted by factors such as transparency of usage, accountability, and unclear explainability, which are fundamental to the legal system (Alaba Ogedengbe, 2024; Enigbokan, 2025). When unexplainable and unaccountable technology influences decisions, addressing these concerns is crucial to ensure that AI technologies are developed and deployed responsibly.

While AI applications have shifted from their theoretical base and laboratory experiments to their practical applications in various dimensions and perspectives, the current focus is now on the safety–critical aspects and the rights associated with them. Critical AI thematic developments, such as the black box structure-based diagnostic system, autonomous vehicles, language model content generation, and work-based algorithms, have raised arguments for liability and compensation. AI inclusion in sensitive areas has caused the emergence of the need for accountability of its processes and activities, and also, considering the fundamental human rights, there is a need for who and what takes responsibility for the actions of AI, in cases of errors, wrong diagnoses and wrong judgments. Hence, the question is: when harm stemming from AI occurs, who is responsible? Will the victims be left without justice? Will the responsibilities shift to the programmers and operators of these AI systems? What are the legal doctrines available on this? This chapter aims to address these issues by drawing on evidence from available legislatures and scholars to understand how answers can be obtained to these valid questions.

The foundation regulatory and doctrinal development of AI accountability and liability has been based on the legal promulgation of the European Union, which is a directive that addresses AI opacity, unpredictability and procedural innovation (Čerka et al., 2015; Fraser & Suzor, 2025; Padovan et al., 2023; Panezi, 2021; Wendehorst, 2020). This EU law has laid the foundation for, and it's at the forefront of, the global address of AI accountability and liability. This Act has legally addressed the procedural innovations of AI, which include the presumptions of causality and defectiveness when victims lack access to key evidence, enhanced judicial powers to order the disclosure of data, logs and systems documentation (Ampovska, 2024;

Fraser & Suzor, 2025; Schütte et al., 2021a) and an expanded definition of AI to cover software and its updates. While the EU AI acts have laid the groundwork for AI liability and accountability, a persistent gap remains in the fragmented national applications of this law due to countries outside the EU. Moreover, their lack of global harmonisation of standards on substantive liability doctrines within the EU member states (Fraser & Suzor, 2025; Hacker & Mauer, 2023; Padovan et al., 2023; Zdraveva, 2024), and the challenges ascribed to causation and faults in high complexities, such as the black box context, are still gaps (Čerka et al., 2015; Li & Schütte, 2024; Padovan et al., 2023; Zdraveva, 2024).

Commentators and analysts of the EU's actions, while commending the significant strides made by the EU in setting precedents to legally address AI-related matters, have also raised concerns regarding the procedural structures. The argument is based on the perception that the procedural structures alone is not sufficient to address the complex responsibility gaps in AI, which suggests the improvement of the Act to be feasible in the adaptive AI systems, and the other jurisdictions' enactment of similar Acts (Li & Schütte, 2024; Truli, 2023; Padovan et al., 2023; Zdraveva, 2024). For instance, scholars have shown the need for the United States to enact regulations governing the AI structure. This argument proceeds from the circumstance that the United States have been supporting the use of AI structure, yet the legal perception regarding its accountability and liability has not been clearly stated. While the US is based on tort law and the court system is structured in an ad-hoc manner, there is a need for a federal AI Act that all states will be subject to. While some studies have assessed and critiqued the EU AI acts, this paper extends the arguments beyond criticism by leveraging past scholarly debates to address how these legal stances can be applied beyond Europe into the global context. Moreover, given that AI accountability and liability are relatively new areas, there are not many scholarly works available. This study aims to fill the gap in literature by contributing to the assessment of the various doctrinal foundations supporting AI accountability and liability. This includes the EU AI Act, the twin directives, and the European Convention on Human Rights (ECHR). Moreover, another novelty of this paper is that it theoretically assesses the practical strategies that can be employed in allocating AI and liability through structures such as compensation schemes, contractual risk management, proportional and shared liability approaches, and governance documents. Based on this, a "strategy and a best practice framework" was conceptually developed to assess these various approaches to AI accountability and liability.

To effectively capture the various related dimensions of these research objectives, this study posed specific research questions, and the discussion section was structured to provide answers to them. These research questions translated to their corresponding research objectives, which were achieved by the end of the chapter.

### 4.1.1 *Research Questions*

This chapter seeks to address the following key research questions:

1. What are the doctrinal foundations of AI accountability and liability?
2. What is the economic perspective on AI accountability and liability as reflected in the compensation model to AI victims
3. In what ways can existing legal and regulatory frameworks evolve to address AI liability?
4. What concrete strategies and best practices can be implemented to promote responsible AI development and deployment?

### *4.1.2 Research Objectives*

These research questions translate to the corresponding research objectives by:

1. Examining the doctrinal foundations of AI accountability and liability
2. Exploring the economic perspectives on AI accountability and liability as reflected in the compensation model to AI victims
3. Examining the legal and regulatory frameworks in addressing AI liability
4. Discussing the strategies and best practices in promoting responsible AI development and deployment.

To address these questions and objectives, this study creates sections and subsections based on doctrinal and economic perspectives of AI liability and accountability, the European Union regulation on AI, the comparative jurisdiction perspectives, the key thematic challenges that emerged from the available scholarly structure, and the recommendations of the policy options available in relations to AI accountability and liability. These are based on the review of prior related papers and grey literature as presented in the methodology section.

## 4.2 Methodology

This paper is based on the past scholarly debates as reflected in relevant databases such as Web of Science and Scopus. Document search was extended to title, abstract and keyword.search string employed was ((“artificial intelligence” OR AI OR “machine learning” OR ML OR algorithm* OR “autonomous system*” OR “autonomous vehicle*” OR “automated decision*” OR “automated decision-making” OR “algorithmic decision*” OR robot* OR “intelligent system*”) AND (liabilit* OR liab* OR compensation OR damages OR remedies) AND (accountab* OR responsib* OR “risk allocation” OR “risk-sharing” OR “risk sharing” OR “risk distribution” OR “proportionate liab*” OR “shared liab*” OR “joint and several liab*” OR “fiduciary dut*” OR “duty to warn” OR “failure to warn” OR “design defect” OR “manufacturing defect” OR “defective product*” OR “safety defect”) AND (“burden of proof” OR causation OR “causal link” OR “causal relationship” OR presumption* OR “rebuttable presumption*” OR “access to evidence” OR "disclosure of evidence" OR "evidence disclosure" OR discovery OR explainab* OR "explainable AI" OR XAI OR transparency OR opacity OR "black box" OR "black-box")).

In Web of Science, 206 documents were found, and from Scopus, 384 documents were found. These papers were systematically reviewed and manually examined to determine their suitability for this paper. AI assistance "Undermind" was also employed in the literature search due to its capability to access semantic scholarships, institutional and grey data relevant to the study. The papers from these various databases were collated, and Covidence was used to remove duplication. After that, papers were assessed for their fit and relevance. The relevant papers included for this chapter are forty-four publications. These papers were studied, reviewed and used as the basis for the discussion section.

## 4.3 Discussion

Based on the review and critique of the existing literature, this section assesses the research questions that have been determined and discusses them. The arguments regarding the doctrinal structure, compensation models, legal and regulatory frameworks, strategies, and best practices were critically discussed.

### *4.3.1 Conceptual Foundations of AI Accountability and AI Liability*

AI accountability concerns assigning responsibility for the outcomes generated by AI systems. This responsibility spans both historical and anticipated AI-related activities (Novelli et al., 2024). These include audits, assessments, oversights and justification of the AI systems' behaviours. Given the complexity and opacity of contemporary AI models, identifying the appropriate party to hold accountable remains a central challenge. Scholars have debated on the stakeholders who should be held responsible for AI behaviour. Some of the suggested stakeholders include the developers of the AI systems, the operators of the AI within the organisations, the organisation using AI, or the collaborations between two or more of the stated stakeholders.

This paper discusses AI accountability and liability from three perspectives. The first is the doctrinal perspective, the second is the economic perspective, and the third is the theoretical perspective. Although these perspectives are intertwined, this study attempts to discuss them as separate entities. Hence, this section aims to assess the first and second research questions as defined in Sect. 1.1, "What *are the doctrinal foundations of AI accountability and liability*?" And "*how do comparative perspectives differ in their approaches to AI accountability and liability*?".

While the doctrinal perspective examines the legal implications of AI accountability, the economic perspective explores the corresponding liability. This involves the discourse on who is liable for AI's wrong diagnoses and the compensation plan for victims. Moreover, AI liability aims to allocate the legal responsibility, causation, incentives, and injunctive remedies once harm occurs as a result of AI behaviour (Beroual, 2025; Čerka et al., 2015; Noto La Diega & Bezerra, 2024; Smith & Fotheringham, 2020). This is based on the need to compensate victims of AI malfunctions and incorrect diagnoses. Hence, the stakeholders who will be held liable for AI behaviours need to be defined. These concepts of AI accountability and liabilities intersect as robust accountability mechanisms, such as data logs, can provide the evidence necessary to trigger legal liability.

### 4.3.2 Doctrinal Perspectives on AI Accountability and Liability

This section critically examines existing literature to assess the first research question, "*What are the doctrinal foundations of AI accountability and liability*?" The available regulations and scholarly judgments have debated whether to recognise AI as a legal person which is subject to litigation, accountability and associated liabilities. They've also debated whether to provide legal creation of a specific sector that focuses on compensation for victims of AI-related activities (Aldmour, 2025; Bashayreh et al., 2021; Nersessian & Mancha, 2020; Wei & Guo, 2025; Zhang, 2025). Other debates have focused on the precise definition of AI, specifically whether software and services should be included within the framework of AI. At the centre of these debates is the European Union (EU), which serves as the foundation for the regulatory structure on AI.

#### AI Accountability and Liability Regulatory

The EU regulatory experiment formed the foundation for regulating AI by promulgating laws and regulations, thus setting a precedent for the world. Prior to the AI law, there were some experiments which are known as the two directives. These are (1) the AI liability directive proposal (2022) and (2) the revised product liability directive proposals (2022).

#### European Union Artificial Intelligence Act (EU AI Act) 2024

The acceptance of AI, coupled with its associated risks, is the major motivator for the promulgation of the EU AI Act. The AI Act was initially proposed in April 2021 as a comprehensive structure to address the AI-related risks. In 2024, the act was officially promulgated. The EU AI Act is deemed to be applicable harmoniously to all EU member states with the aim of controlling AI usage. The EU Act 2024 serves as the regulation on the anticipated risks of AI. The article 3 Sect. 4.1 of the EU AI act defines AI as a "machine-based system that is designed to operate with varying levels of autonomy and that may exhibit adaptiveness after deployment, and that, for explicit or implicit objectives, infers, from the input it receives, how to generate outputs such as predictions, content, recommendations, or decisions that can influence physical or virtual environments." The need for AI-based systems to comply with human rights values has therefore subjected them to accountability (Bas et al., 2024; Ebers, 2024; Graaf & Veldt, 2022; Hacker, 2023; Laux, 2024; Popa, 2024; Wörsdörfer, 2023; Zafar et al., 2025).

Based on the EU AI definition, AI has been classified into four degrees of risk, which range from low-risk to high-risk AI systems. Specifically, these are (1) prohibited risk, (2) high risk, (3) limited risk, and (4) minimal risk. While the Act provides regulations for high-risk individuals to undergo assessment structures, maintain logs, and implement human oversight aimed at mitigating the associated risks, the Act does not offer a direct right to a compensation mechanism. This economic aspect of the AI Act necessitates improved inclusion. Countries proposing to enact their own local jurisdiction AI acts should leverage the gaps in the EU AI Acts and build upon them. China is one country that has proposals on AI acts. Hence, the proposals may be reviewed to fill the existing AI act gaps (Calvano et al., 2025; Graaf & Veldt, 2022; Sovrano & Masetti, 2022).

Regarding the AI risks as presented in the EU AI Act, areas such as medical applications, black box AI, and judicial rulings are deemed to be high-risk. Scholars such as Contini et al. (2024) analysed the AI accountability in the judicial system within the context of the EU. According to the research, AI in Judicial rulings comes after more than a decade of the EU's inclusion of digital systems within its judicial system. Although the usage of AI within the court and judicial proceedings is still relatively low, its application in judicial drafting, prediction of legal decisions, and legal research is very high.

While scholars have examined the AI Act, criticism has been raised against a major gap, which concerns the existence of a "liability gap" (Calvano et al., 2025; Graaf & Veldt, 2022; Sovrano & Masetti, 2022). While the AI Act has addressed the treatment of AI-related risks, it fails to capture AI liability. This is where the question of liability arises: when AI harms people, who is liable for prosecution? And what are the compensation plans for the victim? While the AI Act proposal failed to address gaps, such as liability, two other proposals were issued in 2022: the AI Liability Directive and the revised Product Liability Directives. These two proposals were designed to balance each other.

### European Convention on Human Rights (ECHR)

According to the AI regulations in the EU, AI usage must be subject to the human right values as stipulated in the Charter and the ECHR, which include values related to freedom, democracy, equality and the rule of law. Hence, the member states and countries that want to follow the EU AI acts must subject AI use to the established global human right values. Therefore, the use of AI must not compromise human rights values; rather, it should uphold and respect these values. This perception suggests that AI should be used as assistive technology to support humans, rather than being employed to harm them.

### AI Liability Directive (AILD) Proposal 2022

AILD is the first part of the two AI directives. This serves as the first AI liability proposal, as it is intended to bridge the existing liability gap by assigning responsibility to AI-related harms (Marta et al., 2024). AILD, according to (Duffourc & Gerke, 2023; Li & Schütte, 2024; Marta et al., 2024; Noto La Diega & Bezerra, 2024) proposes the disclosure orders where the court may compel AI providers of high-risk AI systems to disclose all related technical evidence. The proposal also contains the presumption of a causal link, where if the defendant breaches an AI act obligation and harm materialises within the scope of that duty, courts may presume causation unless rebuffed. The third feature of the AILD proposal reveals a minimum level of harmonisation, where member states retain divergent substantive tort rules, thus raising concerns about fragmentation.

AILD is designed to focus specifically on AI systems and aims to transform the legal landscape on manufacturing, providing, designing and deploying AI. Hence, AILD encompasses claims against AI manufacturers, professional providers, and users. While the AILD attempts to harmonise the legal structure regarding AI liability, reduce existing legal uncertainties, and mitigate liability gaps, it still leaves a liability gap in the proposal. This gap has been referred to as the information gap. This gap relates to the accountability for harms caused by AI in situations where the victims are unaware of being harmed. They are the biases and discriminatory behaviour of AI, whose cause may not be known.

For instance, in cases of an AI hiring structure where job seekers are discriminated against based on gender or race and are eliminated from proceeding with the hiring process. Hence, the victims may not be aware of their losses. These information gaps are caused by intrinsic properties of the AI that may be difficult to pinpoint exactly. For instance, it may be due to the complexity and opacity of the AI system. It may also be caused by the environmental complexities, such as the socio-economic intricacies. Scholars have argued and criticised the AILD on the gap that exists in such situations. Hence, while the AILD was designed to reduce the "burden of proof" for the claimant, it has failed to address the biases, thereby shifting more liabilities to the supposed claimants, rather than reducing their liabilities. This has obstructed the argument that the AILD provides transparency in the "burden of evidence" and reduces information flow between the relevant actors and stakeholders, such as the AI users and the manufacturers (Marta et al., 2024).

**AI Responsibility and Liability Regulatory**

**EU AI Act 2024:**

1. prohibited risk
2. high risk
3. limited risk
4. minimal risk

**The Charter and the ECHR**

1. Values related to freedom
2. Democracy
3. Equality
4. The rule of law

**AI liability directive (AILD) proposal 2022**

1. Assigning responsibility to AI-related harms
2. The presumption of a causal link
3. Proposes the disclosure orders
4. Reduce the "burden of proof" for the claimant
5. Existence of a liability gap

**Revised products liability directives (PLD) proposal 2022:**
Inclusion of software and updates as AI products

**Fig. 4.1** AI accountability and liability regulatory. *Source* Authors generated

Revised Products Liability Directives (PLD) Proposal 2022 (3, 34)

While the AILD focuses strictly on AI systems, the revised product liability directives have the key novelties, which include the inclusion of software and updates as AI products (Čerka et al., 2015; Li et al., 2022; Panezi, 2021). Expanded defect presumption where providers implement mandatory documentation, no monetary threshold for property damage and data loss. And a partial reversal of the 10-year-long stop in latent defect cases involving AI-driven updates (Fig. 4.1).

Scholarly Assessments of the Twin Directives (AI Liability and Product Liability Directives)

Based on the scholarly assessments of these twin directives of regulatory experiments, there are mixed perceptions regarding them. (1) First, both are labelled as mere procedural, so they are non-substantive. Second, the procedures were perceived to be half-hearted due to their failure to harmonise duties and standards; hence, the procedures were based more on presumptions and disclosure. Third, from another scholarly perspective, the procedures, according to Li and Schütte (2024), were predicted to generate fragmentation risks due to the future challenges that can arise from different member states' implementation of their legislations. Hence, certainty regarding the exact legal interpretation in each EU member state may be unachievable. Fourth, there are significant gaps in the Act, as noted in other scholarly assessments. These arguments focused on the risks of non-inclusion of the gap existing in the black box AI structure in the Act (Duffourc & Gerke, 2023). For instance, aside from the information gap discussed in the AILD section above, scholars have criticised these two directives as they both failed to capture the potential harms that might be caused by advanced AI structures, such as black-box-based AI. The lack of clarity in the diagnostics in black-box AI, such as the medical AI, was not fully captured in the Act (Duffourc & Gerke, 2023; Li & Schütte, 2024). The complexities in the opaque and vague reasoning of these black box systems may make it impossible to make legal claims with evidence. Hence, since the black box structure may evade the strict and fault-based routes, associated misdiagnoses may leave victims uncompensated. From a legal perspective, scholars have assessed that a defendant can still exploit the technical complexities of AI to rebut causation (Fernández Llorca et al., 2023). Regarding compensation funds, studies argue that in cases where a consistent barrier persists, a statutory compensation fund should be established to ensure victims receive redress (Hacker & Mauer, 2023; Vellinga, 2024). This will minimise the risks experienced by victims.

### 4.3.3 *Economic Perspective on AI Accountability and Liability*

This section seeks to assess the second research question on "*what is the economic perspective on AI accountability and liability as reflected in the compensation model to AI victims?*" The economic classification involves the incentives and risk allocation to the victims of AI, which can be difficult to analyse. While law and economics have conventionally advocated for the liability rule focused on minimising the total social cost, based on accident, precaution, and administrative costs. Whereas some scholars have suggested aligning liability with control, information advantage, and the value chain. These scholars believed that the focus on direct liability may cause the victim may underrepresent the total liabilities caused by the AI (Truli, 2023) thus, incentives may be misallocated. In response to this, scholars such as the studies by (Panezi, 2021) propose a model known as the ecosystem risk pooling, which assesses the collective liability among all the stakeholders and supply chain actors, in addition to contractual re-allocation. The extension of this model was established by Bashayreh et al. (2021) which is known as the international proportional liability framework.

**Product Liability Struggles**

The need for the conventional tort on AI is based on struggles such as the unpredictability of AI, which is based on the model resistance of human intuition, hence causing the victim's inability to prove negligence (Ampovska, 2024; Chamberlain, 2023; Li & Schütte, 2024; Zdraveva, 2024). Another tort base is autonomy and adaptation of the systems, which may eliminate the link between choices and harm. Multiple stakeholders involved, such as the AI developers, providers, and integrators, complicate the liability structure (Beroual, 2025; Truli, 2023). Also, the concept of materiality of the harms, their tangibility and physicality of the harms may fall outside the conventional description of product liabilities (Duffourc & Gerke, 2023; Hacker & Mauer, 2023).

### *4.3.4 Theoretical Approaches to AI Responsibility and Liability*

This section presents scholarly-supported approaches that can be used to continue assessing the second research question and to evaluate the third research question, "*In what ways can existing legal and regulatory frameworks evolve to address AI liability*?" Given that the assessments of the research questions are interwoven, the theoretical approaches also offer economic compensation to AI actors.

While scholars have advocated for a more theoretical approach to the dichotomies between relevant AI stakeholders, especially between AI users and developers/manufacturers, this section aims to provide a comprehensive summary of the available approaches that can be replicated and employed to mitigate AI liabilities. Users within these dimensions are mostly individuals and organisations. Some of the approaches that this study categorises and summarises include the sociotechnical approach, the proportional and shared liability approach, the risk-based and shared stratified approach and the practical strategies approach. While some of these approaches are interwoven, distinct differences exist between them.

### Socio-Technical and Economic Approach

These scholars argued for a more systematic approach to risk analysis by incorporating a structure that covers all the relevant useful periods of the AI through its entire value chain structure (Aldmour, 2025; Hacker & Mauer, 2023; Luiz De Moura & Júnior, 2024; Schütte et al., 2021a; Wagner, 2022). Examples of the system approach include the incentive structure, as previously discussed, and safety principles outlined in the AI Act, particularly regarding risk assessments.

### Proportional and Shared Liability Approach

Another approach, as suggested by some other scholars, is the proportional and shared liability approach (Hacker, 2023; Luiz De Moura & Júnior, 2024; Panezi, 2021; Schütte et al., 2021b). This approach was presented as an alternative option when discussing the existing gaps in the responsibility and liability structure of AI. This is based on the argument of distributed responsibility. Given that the responsibilities among the multiple stakeholders (actors) are different, the liability should also be shared proportionately. These actors include the developer, deployer and operator. By sharing the liability proportionate to their responsibilities, the risk assessment can be spread among multiple stakeholders, and the impact on any one actor will not be overwhelming.

### Risk-Based and Sector-Stratified Approach

This approach has been proposed by scholars aiming to mitigate AI-related risks. The model is based on the liability rules as contained in the AI Act. This approach models the scaling of liability rules based on system risks (Bashayreh et al., 2021; Chamberlain, 2023; Panezi, 2021; Scherer, 2016; Sundaraparipurnan & Potkewitz, 2023; Zhang, 2025). For instance, AI falling within the high-risk range will also be subject to strict liability. This approach is also applicable to sectors that have a strong impact on human rights understanding, such as the medical and legal sectors. Also, sectors that are liable to high risk, such as autonomous vehicle systems, fall within this range (Zhang, 2025). This is because these sectors have a direct impact on human lives, and an AI misdiagnosis, error, or mistake has the potential to cause irreparable harm. By stratifying the high-risk related sectors, the clause of liability for such will be directly in relation to their risks. This perception is supported by legal and economic arguments. In economic terms, the concept "the higher the risk, the higher the return" is a common principle used to assess investments. Based on this perception, this study argues that the AI sectors and systems that fall within the high-risk assessment should also have a high level of liability attached.

**Practical Strategies and Approaches**

Based on the practical approaches in several ecosystems globally, mitigation of risk and allocation of liability have been levelled through the provision of necessary insurance schemes and compensation funds (Erdélyi & Erdélyi, 2020; Vellinga, 2024). In relation to AI liability, scholars have also argued that the liability can be settled by setting up compensation funds and various insurance schemes (Erdélyi & Erdélyi, 2020; Smith & Fotheringham, 2020; Vellinga, 2024). By risk pooling, the establishment of AI-related insurance will serve as a form of compensation where litigation alone cannot adequately cover and provide solutions where the liability cannot be defined with certainty for a specific stakeholder.

In addition, another practical approach is the contractual risk management structure, which is based on the best practices system of explicit and role-sensitive contractual provisions (Custers et al., 2025; Moch, 2024). Provisions of risk management contracts include indemnities, warranties, and allocation clauses. For instance, the smart contract in blockchain is used to manage contracts within the corporate governance structure among various stakeholders, such as management and shareholders. Hence, this study believes that such a contractual structure can also be clearly specified between the relevant AI actors. For instance, the liabilities across the AI supply chain to actors such as the manufacturers, operators, users and all stakeholders should be contractually managed. This will provide legal assistance in the event of litigation and allocation of liabilities.

Furthermore, a practical approach to AI responsibility and liability is the governance document approach. This includes the documentation and organisational risk matrices that align with regulatory standards (Custers et al., 2025; Fraser & Suzor, 2025; Wendehorst, 2020). Clear documentation provides clear processes and evidence necessary for risk assessments. From the perspective of AI responsibility and risk, clear documentation of all related AI behaviours will assist in making informed decisions and driving AI improvements. This will also assist in providing case law on historical behaviours and associated liabilities. Therefore, by replicating the governance documents approach in AI responsibilities and liabilities, risks can be assessed, and liabilities can be mitigated (Fig. 4.2).

### *4.3.5 Comparative Perspectives on AI Responsibilities and Liabilities*

Studies have been conducted in a country context to examine the existing perceptions regarding AI responsibilities and liabilities. The available scholarly works have focused on the United States, European countries, China and Saudi Arabia.

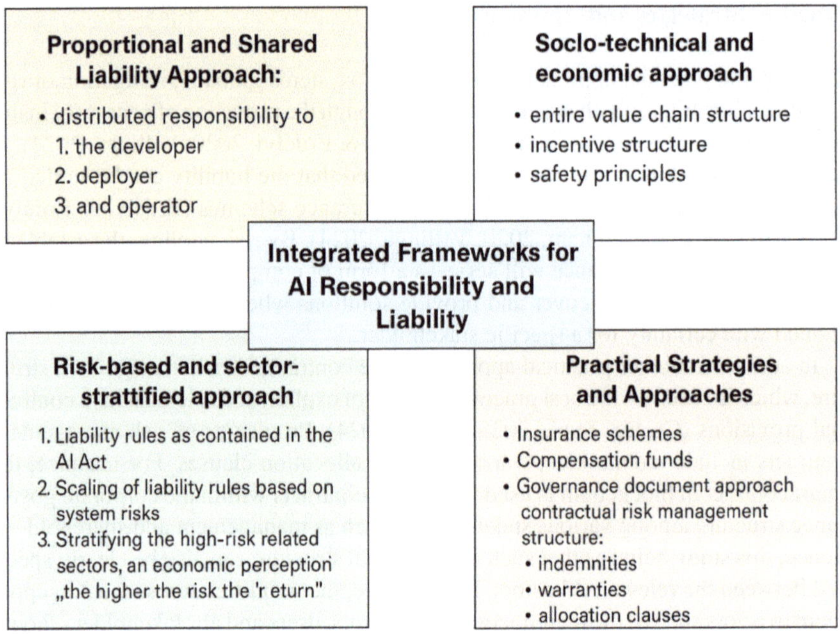


**Fig. 4.2** Integrated framework for AI responsibility and liability. *Source* Authors generated

### United States

Given the widespread use of AI in the United States, it is essential to establish a comprehensive AI law that applies to the entire state. Yet, to date, the United States lacks a federal statute specifically addressing AI-related liability. Aside from the lack of centralised AI Acts, scholars have argued that while the tort law remains decentralised and courts adapt the flexible means of handling cases based on an ad-hoc (case-by-case) basis, it is imperative to leverage the traditional risk assessments within the AI risk assessment structures (Chamberlain, 2023). Hence, the study advocates for the inclusion of this traditional risk assessment as a means of mitigating the anticipated (ex-ante) AI-related risks. Additionally, there exists an immunity for online platforms in US tort law (Section 230), which complicates the call for establishing liability for acts related to AI.

### China

Given the widespread use of AI in China, the legislature has already addressed some AI liability-related concerns, such as local regulations on fully autonomous operations, on which strict manufacturer liability has been imposed (Shenzhen, 2023). Aside from this, according to scholars, there are proposals on the autonomous driving law which aim to shift the liability from users (owners and drivers) to manufacturers (Duffourc & Gerke, 2023; Wei & Guo, 2025). Additionally, proposals for laws on compulsory insurance pools aim to enhance compensation, while mandatory data recorders, such as those in black boxes, are intended to mitigate related risks.

**European Countries**

The EU AI Act (2024) marked a significant stride in AI liability and responsibilities, making Europe a pace setter for the responsible use of AI and the identification of liability. Despite the recent enactment of this Act, scholars have critically assessed it and highlighted gaps in the Legislation. (Godlewska et al., 2020) argued that although the Act have addressed some major points in AI, anticipation regarding inconsistent outcomes in the EU member states should be expected. This is due to the lack of adaptive system concepts in the system. Also, based on the analysis of the proposal (AILD goals) in the Polish setting, without necessary doctrinal reforms, these goals will be hard to achieve. Hence, within the EU framework, there is a need for reformulation of doctrines among member states to support the implementation of the EU AI Acts. Given that AI is increasingly becoming a source of increased danger (Michurin, 2025) has advocated for the increased representation of AI liability in the legislation within the Ukrainian context.

**Saudi Arabia**

While there is limited scholarly discourse on AI responsibility and liability within the Saudi Arabian context, a study by (Aldmour, 2025) recommends integrating AI liability and transparency duties into Sustainable Development Goals 3, 9, and 16 of the Saudi Arabian system.

## 4.4 Criticising AI Accountability and Liability

### *4.4.1 Causation and Evidence in a Black-Box System*

The black box AI structure has been a significant challenge in the legal framework related to AI. This is due to the complex model features of the Blackbox AI. The causal insight into the failures of the system may be difficult to assess as only ad hoc compliance explanations may be provided. Hence, the black-box AI, based on the explainable AI techniques, have remained contested in courts (Grozdanovski, 2025).

### 4.4.2 Non-physical Harms

Scholars have argued that the existence of harms not limited to physicality, which are not yet represented in the AI liability act, is a concern. Harms may be dignitary harms, which can trigger significant damage to socio-economic aspects. Hence, it is important to expand the description of harms and associated liabilities based on the sectoral anti-discrimination statutes (De & Campos, 2024; Nersessian & Mancha, 2020).

### 4.4.3 Ecosystem Modelling

The attribution of risk expectations and the associated compensation have generated some suggestions. For instance, (Panezi, 2021) introduced a model based on the collective risk pools with contractual back allocation similar to the industrial product-safety approach. Whereas (Fraser & Suzor, 2025) The model is like the foreseeable and reasonable care approach, focusing on the organisation being responsible for isolated errors. Hence, the best approach to liability and compensation is still contested.

### 4.4.4 Scope of Strict Versus Fault-Based Liability

While Wagner (2022) advocated for liability focusing strictly on the manufacturers, Wendehorst (2020) advocated for a more lenient approach to manufacturers, as either or a combination of the operators, users, and organisations may be guilty of misuse; hence, users of high-risk systems that ignore manufacturers' control should be responsible for the associated liability.

### 4.4.5 Compensation

To date, the economic modelling of compensation remains unclear. Hence, there is a need for mandatory insurance and compensation funds to be set up for high-risk AI and for AI risks whose consistency of occurrence has been determined to be high. These challenges, as summarised by this chapter, have been presented in the Fig. 4.3.

**Fig. 4.3** Critical issues in AI accountability and liability. *Source* Author's compilation

**Critical Issues in AI Accountability and Liability**

1. Causation and evidence in a black-box system
2. Ecosystem Modelling
3. Non-physical harms
4. Scope of strict versus fault-based liability
5. Compensation

## 4.5 AI Responsibility and Liability: What is the Way Forward?

After assessing the scholarly and doctrinal arguments on AI responsibility and liability, it can be inferred that there is no conclusive direct answer, as the debate has generated diverse perceptions, suggestions, and additional arguments. Hence, this has created a significant gap that needs to be filled. It is imperative for this study to summarise the arguments and give a suggestion. This section discusses the author's perception based on the scholarly assessment as explained in this chapter. This aims to provide answers to all the research questions, particularly offering suggestions for question four: "*What concrete strategies and best practices can be implemented to promote responsible AI development and deployment?*".

First, this chapter suggests that further empirical studies may be conducted in this area. An example is the simulation of a real-life model. By replicating theoretical models in practical simulated scenarios, there may be more clarity on AI responsibility and liability. For instance, the thematic challenge of this study shows emerging themes such as compensation. By empirically replicating the economic models in a simulated environment, the most effective method of compensation can be determined. Additionally, there may be a need for a combination of various available economic models to compensate AI victims. For instance, there may be a need to include the enforcement of mandatory insurance, along with the establishment of a compensation fund for potential victims. The inclusion of both models may serve as a strong mitigation against AI-related losses to victims.

Moreover, based on the existing arguments, it can be reasonably concluded that the current laws, standards, and regulations regarding AI responsibility and liability are presently insufficient. Aside from the EU AI Act and the two twin directives, there appear to be limited regulations globally addressing this issue. Since AI usage is increasingly adopted by users globally, it is imperative to mitigate associated risks and reduce harms and victimisation. Hence, it is advised that there should be a global address of the legal issues surrounding AI.

While there is a need for the establishment of global standards on AI responsibility and liability, the doctrinal and economic models regarding AI responsibility and liability should be incorporated into the global standard-setting bodies, such as the International Federation of Accountants (IFAC) and other relevant organisations.

There is a need for the domestication of such standards to reflect the specific regions in which they are to be implemented. For instance, the issue of litigation and procedural orders related to AI should be addressed locally by each country. This perception is to address the issues peculiar to each jurisdiction. Hence, AI-related legal matters should be grounded in the human rights framework and the constitutional structure of each country.

Regarding the allocation of AI liability, there are ongoing debates about who should be held responsible for the liability arising from AI-related harms. Although this was a gap as it was not explicitly addressed by the EU AI Acts, the twin directives proposals are based on liability, as explained earlier in the chapter. While the revised product liability directive has been proposed and is awaiting approval, the AI liability directive was withdrawn in February 2025 due to a lack of consensus on the presumption of causation.

Hence, scholars have presented various perspectives on the liable actors, while some argue that the manufacturers of such AI should be held accountable, while others believe that the operators may make errors related to implementation. Hence, this paper aligns with the doctrinal basis. AI acts may be replicated in other countries by including this gap in the domestic jurisdiction basis. Additionally, responsibilities related to AI, along with the corresponding liabilities, should be clearly stated before the AI is made available for use. Clauses regarding AI-related matters should be drafted in accordance with the applicable AI Acts and potential global standards, as interpreted by local jurisdictions. Hence, satisfying the issue of responsibility and liability clauses should be achieved before AI is released to the public. If there is no clarity on these, the manufacturer should be liable. Hence, this study believes that the legal standards related to AI should be addressed by each country in accordance with human rights principles. Hence, the promulgation of laws, standards, and regulations regarding AI responsibility and liability is of utmost importance.

Additionally, regarding AI risks, this study suggests that, based on the EU AI Act, which categorises AI risk into varying levels of risk, ranging from unacceptable to low risks, all AI systems globally should be ethically classified into these risk levels. Aside from the lowest risk on the threshold of classification, while unacceptable risks, such as babysitting, should not be allocated to AI systems, related activities in this regard should be carried out by humans. High AI risks should be subject to transparency and human oversight. Given that these AIs are useful for humans, humans should act as their administrators, and they must be submitted to human operation based on human rights standards. This aims to mitigate the associated high risks and irreversible harms that may be caused by the riskiness of AI.

For instance, automated vehicles should be transitioned to full human operations, and matters related to medical, black-box, and legal AI should be overseen by humans. Therefore, while AI serves as an assistive technology to humans, it must be subjected to human control and administration. Expert administrators should be trained to handle these matters. For instance, based on actor-network theory, it can be translated into how the administrative, or human, factor cooperates with the network, or AI, to carry out a successful task. While the technology contributes by offering a workflow and other digital guides, or by automating tasks that have previously been done manually by humans, it aids humans in carrying out tasks.

Hence, technology and law are expected to function together with the objective of achieving fair procedures. AI should be designed in accordance with legal and ethical standards and principles. They should also be subjected to the national constitution and international standards on human rights. For instance, in German courts, an AI system known as Smart Sentences is used. The AI was designed to analyse case law across time and jurisdictions of the German courts. While analysing, the AI was subjected to human administration, as reflected in the judges' supervision of it and in the categorisation of case law.

Finally, AI accountability should be viewed as instilling values into AI based on systemic values and interests. For instance, AI used within an organisation should be designed and embedded with the organisation's values. This will foster alignment of activities (e.g., in a translation firm, speech-to-text can be embedded into AI design). In summary, while AI may reduce the need for human operations, it also creates new jobs. People need to be trained to become expert operators and administrators of AI. Expertise in this sense leads to the timely recognition of AI's incorrect diagnoses and errors, thereby reducing the associated harms, victimisation, and liability. These suggestions are summarised in Fig. 4.4 titled "key strategies for responsible AI accountability and liability". The purpose of summarizing them is to classify all the suggested strategies under relevant subheadings. This will help readers understand the entire chapter more easily and interpret it more effectively.

## 4.6 Conclusion

This chapter addresses concerns related to AI accountability and liability by examining the discourse of available scholars, AI-related proposals, and the EU AI acts of 2024. The EU twin directives (the two proposals in 2022) reflect the most advanced attempts to examine AI accountability and liabilities in the present world. While the EU AI acts and proposals attempts to modernise the AI related remedies, scholars have criticise the existing gaps in the system which include the harmonization capability among all the member states, given that in some of these countries, the available legislatures may not be reasonably sufficient to enact the act and the interpretation, based on the different legal framework applicable in each country. This study also attempts to examine the comparison of AI perspectives across various countries, including the United States, China, European countries, and Saudi Arabia. While the United States is based on Tort law and each state has an ad-hoc court system, there currently lacks a federal law to address AI accountability and liability. Additionally, there are legal issues that could contradict the proposed AI law. For instance, the law supporting online platforms may contradict AI acts. In China, while local legislatures exist for high-risk AI, there are currently proposals for other forms of AI. In Saudi Arabia, although a scholarly discourse exists, it is suggested that AI liabilities be incorporated into some of the existing SDG programs. This study also examines the

**Fig. 4.4** Key strategies for responsible AI accountability and liability. *Source* Author's generated

discourse on the ecosystem modelling of the AI liability structure. While manufacturers may be responsible for AI errors, in situations where users experience harm due to the misuse of systems, especially when the manufacturer clearly states the direction for use, the manufacturers are not liable. Additionally, compensation for liabilities was discussed in this study. Models have been created by scholars, and this study suggests that high-risk AI should have mandatory insurance and compensation funds allocated to potential victims. The clause of harms should also be extended to non-physical harms. Although this paper attempts to cover major areas in AI accountability and liability, limitation exists. For instance, this study only examines the prior body of literature and grey areas; there is a need for empirical assessment of AI accountability and liability. Future studies can therefore empirically assess this topic.

## References


Alaba Ogedengbe, F. (2024). Investigating the influence of IT inaccessibility and social pressure on employees shadow cloud IT usage during the COVID-19 pandemic MCO period. *International Journal of Business Information Systems, 47*(4), 1.

Aldmour, R. (2025). Civil liability for damages caused by artificial intelligence in light of sustainable development goals "SDG3, 9 & 16" "A legal analysis within the Saudi civil transactions system. *Journal of Lifestyle and SDGs Review, 5*(5), e06197. https://doi.org/10.47172/2965-730x.sdgsreview.v5.n05.pe06197

Ampovska, M. (2024). European Union civil liability frameworks in the age of artificial intelligence: Assessing current regimes and future prospects. *Vestnik Sankt-Peterburgskogo Universiteta. Pravo, 15*(2), 466–482. https://doi.org/10.21638/spbu14.2024.210

Bas, G., Salinas, C., Tinoco, R., & Sevilla, J. (2024). The EU AI Act: A pioneering effort to regulate frontier AI? *Inteligencia Artificial, 27*, 55–64. https://doi.org/10.4114/intartif.vol27iss73pp55-64

Bashayreh, M., Sibai, F. N., & Tabbara, A. (2021). Artificial intelligence and legal liability: Towards an international approach of proportional liability based on risk sharing. *Information and Communications Technology Law, 30*(2), 169–192. https://doi.org/10.1080/13600834.2020.1856025

Beroual, N. (2025). AI and civil liability: Contrasting Algerian legislation with the European Union's regulatory approach. *Science, Education and Innovations in the Context of Modern Problems, 8*(5), 133–143. https://doi.org/10.56334/sei/8.5.15

Calvano, M., Curci, A., Desolda, G., Esposito, A., Lanzilotti, R., & Piccinno, A. (2025). Building Symbiotic AI: Reviewing the AI Act for a Human-Centred, Principle-Based Framework. ArXiv, abs/2501.08046. https://doi.org/10.48550/arXiv.2501.08046

Čerka, P., Grigienė, J., & Sirbikytė, G. (2015). Liability for damages caused by artificial intelligence. *Computer Law and Security Review, 31*(3), 376–389. https://doi.org/10.1016/j.clsr.2015.03.008

Chamberlain, J. (2023). The risk-based approach of the European Union's proposed artificial intelligence regulation: Some comments from a tort law perspective. *European Journal of Risk Regulation, 14*(1), 1–13. https://doi.org/10.1017/err.2022.38

Contini, F., Ontanu, E. A., & Velicogna, M. (2024). AI accountability in judicial proceedings: An actor–network approach. *Laws, 13*(6). https://doi.org/10.3390/laws13060071

Custers, B., Lahmann, H., & Scott, B. I. (2025). From liability gaps to liability overlaps: Shared responsibilities and fiduciary duties in AI and other complex technologies. *AI and Society, 40*(5), 4035–4050. https://doi.org/10.1007/s00146-024-02137-1

De, M., & Campos, L. (2024). *Comments on the article titled "The regulation of AI liability in Europe: a critical overview of two recent Directive Proposals-the (new) ALD and the (revised) PLD" by Beatriz Garcia*. E-Publica.

Duffourc, M. N., & Gerke, S. (2023). The proposed EU directives for AI liability leave worrying gaps likely to impact medical AI. *NPJ Digital Medicine*. https://doi.org/10.1038/s41746-023-00823-w

Ebers, M. (2024). Truly risk-based regulation of artificial intelligence how to implement the EU's AI Act. *European Journal of Risk Regulation*. https://doi.org/10.1017/err.2024.78

Enigbokan, O. (2025). Examining the potential challenges of artificial intelligence in statelessness determination from a human rights perspective. *International Human Rights Law Review*. https://doi.org/10.1163/22131035-14020001

Erdélyi, O. J., & Erdélyi, G. (2020). The AI liability puzzle and a fund-based work-around. In *Proceedings of the AAAI/ACM conference on AI, ethics, and society* (pp. 50–56). https://doi.org/10.1145/3375627.3375806

Fernández Llorca, D., Charisi, V., & Hamon, R. (2023). Liability regimes in the age of AI: A use-case driven analysis of the burden of proof. *Journal of Artificial Intelligence Research, 76*, 1.

Fraser, H. L., & Suzor, N. P. (2025). Locating fault for AI harms: A systems theory of foreseeability, reasonable care and causal responsibility in the AI value chain. *Law, Innovation and Technology, 17*(1), 103–138. https://doi.org/10.1080/17579961.2025.2469345

Godlewska, M., Morawska, S., & Banasik, P. (2020). Civil liability for artificial intelligence products versus the sustainable development of CEECs: Which institutions matter? *Ruch Prawniczy, Ekonomiczny i Socjologiczny, 82*(2), 179–192. https://doi.org/10.14746/rpeis.2020.82.2.13

Graaf, T. de, & Veldt, G. (2022). The AI act and its impact on product safety, contracts and liability. *European Review of Private Law*. https://doi.org/10.54648/erpl2022038

Grozdanovski, L. (2025). The explanations one needs for the explanations one gives—The necessity of explainable AI (XAI) for causal explanations of AI-related harm: Deconstructing the "refuge of ignorance" in the EU's AI liability regulation. *International Journal of Law, Ethics, and Technology*. https://doi.org/10.2139/ssrn.4740419

Hacker, P. (2023). AI regulation in Europe: From the AI act to future regulatory challenges. In *Oxford Handbook of Algorithmic Governance of Law*. Oxford University Press. https://carnegieendowment.org/2023/02/14/lessons-from-world-s-two-experiments-in-ai-

Hacker, P., & Mauer, M. (2023). *The European AI liability directives-critique of a half-hearted approach and lessons for the future*.

Laux, J. (2024). Institutionalised distrust and human oversight of artificial intelligence: Towards a democratic design of AI governance under the European Union AI Act. *AI and Society, 39*(6), 2853–2866. https://doi.org/10.1007/s00146-023-01777-z

Li, S., Faure, M., & Havu, K. (2022). Liability rules for AI-related harm: Law and economics lessons for a European approach. *European Journal of Risk Regulation, 13*(4), 618–634. https://doi.org/10.1017/err.2022.26

Li, S., & Schütte, B. (2024). The proposed EU artificial intelligence liability directive does/will its content reflect its ambition? *Technology and Regulation*. https://doi.org/10.26116/techreg.2024.014

Luiz De Moura, J., & Júnior, F. (2024). Algorithmic torts: The role of explainability. *Brazilian Journal of Law, Technology and Innovation*. https://orcid.org/0000-0002-0192-2336

Marta, Z., Mokander, J., Novelli, C., Casalari, F., Taddeo, M., & Floridi, L. (2024). The EU AI liability directive (AILD): Bridging information gaps. *AI and Society, 39*(4), 1871–1882. https://doi.org/10.1007/s00146-023-01635-y

Michurin, I. (2025). Subjects of civil liability for damage caused by the use of artificial intelligence under the legislation of the Eu and Ukraine. *University Scientific Notes, 4*(106), 4–13. https://doi.org/10.37491/UNZ.106.1

Moch, E. (2024). Liability issues in the context of artificial intelligence: Legal challenges and solutions for AI-supported decisions. *East African Journal of Law and Ethics, 7*(1), 214–234. https://doi.org/10.37284/eajle.7.1.2518

Nersessian, D., & Mancha, R. (2020). From automation to autonomy: Legal and ethical responsibility from automation to autonomy: Legal and ethical responsibility gaps in artificial intelligence innovation gaps in artificial intelligence innovation. *Michigan Technology Law Review Michigan Technology Law Review Article, 3*, 2021. https://repository.law.umich.edu/mtlr. https://repository.law.umich.edu/mtlr/vol27/iss1/3

Noto La Diega, G., & Bezerra, L. C. T. (2024). Can there be responsible AI without AI liability? Incentivizing generative AI safety through ex-post tort liability under the EU AI liability directive. *International Journal of Law and Information Technology*. https://doi.org/10.1093/ijlit/eaae021

Novelli, C., Taddeo, M., & Floridi, L. (2024). Accountability in artificial intelligence: What it is and how it works. *AI and Society, 39*(4), 1871–1882. https://doi.org/10.1007/s00146-023-01635-y

Ogedengbe, F. A., & Adelowotan, M. O. (2025). Revolutionising corporate governance: Blockchain's transformative impact and potential. In *Frontiers in Blockchain* (Vol. 8). Frontiers Media SA. https://doi.org/10.3389/fbloc.2025.1654633

Padovan, P. H., Martins, C. M., & Reed, C. (2023). Black is the new orange: How to determine AI liability. *Artificial Intelligence and Law, 31*(1), 133–167. https://doi.org/10.1007/s10506-022-09308-9

Panezi, A. (2021). Liability rules for AI-facilitated wrongs: An ecosystem approach to manage risk and uncertainty. *Social Science Research Network.* https://apnews.com/article/homicide-arizona-transportation-archive-

Popa, D. M. (2024). Multilevel oversight of AI systems in line with the AI Act. *AI Policy Exchange Forum.* https://doi.org/10.63439/xefy3802

Scherer, M. U. (2016). Regulating artificial intelligence systems: Risks, challenges, competencies, and strategies. *Harvard Journal of Law & Technology, 29*(2). http://www.theguardian.com/technology/2014/sep/12/artificial-intelligence-data-

Schütte, B., Majewski, L., & Havu, K. (2021a). Damages liability for harm caused by artificial intelligence-EU law in flux damages liability for harm caused by artificial intelligence-EU law in flux. *Helsinki Legal Studies Research Paper, 69*, 35. http://www.ssrn.comElectroniccopyavailableat. https://ssrn.com/abstract=3897839

Schütte, B., Majewski, L., & Havu, K. (2021b). *University of Helsinki faculty of law damages liability for harm caused by artificial intelligence-EU law in flux damages liability for harm caused by artificial intelligence-EU Law in Flux.* http://www.ssrn.comElectroniccopyavailableat. https://ssrn.com/abstract=3897839

Smith, H., & Fotheringham, K. (2020). Artificial intelligence in clinical decision-making: Rethinking liability. *Medical Law International, 20*(2), 131–154. https://doi.org/10.1177/0968533220945766

Sovrano, F., & Masetti, G. (2022). Foreseeing the impact of the proposed AI Act on the sustainability and safety of critical infrastructures. *Proceedings of the 15th International Conference on Theory and Practice of Electronic Governance.* https://doi.org/10.1145/3560107.3560253

Sundaraparipurnan, N., & Potkewitz, M. (2023). *A risk-based approach to assessing liability risk for AI-driven harms considering EU liability directive Self-assessment of liability risk for AI-driven harms.*

Truli, E. N. (2023). Non-contractual liability in the context of artificial intelligence: The long way to new EU legislative tools. *European Review of Private Law*, 35–56. https://doi.org/10.54648/erpl2023002

Vellinga, N. E. (2024). Rethinking compensation in light of the development of AI. *International Review of Law, Computers and Technology, 38*(3), 391–412. https://doi.org/10.1080/13600869.2024.2324554

Wagner, G. (2022). Liability rules for the digital age—Aiming for the Brussels effect. *Journal of European Tort Law, 13*(3), 191–243. https://doi.org/10.1515/jetl-2022-0012

Wei, X., & Guo, C. (2025). A comparative legal study on the attribution of liability for autonomous driving accidents in China and Germany. *Country, Area and Advanced Technology.* https://doi.org/10.37420/j.caatj.2025.003

Wendehorst, C. (2020). Strict liability for AI and other emerging technologies. *Journal of European Tort Law, 11*(2), 150–180. https://doi.org/10.1515/jetl-2020-0140

Wörsdörfer, M. (2023). Mitigating the adverse effects of AI with the European Union's artificial intelligence act: Hype or hope? *Global Business and Organizational Excellence.* https://doi.org/10.1002/joe.22238

Zafar, S., Kelly, J., Heidemann, L., & Mata, N. (2025). Leveraging existing road-vehicle standards to address EU AI Act compliance. *2025 IEEE/ACM International Workshop on Responsible AI Engineering (RAIE)*, 74–81. https://doi.org/10.1109/RAIE66699.2025.00017

Zdraveva, N. (2024). *Odgovornost za štetu prouzrokovanu upotrebom sistema veštačke inteligencije u pravu Evropske unije – stanje i izazovi.* 195–218. https://doi.org/10.51204/internet_dijalog_2410a

Zhang, R. (2025). Autonomous vehicles: Legal governance of civil liability risks. *Lecture Notes in Education Psychology and Public Media, 96*(1), 108–114. https://doi.org/10.54254/2753-7048/2025.bo24130

# Chapter 5
# Data Privacy and Security

**Nusirat Ojuolape Gold and Tasneem Mahmood**

**Abstract** In an era where Artificial Intelligence (AI) is proliferating every system with processes that rely heavily on large amounts of personal and sensitive data, data privacy and security have become a central concern for ethical AI governance. This chapter explores this evolving landscape, particularly the AI-driven data processing within the rapidly evolving digital and regulatory landscapes of the Sub-Saharan African context. The chapter highlights the peculiarities surrounding AI-system privacy and security challenges. Drawing on the contextual integrity, social control, information boundary, and ethical decision-making theories, this chapter explores how Privacy-Enhancing Technologies (PETs) and governance approaches can reduce risks arising from the vast data processing and algorithm decision-making. Employing a qualitative integrative review approach that synthesizes recent scholarly work, policy frameworks, and regional initiatives, the chapter identifies and addresses the existing challenges faced with balancing data-driven innovation with robust privacy protections and suggests actionable roadmaps for integrating privacy and security principles into AI system development. The chapter synthesis also highlights recurrent issues like fragmented regulatory frameworks, limited infrastructural facilities, resource constraints, and gaps in capacity building, underscoring opportunities for responsible AI adoption through context-specific governance and technical safeguards that use PETs such as differential privacy, end-to-end encryption, federated learning, privacy-by-design approaches, and homomorphic encryption that enhances security while maintaining AI's functionality. Therefore, ensuring AI systems remain accountable, transparent, and aligned with user rights. Through this integrative approach, the chapter reinforces the need for a multidisciplinary strategy combining law, technology, and policy with designing AI ecosystems that safeguard privacy while enabling responsible technological advancements. The chapter, therefore, concludes with practical recommendations for integrating AI innovations

N. O. Gold (✉)
Department of Commercial Accounting, University of Johannesburg, Johannesburg, South Africa
e-mail: ngold@uj.ac.za; nusirat.gold@kwasu.edu.ng

T. Mahmood
Department of Accountancy, College of Business and Economics, University of Johannesburg, Johannesburg, South Africa
e-mail: tmahmood@uj.ac.za

 
M. Adelowotan and H. Coovadia (eds.), *AI and Accountability*, CSR, Sustainability, Ethics & Governance, https://doi.org/10.1007/978-3-032-20091-4_5

with strong data governance and ethical accountability for the Sub-Saharan African context.

## 5.1 Introduction

Data privacy and security have been steering constant debate globally owing to the rapid advancement in technologies, which has led to significant increases in data generation, gathering, and processing. While data security is concerned with preventing unauthorized access, alteration, or loss of personal information, data privacy is particular with an individual's control over the collection, usage, sharing, and deletion of personal information. The widespread adoption of artificial intelligence (AI) systems across public and private establishments has increased the scope and stakes of data privacy and security. This is particularly owing to their reliance on vast, diverse datasets and continuous model retraining. The scale and opacity further increase the likelihood for re-identification, erroneous conclusions, and misuse of personal information (Munung et al., 2024; Zaidan & Ibrahim, 2024).

AI-based models frequently integrate health, financial, mobile, and geolocation data to produce insightful results. They have also opened new possibilities for data misuse, re-identification, and inference of sensitive attributes. For instance, in Africa, particularly Sub-Saharan Africa, due to fragmented data infrastructure, lack of regulatory harmonization, and weak technical capability to implement strong privacy-by-design strategies, risks of data misuse and privacy breach are exacerbated (Ayana et al., 2024; Effoduh et al., 2024; Plantinga et al., 2024). This does not deny the fact that AI promises unique opportunities that can reshape different sectors, including the educational landscape, agriculture, businesses, finance, and healthcare globally. But, the benefits can only be attained if data practices are reliable and individual rights are protected (Coovadia et al., 2025; Mienye et al., 2024).

Although governments and organizations across SSA are eager to leverage AI to further advance their goals in each of these sectors as recent evidence shows that a growing number of countries within the region have been coming up with their own data protection laws. While this is commendable, the enforcement of such laws, public awareness of data privacy rights, and the strength of regulatory standards remain inconsistent across the region. Besides, it is crucial to note that when privacy and security failed to be ingrained by design, the same data flows that ought to foster AI's benefit would end up threatening public trust and individual rights (Mienye et al., 2024; Munung et al., 2024). Since the geographical landscape varies across countries, with some regions having active regulators and contemporary data protection laws, others are yet to establish basic legal frameworks (Munung et al., 2024; Plantinga et al., 2024). This has led to cross-border regulatory friction for AI systems, thereby creating difficulty for scaling data-driven solutions across the regions (Africa Data Protection Report, 2024; Musoni, 2024).

As countries within the continent have begun recognizing the significance of safeguarding personal and sensitive data, issues, especially those about data sovereignty, cybersecurity vulnerabilities, and trust in institutions, persist. Recent technological developments, popularly referred to as PETs such as Differential Privacy (DP) and Federated Learning (FL), offer useful tools to mitigate privacy risks while allowing for insightful data analytics. Yet, poor governance mechanisms to promote PETs uptake, limited infrastructure, uneven technical skills, and cost concerns are some of the factors that have been hindering adoption in SSA (ISACA, 2024; Tayych & Al-Jumaili, 2024). Hence, the need for regionally relevant guidelines on integrating privacy and security into AI lifecycles is highlighted by these governance and capacity gaps.

SSA is faced with a dual challenge: First is that AI applications depend largely on cross-sectoral data without consistently incorporating privacy-by-design and security-by-design principles; and second is the regional differences in organizational and regulatory capabilities to operationalize such design principles. The outcome is a recurring conflict between two policy goals, i.e., using AI for development and safeguarding citizens' data rights, one that is made worse by disjointed data protection laws, a slow adoption of PETs, and financial limitations that compromise risk management and organizational compliance. This misalignment erodes public trust, limits the sustainable scaling of AI solutions throughout SSA, and puts people at risk for harm (privacy violations, discriminatory inferences) (Lawyers Hub, 2023; Munung et al., 2024).

Given the foregoing issues and conditions, this chapter seeks to answer a very pertinent question: How can SSA companies and government establishments implement strong data privacy and security measures throughout the AI design lifecycle, employing workable technical, organizational, and governance measures to facilitate reliable, privacy protection-compliant AI deployment? To answer this vital question, the chapter focused on SSA and proceeded with the following objectives.

(i) Clarify current definitions and differences between data privacy and data security in AI systems.
(ii) Outline privacy and security risks associated with ethical and legal issues arising from AI deployment, including sectoral risks and priorities
(iii) Assess existing PETs and governance mechanisms
(iv) Propose a workable governance strategy that synchronizes technical PETs with organisational processes and emerging regional legal mandates like the Protection of Personal Information Act (POPIA) and other African data protection guidelines.
(v) Suggest practical roadmaps for organizations, businesses, and policymakers in SSA to integrate privacy and security by design into AI system design, while accounting for local constraints and regional opportunities

The chapter discusses and suggests how ethical AI governance can safeguard data privacy and security in SSA by drawing from four interrelated theories: contextual integrity, information boundary, ethical decision-making, and social control. Collectively, they inform the chapters' core argument that maintaining data privacy and security in an AI-driven environment necessitates striking a balance between individuals' autonomy, ethical governance, and contextual regulation.

The chapter contributes uniquely to regional discourse in multiple ways. (a) It synthesizes the most recent scholarly literature and key practitioner resources on the realities facing SSA. (b) By linking technical trade-offs (such as privacy vs. model utility) to practical organizational constraints, the chapter evaluates the operational viability of PETs and governance measures specifically for SSA organizations. (c) It provides a pragmatic governance roadmap that unifies recommended practices with regional legal regimes (particularly POPIA and emerging continental initiatives) and assigns responsibilities to the board, IT, legal, and operational teams. By doing this, the chapter goes beyond theoretical recommendations and offers actionable context-specific guidance.

The chapter is justified and deemed critical for three reasons. First, because the use of AI in SSA is gaining widespread adoption, the institutional and technological framework for safeguarding the personal information of users is still in its infancy. This, therefore, presents urgent ethical and legal challenges for both individuals and institutions (Plantinga et al., 2024). Second, although there are PETs, there is a lack of documentation regarding their practical application in cross-jurisdictional and low-resource African contexts; practitioners require guidelines that specifically address infrastructure, skill, and cost limitations (ISACA, 2024). Third, harmonized, practical guidelines that bridge the gaps between data protection impact assessments (DPIAs), PETs, board oversight, vendor due diligence, and regulator engagement could significantly limit privacy harms and increase stakeholder trust, opening the door to safer AI for development objectives (Africa Data Protection Report, 2024). Overall, the chapter responds to an urgent call for regionally relevant guidance: SSA faces unique trade-offs between harnessing AI for development and protecting citizens' rights. And without context-sensitive governance, AI deployment risks amplifying inequality, undermining privacy protection, or enabling intrusive surveillance (Alaran et al., 2025; Masinde et al., 2025).

The rest of the chapter is structured as follows: Section 5.2 focuses on literature discussion with particular focus on the different definitions of privacy and security; next, map privacy and security risks across different sectors including finance and public services in SSA; next section discusses PETs, governance tools, and their suitability; this is followed by the theoretical foundation; then the methodology. The next section presents a stakeholder-centric governance roadmap with short to long-term prioritized actions, and the next section provides policy recommendations for regulators and capacity-building actions for practitioners. The final section discusses pathways that SSA companies can employ to operationalize privacy and security throughout the AI lifecycle.

## 5.2 Literature Review

### *5.2.1 Conceptual Definitions*

The application of deep learning algorithms in AI is significantly enhancing efficiency and business processes. The advancement has dramatically accelerated data generation across individual, enterprise, and institutional levels. Previously, personal information seemed to be a very simple term, but with technological advancement, particularly the fourth industrial revolution (4IR), its boundaries became blurred, making it increasingly complex to define (Masinde et al., 2025). More importantly, the rise of Internet of Things (IoT), AI, and other pervasive data collection tools reinforces that personal information now extends far beyond traditional identifiers like names, phone numbers, and addresses (Cheng et al., 2022).

Data privacy simply refers to the rights, practices, and principles governing the collection, processing, storage, and protection of personal information. It has to do with who can access, use, share, and manage personal information and under what conditions. Data privacy protection is also a way to protect personal data from unauthorized use, access, and manipulation (Mosaiyebzadeh et al., 2023). Its main goal is to guarantee that users maintain control over their personal data and that it is used in a way that complies with individuals' consent and contextual expectations. At the center of privacy are rules, consent, legitimate purposes, and the preservation of users' informational autonomy. For instance, whether an organization is permitted to gather or deduce sensitive information from data or whether it is permitted to share records with third parties (Conduah et al., 2025; Martin & Zimmermann, 2024). Data security, on the other hand, relates to technical and organizational measures safeguarding an individual's data against unauthorized access, alteration, loss, or disclosure (Al-Kharusi et al., 2024). While privacy regulates how and why data may be used, security is concerned with ensuring confidentiality, integrity, and availability throughout the data lifecycle (storage, transmission, processing). These obligations are different but still complementary because strong security is necessary for privacy; however, security by itself does not guarantee that data will be used in an ethical or privacy-compliant manner. Besides, this distinction is very important for AI systems as they raise the stakes of both concepts. First, even in situations where datasets are supposedly "anonymized," the efficacy of AI often relies on combining and connecting disparate datasets, raising the possibility of privacy violations like re-identification or inference of sensitive attributes (Martin & Zimmermann, 2024). Second, research has stressed that AI generally brings about unique security threats that target models and data pipelines, which the traditional IT security techniques might not be able to handle (Alhitmi et al., 2024; Al-Kharusi et al., 2024). Examples of such threats include model inversion, membership inference, and backdoor attacks. Hence, organizations must be ready to deal with two interrelated issues, namely: protecting data and AI artifacts from harm and limiting AI's use of data in a way that safeguards individuals' rights and expectations.

The Organization for Economic Co-operation and Development (OECD), 2023, defines AI governance as a multi-stakeholder framework for ensuring AI systems are inclusive, human-centered, transparent, robust, and accountable. It entails the policies, procedures, regulations, and organizational strategies guiding the development, usage, and oversight of AI systems, so that they are safe, reliable, lawful, and conform to societal laws and values. It covers accountability procedures, standards, audits, transparency needs, and risk management techniques. Recent analysis of governance under the European Union (EU) AI Act highlighted the regulatory procedures necessary for controlling AI threats across sectors (European Union, 2024).

Ethical AI governance, on the other hand, is almost similar to AI governance but refers to the design, deployment, and use of AI systems in a manner that aligns with moral values, norms, priorities, fairness, accountability, transparency, and societal well-being (Plantinga et al., 2024). Ethical AI has been explained using principles of beneficence, non-maleficence, autonomy, fairness, and explicability (Floridi & Cowls, 2022). It therefore addresses concerns relating to bias mitigation, fairness issues, transparency, inclusivity, and damage prevention. It is more of a value-driven principle than legal frameworks and focuses on what organizations ought to do, even if regulations do not explicitly require them. The concept underpins a variety of international frameworks for AI governance, including the OECD AI Principles, the EU Ethics Guidelines for Trustworthy AI, and the Institute of Electrical and Electronics Engineers (IEEE) Global Initiative on Ethics of Autonomous and Intelligent Systems (Plantinga et al., 2024).

In a nutshell, data privacy safeguards individuals' information, AI governance protects society by regulating AI systems and activities of stakeholders, and Ethical AI guards societal values and principles, ensuring the AI system is fair, reliable, and beneficial.

### *5.2.2 Theoretical Underpinning*

This chapter anchors its analysis on four interrelated theories that collectively explain how AI systems protect personal information. Nissenbaum's (2004) Contextual Integrity theory (CIT) provides the normative foundation with which this chapter explains why several AI-driven privacy issues arise. AI systems often deviate from predicted contextual information flows by aggregating data in opaque ways, profiling across contexts, and repurposing data. This theory is particularly useful in explaining how organizational settings, with their unique norms and relational dynamics, must adapt their data-handling practices to preserve confidentiality and trust. This theory emphasizes how crucial it is to match technological design with contextual consent and fairness in AI environments where data is reused and transferred across domains. It therefore applies to the definition, problems, and PETs sections to demonstrate how privacy violations occur when AI systems fail to conform with contextual norms (For instance, health vs financial data usage).

The second is the Information Boundary theory (IBT), a synthesis of Petronio (1991)'s communication boundary management and privacy. This theory explains how individuals establish and manage boundaries around their personal information, particularly in digital environments (Conduah et al., 2025). i.e., how people control the flow of their personal data by creating psychological and social boundaries. The theory, therefore, posits that people establish informational spaces with clear boundaries to preserve their privacy, and they feel uneasy when these boundaries are crossed. The theory emphasizes that privacy breaches often happen when control over these boundaries is lost. As a result, the theory complements this by explaining how people manage the disclosure of personal information. This is of relevance to AI systems that collect user data without explicit consent. We apply this theory systematically to issues pertaining to consent failures, data minimization problems, and zero-knowledge proofs (ZKPs), demonstrating how PETs can strengthen or protect personal boundaries in settings with fragmented regulatory mechanisms.

In order to offer an analytical account of how organizations behave, particularly those in the SSA, and why they sometimes choose to employ weak encryption and insecure data practices, the chapter also employs the Ethical Decision-making theory. Organizations within the SSA region sometimes choose this form of practice due to moral disengagement, misaligned incentives, or even cost–benefit biases. Trevino (1986) sheds light on how organizations and developers make moral decisions regarding the collection, storage, and use of data. It highlights how decisions about privacy are influenced by personal values, corporate culture, and ethical environments. This chapter's AI governance and roadmap sections integrate this theoretical perspective to support the need for accountability frameworks, audits, and duty-of-care procedures.

Hirschi (2017) Social Control theory (SCT) offers the backbone for governance-based recommendations. This theory, while strengthening the regulatory aspect, emphasizes the importance of formal control measures (i.e., oversight, accountability, regulation, and compliance) and informal control measures (professional codes of conduct and social norms) that influence responsible data behaviours and safe data environments. This theory is applied to the SSA governance roadmap, demonstrating how strong enforcement strategies, societal norms, and sectoral standards reduce privacy-violating behaviour.

Collectively, these theories provide a comprehensive framework that combines social norms, institutional governance, organizational responsibility, and individual ethics to explain how data security and privacy can be successfully incorporated into AI systems. The theories are woven throughout the sections of the chapter to explain (a) the behaviour of stakeholders when handling sensitive data, (b) why privacy and security concerns do arise, and (c) what governance and technical strategies are required to align AI systems with ethical norms and contextual expectations (Fig. 5.1).

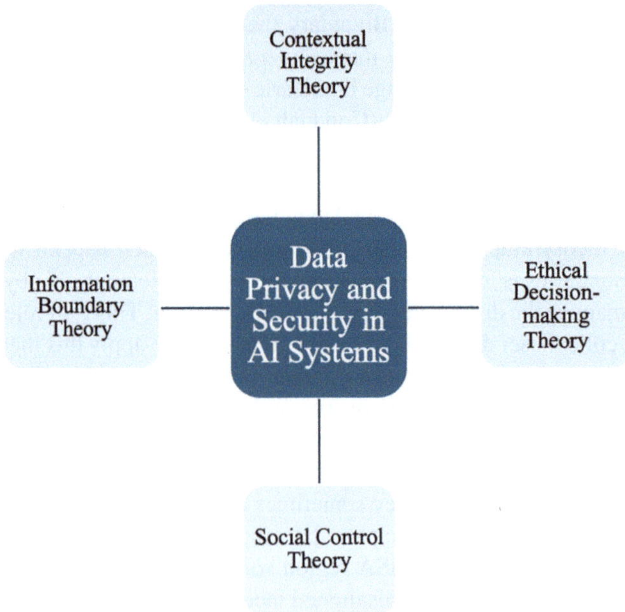


**Fig. 5.1** Theoretical framework

## 5.3 Methodology

### *5.3.1 Research Approach*

The chapter explores data privacy and security concerns in SSA's AI governance employing a structured qualitative research design based on an integrative literature review approach, which synthesizes recent scholarly research, policy frameworks, and regulatory standards from different sources, including databases like Web of Science (WoS), Scopus, IEEE Xplore, and Google Scholar, suitable for conceptual discourse in the emerging SSA setting. This approach is ideal to systematically analyze recent contemporary literature on data privacy, data security, AI governance, and ethics to derive a coherent analytical framework tailored for the SSA context.

### *5.3.2 Sample Selection Criteria*

Documents employed for this chapter were sourced mainly from peer-reviewed journal articles, policy documents such as those from OECD, EU, and South African POPIA, and other relevant institutional reports. To ensure recency and contemporary relevance, the chapter focused mainly on scholarly articles and published documents within the last five years, owing to the rapid technological and regulatory policy developments.

**Inclusion Criteria**

(i) The chapter considered journal articles, including book chapters, that are focused on data privacy, security, AI governance, and institutional policy guidelines relevant to SSA digital ecosystems and comparable emerging economies.
(ii) We also considered empirical and theoretical studies relevant to PETs
(iii) Articles and policy documents must be published in English.

**Exclusion Criteria**

(i) Articles published before 2020 with no relevance to privacy, security, AI governance, ethical AI, and SSA.
(ii) Research papers and policy documents that focus exclusively on developed countries without generalizability to other contexts.

### *5.3.3 Data Extraction and Thematic Development*

The extracted articles were coded for recurrent themes about (i) definitions, (ii) challenges, (iii) PETs, (iv) AI governance strategies and accountability, and (v) SSA AI governance regulation and ethical principles using a structured coding process guided by the thematic analysis of (Braun & Clarke, 2023; Byrne, 2022). The codes were iteratively grouped into high-order themes, with four interwoven theoretical lenses guiding the analytical interpretation rather than mere descriptive groupings. For instance, to justify the arguments, "contextual privacy violations" were analysed through CIT, while "weak institutional enforcement" was interpreted through SCT. This approach ensured that selected themes were conceptually robust and theoretically grounded. This consequently helped in shaping the entire chapter structure through conceptual definitions, privacy and security challenges identification, PETs analysis, highlighting of governance mechanisms and instruments, and finally suggesting pathways for developing a roadmap tailored to the SSA context. This methodological approach helps to ensure that the chapter is transparent, allows for replicability, and theoretical rigour.

## 5.4 Data Privacy and Security Challenges in AI Systems

AI systems face a lot of significant risks pertaining to data privacy globally due to large, diverse datasets and continuous model development. In SSA, it is even more pronounced because it intersects with a series of interconnected issues like resource constraints, weak enforcement and regulatory fragmentation, cross-jurisdictional transfer, capacity and infrastructure limitations, technical vulnerabilities specific to AI models, and sectoral sensitivity of data in areas like health or finance, and supply-chain/vendor risks. Hence, this raises the risk of privacy violations and security failures. Therefore, organizations seeking to deploy AI systems must understand each of these technologies (i.e., PETs) and their challenges.

PETs are a series of technologies that offer protection to personal privacy, such as providing anonymity by allowing individuals to decide on the disclosure of their personal data and allowing organizations an avenue to personalize AI services for customers without compromising their privacy (CIPL, 2025; Mosaiyebzadeh et al., 2023; OECD, 2023). They equally aid organisations in enforcing their own privacy policies and practices. Hence, they are essential tools for handling personal data distribution in international public spaces. While PETs provide technical mitigation for privacy, research has also shown that they come with some trade-offs. Based on these, the AI governance framework needs to consider both boundary management and contextual integrity aspects of privacy challenges. This is crucial because the challenges need transparent data handling procedures, explainable AI models, and context-specific consent measures that restore individuals' trust and autonomy in the digital ecosystems. Below are common PETs, their benefits, and challenges.

(i) **Differential Privacy (DP)**

DPs are a type of PETs that introduce statistical noise to datasets/queries to prevent individual identification from databases using aggregation functions like mean, sum, or variance (Auñón et al., 2024; Tayyeh & Al-Jumaili, 2024). This noise makes it difficult to distinguish an individual's contribution, guaranteeing a certain level of privacy for some queries, consequently preserving statistical properties in the global dataset. While it guarantees individual privacy, it also allows organizations to exchange or analyze data (Su, 2025). Despite its benefits, it involves lots of compromises in reality because the more privacy that is applied to a dataset, the less relevant the data gets (CIPL, 2025).

The risk with DP when viewed from the perspective of contextual integrity theory (CIT) is that it helps to maintain appropriate information flows by minimizing identifiable connections. Yet, organizations might reduce their effectiveness, especially when they expose data anyhow, with the DP reducing the model's utility drastically, underscoring the need for governance oversight.

(ii) **Federated Learning (FL)**

FL is another promising PETs overcoming privacy concerns, particularly in health and finance sectors (Mosaiyebzadeh et al., 2023) because it gives room for model training across distributed datasets or devices without necessarily moving the raw data to a central server, giving users domestic control over their data, consequently minimizing centralized data risk (Abbas et al., 2024). It allows multiparty model training while maintaining privacy (CIPL, 2025). Despite the opportunity this technology offers, it still exposes users to vulnerabilities like model update and data leakages, trouble coordinating across multiple nodes, and stragglers in low-connectivity areas (CIPL, 2025; Mosaiyebzadeh et al., 2023; OECD, 2023). Meanwhile, in SSA, infrastructural gaps and variations in connectivity reduce its feasibility.

While this seems like a benefit in terms of boundary control and local data retention, especially given SSA's reality for data sovereignty, without an effective governance framework and strong regulatory enforcement, it may lead to unintended exposure. Highlighting the need for ethical decision-making and social control aligns with ethical decision-making theory and social control theory.

(iii) **Secure Multi-Party Computation (SMPC) and Synthetic Data**

With SMPC, multiple parties can have access to their combined data without revealing its contents to one another (ISACA, 2024) because it estimates joint functions on their private inputs without sharing the inputs themselves. This technology utilizes a cryptographic technique termed "secret sharing", in which the data of each participating party is divided into pieces and given to the other parties. Synthetic data, on the other hand, is artificially generated data similar to real data (CIPL, 2025) but without direct identifiers, minimizing privacy risks while enabling analytics (Feretzakis et al., 2024). Despite these technologies' presumed benefits, SMPC requires a reliable network coupled with huge coordination, while synthetic data are susceptible to re-identification attacks and can produce bias if the underlying data itself is biased (OECD, 2023).

Both technologies support contextual flows and information boundary aligning with contextual boundary (CIT) and information boundary (IBT) theories. Both reinforce governance mechanisms that prioritize accountability in SMPC arrangements and fairness in synthetic data design.

(iv) **Homomorphic Encryption (HE)**

Similar to the SMPC, HE allows performing computations on encrypted data instead of raw data, providing a higher level of protection by ensuring that sensitive contents remain encrypted during data processing, thereby preserving confidentiality (Auñón et al., 2024; Feretzakis et al., 2024). Hence, this helps in addressing model-centric risks in AI pipelines. According to CIPL (2025), HE can be employed to encrypt models themselves, ensuring that both the data and the models remain private while model validation, deployment, and collaborative model training are ongoing. Their challenges, however, stem from the fact that they are computationally intensive, owing to their computation costs, cannot offer input privacy for more than a single party, often needing cryptographic expertise for their development, and security may not be guaranteed, especially if an adversary gets decryptions of some cipher texts (ISACA,

2024). Besides, for resource-constrained contexts like SSA countries, aside from demanding higher costs, it has scalability issues and is often impractical for large real-time models.

Meanwhile, when viewed from the lens of social control, its benefits offer strong security protections, yet if it were to be deployed for local infrastructure, governance must prioritize its realistic uses and refrain from over-promising.

(v) **Zero-Knowledge Proof (ZKP)**

This form of PETs is a cryptographic method employed to prove knowledge about data without revealing the data itself, deployed for decentralized identity and authentication management (ISACA, 2024). For instance, a ZKP-based identity solution can verify a user's identity and detect their citizenship without them having to provide their passport information; likewise, it could perform age verification without them needing to disclose their date of birth. Also, in the health sector, the model offers data protection constraints by withholding their actual record. The technology offers benefits like facilitating secure transactions and verification schemes because data is not stored in any centralized location, thereby protecting it from cyberattacks (ISACA, 2024; Singh et al., 2022).

Despite their presumed benefit, they require strong technical expertise, heavy cryptographic computation knowledge, and scalability issues that restrict their use for practical cases needing prompt response in real-time AI systems. Furthermore, verifying and generating proofs with ZKPs applications can be computationally intensive with requiring a strong trust anchor (i.e., digital identity infrastructure). Hence, their deployment in developing contexts like SSA countries is currently difficult to meet and has limited applicability in areas like blockchain technology. When viewed from the lens of the information boundary, it aligns with the principle of "knowing without seeing" and enforcing data minimization. It also aligns with the contextual integrity principles because it ensures only relevant data is disclosed without legitimate limit.

Collectively, while these PETs offer strong protection tools, their effectiveness, particularly in SSA, rests on an appropriate technological context and appropriate integration into governance frameworks. Hence, it is worth noting that they may not serve as stand-alone promising solutions, rather must be combined with governance frameworks that reflect the realities of SSA countries, particularly their regulatory environments, technological capabilities, and stakeholder expectations (Table 5.1).

## 5.5 AI Governance and the Safeguard of Data Privacy and Security in SSA

Effective AI governance offers institutional mechanisms to protect data privacy and security and ethical support necessary for translating ethical principles like fairness, transparency, and accountability into actionable protection practices. In the context of SSA, governance efforts needed for AI-driven data privacy and security

**Table 5.1** PETs summary, benefits, and challenges

| PETs | Benefits | Challenges | Suitability for SSA |
|---|---|---|---|
| Differential privacy | Enables data sharing and guarantees privacy | Computational demands and privacy trade-offs | Although useful for regulatory compliance, it requires capacity for full functionality |
| Federated learning | Allows for boundary control due to local data retention | Needs strong connectivity and may produce coordination risks; likewise, update leakages | Requires strong infrastructure development, although it may be a good fit for data sovereignty |
| Secure multi-party computation (SMPC) and synthetic data | Multiparty analytics without sharing raw data, bias-reduced training | It can be very complex owing to its reliance on initial data quality | Where the governance framework is very strong, it can be very useful for AI projects across collaborative regions |
| Homomorphic encryption (HE) | Guarantees strong confidentiality as data remains encrypted during processing | Requires huge computation cost, scalability constraints, and slow performance | Has potential for cloud-based contexts with adequate support |
| Zero-knowledge proof (ZKP) | Guarantees confidentiality as it allows for secure transactions and verification claims without disclosing user data. Also, it prevents cyberattacks | Complex implementation requires significant technical expertise, scalability issues, and limited application in blockchain technologies | Appropriate for contexts requiring verifiable trusts like Fintech and digital ID |

are of particular concern owing to fragmented regulations and institutional frameworks, weak infrastructural capabilities, and a low level of digital literacy (World Bank, 2025). Hence, governance efforts, especially in SSA settings, must go beyond compliance-based regulation to include value-based approaches grounded in ethical reasoning and accountability, aligning with social norms and institutional contexts within which the AI system operates. This will ensure appropriate data flow across institutions, particularly for cross-border data exchanges prompted by cloud-based AI systems. Aligning this also to the ethical decision theory reinforces that ethical outcomes depend on awareness, judgment, and moral behaviour, which collectively inform the decisions surrounding AI data gathering, storage, and use. For instance, organizations must assess the ethical implications of AI models trained on sensitive or biased data, making sure that ethical deliberations come before technological implementation. Although quite a few SSA countries have enacted privacy laws, like South Africa has their POPIA enacted in 2020, Nigeria has the Data Protection Act (DPA) enacted in 2023, and Kenya DPA enacted in 2019, yet their integration into AI oversight is still quite limited. This is because in most of the AI systems, explicit accountability frameworks pertaining to who owns, controls, audits, or rectifies algorithmic misuse are often absent (International Telecommunication Union, 2025).

At the institutional level, social control theory reinforces the need for societal measures like legal sanctions, governance codes, and oversight committees to regulate AI-driven behaviour. In SSA, this translates into strengthening the mandates of data protection authorities, enforcing corporate accountability through AI ethics boards, and embedding privacy impact assessments within national digital strategies. These governance actions are vital as they create a structured environment where ethical decision-making is reinforced by institutional controls, ensuring that privacy and security principles are consistently upheld.

### *5.5.1 Institutionalizing AI Governance for Privacy and Security*

While a strong governance framework is required for AI systems deployment globally, the functionality and effectiveness of PETs, particularly in SSA, require integrating three core pillars, namely: Regulatory frameworks, technical safeguards, and organisational accountability. These core pillars guarantee governance structures that uphold accountability and compliance for operating PETs.

(i) ***Regulatory framework and cross-border data governance:*** Owing to the frequent cross-border processing of data by AI models, it is often difficult to enforce local privacy laws. For instance, while the African Union's Convention on Cyber Security and Personal Data Protection (Malabo Convention, 2025) was entered into force on 8th June 2023, with about 15 African Union (AU) member states legally applying it within their jurisdiction, its influence/applicability is still limited due to several countries including South Africa which is a major country yet to ratify it (Malabo Convention, 2025). Therefore, the United Nations Economic Commission for Africa (UNECA) (2025) recommended that to standardize PETs adoption, promote trust, and encourage innovation in SSA, it is vital for countries within the SSA to regionally harmonize AI data laws and this can be backed by "Smart Africa Alliance" and "African Continental Free Trade Area (AfCFTA)" digital trade protocols.

(ii) ***Technical safeguards***: The use of PETs in public and commercial AI systems, particularly for those in the financial and healthcare sectors, it is important that AI models be institutionalized by governance to safeguard sensitive customer data. For instance, implementing FL and DP in AI models for these domains, incorporating data protection into the system architecture, supports the information boundary theory. A typical example can be found in South Africa's Information Regulator (IRSA), which has started offering technical audit advice for credit scoring systems that use AI (Information Regulator of South Africa, 2026).

(iii) ***Organisational accountability***: For an effective governance mechanism, it is crucial to ensure that the AI-based privacy accountability reflects principles in the King IV code of Corporate governance (IoDSA, 2022). For instance, it should reflect how responsibilities are assigned to the Chief Data Officers (CDOs), mandating the audit of algorithms, and keeping track of data provenance. This aligns with the social control theory, upholding responsible behaviour through sanctions, ethical, and compliance frameworks.

### 5.5.2 Practical Governance Roadmap for Integrating PETs into Policy and Practice

It is vital to ensure the governance of AI pertaining to privacy and security, particularly in SSA-focused organizations and businesses, through value-based reasoning processes that strike a balance between innovation and ethical responsibility. Below in Table 5.2, we provide a structured governance road map aligning PETs with governance actions.

Collectively, these mechanisms operationalize ethical governance by aligning organizational behaviour with social norms and institutional enforcement, ensuring that data privacy and security are not reactive measures but integral features of AI governance systems. In short, to build a sustainable roadmap for data privacy and security governance in SSA, it is important to integrate and consider all issues about contextual integrity, information boundary management, ethical decision-making, and social control. The contextual integrity aspect would ensure that AI data practices respect local norms and values. The information boundary aspect would empower individuals to manage their data rights, while the ethical decision-making aspect would foster moral reasoning among policymakers and corporate actors. Finally, the social control aspect would help to enforce accountability through institutional oversight.

Overall, we recommend a privacy and security design that prioritizes cultural alignment by integrating AI systems that reflect the realities and contextual norms of African societies, thereby guaranteeing ethical data flows. For user empowerment, we recommend developing AI systems that consider management tools consent and privacy dashboards, which offer users control over their data. To strengthen institutional capabilities, it is vital to confer more power on organisations/bodies in charge of regional data protection. For instance, expand the authority of the organisation in charge of the African Union Data Policy. Furthermore, to encourage ethical leadership, it is crucial to educate leaders in privacy governance and AI design ethics while also encouraging the continental alignment of AI ethics and data governance regulations to guarantee uniformity and interoperability.

Finally, to maintain AI privacy and security, SSA needs to invest in the following:

(a) Regulatory sandboxes for testing PETs-based AI models before market release and public deployment.

**Table 5.2** Governance road map, PETs and governance actions

| Governance level | Aim | Key actions | Applicable theory |
|---|---|---|---|
| Regional harmonization | To encourage cross-border AI data sharing and promote compliance | Harmonize using the digital policy protocols of AU AfCFTA and Smart Africa. This will foster regional frameworks for managing cross-border data sharing | Echoes the contextual integrity theory |
| Policy development | To create clear AI privacy guidelines | Create national AI policies that integrate current privacy laws with PETs standards like DP, FL, and ZKP. Also, create AI ethics and data governance councils for both national and organizational levels | Also echoes the contextual integrity theory |
| Organisational integration | To build oversight and establish internal accountability | Require the establishment of internal AI ethics committees, PETs compliance checks, and DPIAs before AI system deployment | Echoes the social control theory |
| Creating awareness and capacity building | To improve the culture of ethics and skills | Provide training on AI governance for data officers, including analysts and regulators | Also echoes the social control theory |
| Technical implementation | To integrate PETs in the AI design | Mandate the adoption of DP, FL, and HE in AI data flows | Echoes the information boundary theory |
| Monitoring and audit | Maintain transparency and promote accountability through professional and legal sanctions for non-compliance | Implement third-party oversight, ZKP-based compliance verification, and AI audit trails into public reporting and practice | Echoes the ethical decision-making theory |

(b) A unified African AI governance framework that combines cybersecurity, innovation, and data ethics under shared regional guidelines.
(c) Public–private partnerships (PPPs) to build technical PETs capacity

These imperatives support digital inclusion, data sovereignty, and ethical governance as pillars of sustainable development, aligning with the African agenda's 2063 (Agenda, 2063: The Africa We Want, 2025).

## References


Abbas, S. R., Abbas, Z., Zahir, A., & Lee, S. W. (2024). Federated learning in smart healthcare: A comprehensive review on privacy, security, and predictive analytics with IoT integration. *Healthcare (Switzerland), 12*(24), 2587. https://doi.org/10.3390/healthcare12242587

Africa Data Protection Report. (2024). https://www.africadataprotection.org/africadataprotection_report_en_december_2024.pdf

Agenda 2063: The Africa We Want, African Union 1. (2025). https://au.int/en/agenda2063/overview

Alaran, M. A., Lawal, S. K., Jiya, M. H., Egya, S. A., Ahmed, M. M., Abdulsalam, A., Haruna, U. A., Musa, M. K., & Lucero-Prisno, D. E. (2025). Challenges and opportunities of artificial intelligence in African health space. *Digital Health, 11*, 1–7. https://doi.org/10.1177/20552076241305915

Alhitmi, H. K., Mardiah, A., Al-Sulaiti, K. I., & Abbas, J. (2024). Data security and privacy concerns of AI-driven marketing in the context of economics and business field: An exploration into possible solutions. *Cogent Business and Management, 11*(1), 2393743. https://doi.org/10.1080/23311975.2024.2393743

Al-Kharusi, Y., Khan, A., Rizwan, M., & Bait-Suwailam, M. M. (2024). Open-source artificial intelligence privacy and security: A review. *Computers, 13*(12), 311. https://doi.org/10.3390/computers13120311

Auñón, J. M., Hurtado-Ramírez, D., Porras-Díaz, L., Irigoyen-Peña, B., Rahmian, S., Al-Khazraji, Y., Soler-Garrido, J., & Kotsev, A. (2024). Evaluation and utilisation of privacy enhancing technologies—A data spaces perspective. *Data in Brief, 55*, Article 110560. https://doi.org/10.1016/j.dib.2024.110560

Ayana, G., Dese, K., Daba Nemomssa, H., Habtamu, B., Mellado, B., Badu, K., Yamba, E., Faye, S. L., Ondua, M., Nsagha, D., Nkweteyim, D., & Kong, J. D. (2024). Decolonizing global AI governance: Assessment of the state of decolonized AI governance in Sub-Saharan Africa. *Royal Society Open Science, 11*(8), Article 231994. https://doi.org/10.1098/rsos.231994

Braun, V., & Clarke, V. (2023). Toward good practice in thematic analysis: Avoiding common problems and be(com)ing a knowing researcher. *International Journal of Transgender Health, 24*(1), 1–6. https://doi.org/10.1080/26895269.2022.2129597

Byrne, D. (2022). A worked example of Braun and Clarke's approach to reflexive thematic analysis. *Quality and Quantity, 56*(3), 1391–1412. https://doi.org/10.1007/s11135-021-01182-y

Cheng, X., Su, L., Luo, X., Benitez, J., & Cai, S. (2022). The good, the bad, and the ugly: Impact of analytics and artificial intelligence-enabled personal information collection on privacy and participation in ridesharing. *European Journal of Information Systems, 31*(3), 339–363. https://doi.org/10.1080/0960085X.2020.1869508

CIPL. (2025). Privacy-enhancing and privacy-preserving technologies in AI: Enabling data use and operationalizing privacy by design and default. In *Center for Information Policy Leadership* (Issue March). https://www.informationpolicycentre.com/uploads/5/7/1/0/57104281/cipl_pets_and_ppts_in_ai_mar25.pdf

Conduah, A. K., Ofoe, S., & Siaw-Marfo, D. (2025). Data privacy in healthcare: Global challenges and solutions. *Digital Health, 11*, 1–19. https://doi.org/10.1177/20552076251343959

Coovadia, H., Marx, B., Botha, I., & Gold, N. O. (2025). Building an ethical artificial intelligence corporate governance framework for the integration of emerging technologies into business processes. *South African Journal of Accounting Research*. https://doi.org/10.1080/10291954.2025.2523661

Effoduh, J. O., Akpudo, U. E., & Kong, J. D. (2024). Toward a trustworthy and inclusive data governance policy for the use of artificial intelligence in Africa. *Data and Policy*. https://doi.org/10.1017/dap.2024.26

European Union. (2024). Artificial Intelligence Act Texts: Regulation (EU) 2024/1689 of the European Parliament and of the Council of 13 June 2024. *Official Journal of the European Union, 1689*(3), 1–144. http://data.europa.eu/eli/reg/2024/1689/oj

Feretzakis, G., Papaspyridis, K., Gkoulalas-Divanis, A., & Verykios, V. S. (2024). Privacy-preserving techniques in generative AI and large language models: A narrative review. *Information (Switzerland), 15*(11), 697. https://doi.org/10.3390/info15110697

Floridi, L., & Cowls, J. (2022). A unified framework of five principles for AI in society. *Machine Learning and the City: Applications in Architecture and Urban Design, 1*(1), 535–545. https://doi.org/10.1002/9781119815075.ch45

Hirschi, T. (2017). *Causes of delinquency*. Taylor and Francis. https://doi.org/10.4324/9781315081649

Information Regulator of South Africa. (2026). *Information regulator South Africa 2025/2026 annual performance plan*. https://inforegulator.org.za/wp-content/uploads/2025/08/2025-2026-Annual-Performance-Plan.pdf

International Telecommunication Union. (2025). *State of digital development and trends in the Africa region: Challenges and opportunities* (Issue April).

IoDSA. (2022). *Understanding King IV and what it is intended to achieve—Institute of Directors in Southern Africa (IoDSA)*. IodSA in the Press. https://www.iodsa.co.za/news/389613/Understanding-King-IV-and-what-it-is-intended-to-achieve.htm

ISACA. (2024). *Exploring practical considerations and applications for privacy enhancing technologies*. ISACA. https://www.isaca.org/resources/white-papers/2024/exploring-practical-considerations-and-applications-for-privacy-enhancing-technologies?

Lawyers Hub. (2023). Africa privacy report 2023/2024: A review of policy trends and digital frontiers in Africa's data protection landscape. In *a Lawyers Hub Publication*. https://www.lawyershub.org/DigitalResources/AfricaPrivacyReport2023-24/AfricaPrivacyReport2023-2024.pdf?

Malabo Convention. (2025). African union convention on cyber security and personal data protection. *Michalsons*. https://doi.org/10.1017/ilm.2016.3

Martin, K. D., & Zimmermann, J. (2024). Artificial intelligence and its implications for data privacy. *Current Opinion in Psychology, 58*, Article 101829. https://doi.org/10.1016/j.copsyc.2024.101829

Masinde, J., Mugambi, F., & Muthee, D. W. (2025). Big data and personal information privacy in developing countries: Insights from Kenya. *Frontiers in Big Data, 8*, 1532362. https://doi.org/10.3389/fdata.2025.1532362

Mienye, I. D., Sun, Y., & Ileberi, E. (2024). Artificial intelligence and sustainable development in Africa: A comprehensive review. *Machine Learning with Applications, 18*, Article 100591. https://doi.org/10.1016/j.mlwa.2024.100591

Mosaiyebzadeh, F., Pouriyeh, S., Parizi, R. M., Sheng, Q. Z., Han, M., Zhao, L., Sannino, G., Ranieri, C. M., Ueyama, J., & Batista, D. M. (2023). Privacy-enhancing technologies in federated learning for the internet of healthcare things: A survey. *Electronics (Switzerland), 12*(12), 2703. https://doi.org/10.3390/electronics12122703

Munung, N. S., Staunton, C., Mazibuko, O., Wall, P. J., & Wonkam, A. (2024). Data protection legislation in Africa and pathways for enhancing compliance in big data health research. *Health Research Policy and Systems, 22*(1), 145. https://doi.org/10.1186/s12961-024-01230-7

Musoni, M. (2024). *Envisioning Africa's AI governance landscape in 2024—ECDPM Briefing Note 177* (Issue 177).

Nissenbaum, H. (2004). Privacy as contextual integrity. *Washington Law Review, 79*(1), 119–157. https://heinonline.org/hol-cgi-bin/get_pdf.cgi?handle=hein.journals/washlr79&section=16

OECD. (2023). Emerging privacy-enhancing technologies: Current regulatory and policy approaches. In *OECD digital economy papers* (no. 351). https://doi.org/10.1787/bf121be4-en

Petronio, S. (1991). Communication boundary management: A theoretical model of managing disclosure of private information between marital couples. *Communication Theory, 1*(4), 311–335. https://doi.org/10.1111/j.1468-2885.1991.tb00023.x

Plantinga, P., Shilongo, K., Mudongo, O., Umubyeyi, A., Gastrow, M., & Razzano, G. (2024). Responsible artificial intelligence in Africa: towards policy learning. *Data and Policy*. https://doi.org/10.1017/dap.2024.60

Singh, N., Dayama, P., & Pandit, V. (2022). Zero knowledge proofs towards verifiable decentralized AI pipelines. *Lecture Notes in Computer Science, 13411 LNCS*, 248–275. https://doi.org/10.1007/978-3-031-18283-9_12

Su, W. J. (2025). A statistical viewpoint on differential privacy: Hypothesis testing, representation, and Blackwell's theorem. *Annual Review of Statistics and Its Application, 12*(1), 157–175. https://doi.org/10.1146/annurev-statistics-112723-034158

Tayyeh, H. K., & Al-Jumaili, A. S. A. (2024). Balancing privacy and performance: A differential privacy approach in federated learning. *Computers, 13*(11), 277. https://doi.org/10.3390/computers13110277

Trevino, L. K. (1986). Ethical decision making in organizations: A person-situation interactionist model. *The Academy of Management Review, 11*(3), 601. https://doi.org/10.2307/258313

United Nations Economic Commission for Africa. (2025). *United nations economic commission for Africa: Economic report*. United Nations. https://www.uneca.org/economic-report-on-africa-2025

World Bank. (2025). Building trustworthy artificial intelligence: Frameworks, applications, and self-assessment for readiness. In *World bank* (Issue September). https://doi.org/10.1596/43656

Zaidan, E., & Ibrahim, I. A. (2024). AI governance in a complex and rapidly changing regulatory landscape: A global perspective. *Humanities and Social Sciences Communications, 11*(1), 1–18. https://doi.org/10.1057/s41599-024-03560-x

# Chapter 6
# AI Autonomy, Control, and Human Oversight

**Fowokemi Alaba Ogedengbe and Nusirat Ojuolape Gold**

**Abstract** Advances in Artificial Intelligence (AI) have brought the autonomy, control, and human oversight of AI systems to the forefront of debate. As traditional roles are shifting to machines making independent or semi-autonomous decisions, these enhancements are increasing efficiency and performance. However, there have been concerns that machine autonomy could amplify bias that may result in serious financial, legal, or reputational harm at the expense of human rights. This has led to a series of campaigns promoting the safe deployment and ethical use of AI systems to foster accountability, transparency, and oversight. This chapter explores how autonomous AI systems can be governed responsibly throughout their lifecycle. To achieve the research intent, the chapter employs a literature review methodology to explore the nuances of AI autonomy, its control mechanisms, and a model for effective human oversight, thereby ensuring the responsible development and deployment of AI that enhances societal trust. Academic databases such as Scopus and Web of Science were used for data collection. Five research objectives were assessed and presented in the discussion section. This reveals the findings from the dataset as reflected in the varying forms of machine autonomy and prominent controls guiding AI deployment. The chapter also provided insights into emerging regulations from within Africa and suggested solution pathways. The chapter contributes to ongoing debates on protecting human rights from the challenges surrounding the use of autonomous AI in various business sectors.

---

F. A. Ogedengbe (✉)
Department of Accountancy, College of Business and Economics, University of Johannesburg, Johannesburg, South Africa
e-mail: fogedengbe@uj.ac.za; ogedfowokemi@gmail.com

N. O. Gold
Department of Commercial Accounting, College of Business and Economics, University of Johannesburg, Johannesburg, South Africa
e-mail: ngold@uj.ac.za



M. Adelowotan and H. Coovadia (eds.), *AI and Accountability*, CSR, Sustainability, Ethics & Governance, https://doi.org/10.1007/978-3-032-20091-4_6

## 6.1 Introduction

The rapid advancements in artificial intelligence (AI) have brought the concepts of autonomy, control, and human oversight to the forefront of AI debate. Modern AI systems operate along a spectrum of autonomy, ranging from narrow automation that depends on human decision-makers to semi-autonomous systems that require supervision, and finally to independent systems that make autonomous decisions with minimal human involvement. Similarly, AI is reshaping organisational decision-making by transforming traditional roles and tasks into the deployment of algorithmic systems for specific purposes. Some of these purposes include service delivery, credit scoring, automated trading, supply chain optimisation, predictive maintenance, recruitment, compliance monitoring, and customer engagement, thereby transferring routine and strategic decisions from humans to integration of machines with humans (Breidbach, 2024; Przegalinska et al., 2025). These technological advancements promise substantial benefits, including improved operational efficiency and performance, economic growth, increased comfort, enhanced safety through crime detection, and sustainability improvements (Enigbokan, 2025; Ogedengbe & Adelowotan, 2025; Zaidan & Ibrahim, 2024). Furthermore, in areas like education and health care, AI is capable of fostering social development, better quality outcomes, improve diagnostic accuracy, and workflow efficiency (Ogedengbe, 2024; Alhosani & Alhashmi, 2024; Khosravi et al., 2024; Ogedengbe, 2024; Sharma, 2024).

The AI systems generally operate along a spectrum of autonomy, ranging from a narrow decision-support to taking actions with limited human input (Zaidan & Ibrahim, 2024). While its development and deployment are still gaining traction, scholarly debates have highlighted the need to ensure its benefits do not come at the expense of human rights. This is justified by the concerns about ensuring their safe, accountable and ethical use. As AI deployments intensify, risks of errors owing to persistent biases are being amplified, which may result in serious financial, legal, or reputational harms, transparency gaps, and regulatory challenges (Cheong, 2024; Langer et al., 2025a, 2025b, 2025c). Hence, AI autonomous capabilities are still questionable (Ferl, 2024). It is therefore imperative to understand the nuances of AI autonomy, the mechanisms for its control, and the model for effective human oversight to ensure responsible AI developments and societal trust (Engin, 2025; Fernández & Moratinos, 2021; Methnani et al., 2021a, 2021b).

Moreover, as AI systems continue to be integrated into economic decisions within the organisation, there has been a gap in understanding how the autonomous technologies are governed responsibly throughout their lifecycle (Papagiannidis et al., 2025). There is therefore a need to understand the organisation's ability to retain meaningful human control (MHC) over AI activities, rather than mere symbolic compliance (Robbins, 2024). The central challenge lies in the governance gap between the pace of AI deployment in businesses and the readiness of oversight frameworks within firms and regulatory systems.

For organisations, the question is not just whether AI can optimise operations, but also who will be held liable when autonomous systems fail: the firm, managers, or the

AI developer? Justification for this debate is evidence in AI liability patterns, such as discriminatory hiring algorithms, automated financial trading that steers market disruption, vague supply-chain models that leave suppliers unable to perform effectively, and legal teams unable to conduct due diligence (Breidbach, 2024; Butler, 2025). These highlight the risks associated with AI usage when oversight is weak or symbolic. Thus, warranting regulatory scrutiny. In response to these, evolving governance instruments such as the EU AI Act, the U.S. FDA's guidance on algorithmic products, and international standardisation efforts reinforce the need for meaningful human oversight, particularly for high-risk AI systems (Chee, 2025; Kusche, 2024). Despite the series of campaigns for AI control, many firms still lack the internal capacity to operationalise the oversight requirements, leaving them exposed to reputational, financial, and legal risks (Kusche, 2024).

This chapter aims to provide a synthesis between the increasing autonomy of AI systems and the governance mechanisms necessary to ensure the systems operate safely, accountably, and fairly in critical decision-making roles, particularly in high-risk sectors such as healthcare and autonomous vehicles.

### *6.1.1 Research Objectives*

Specifically, the chapter addresses the following objectives.

(i) Explore the conceptual, philosophical, and sectoral taxonomies of AI autonomy.
(ii) Investigate control strategies for artificial intelligence
(iii) Explore human oversight models and ethical considerations
(iv) Examining the ethical frameworks and practical governance of AI
(v) Exploring the best practices for Human–AI interfaces

This chapter synthesises current research, sectoral practices, and emerging legal and ethical frameworks, providing a comprehensive overview of these interrelated domains through a literature review approach. In the subsequent sections, we present the methodology, followed by a structured discussion section and its subsections, and conclude with the conclusion section.

## 6.2 Methodology

A systematic literature review was conducted on this topic. Databases such as Scopus and Web of Science were employed to get relevant papers. First, the author utilises all relevant keywords and synonyms to construct a comprehensive search string, thereby capturing a broad range of literature. After careful consideration, the keyword used is ((“artificial intelligence” OR AI OR “machine learning” OR “autonomous system*” OR “autonomous agent*” OR “autonomous vehicle*” OR “autonomous robot*” OR "automated decision*" OR "automated decision-making" OR "algorithmic decision*" OR "intelligent system*" OR "AI system*") AND (autonom* OR "self-learning" OR "self learning" OR "self-adaptive" OR "self adaptive" OR "adaptive system*" OR "black-box" OR "black box") AND ("human oversight" OR "human-in-the-loop" OR "human in the loop" OR "human-on-the-loop" OR "human on the loop" OR "human-in-command" OR "human in command" OR "meaningful human control" OR "meaningful control" OR "human control" OR "operator control" OR "human supervision" OR "human supervisor*" OR monitoring OR oversight OR "human intervention" OR "ability to intervene")).

This search string was employed in data search on the two major academic databases, that is web of science and Scopus. The initial search data was from June 2025. This search was updated on November 30, 2025. According to Web of Science and Scopus, 5451 and 14,779 publications were identified, respectively. On Scopus, the search was extended to titles, abstracts and keywords. To focus on relevant papers, in Web of Science, the search string was extended to include "TITLE-ABS-KEY" which reduced the papers to 64 publications. On Scopus, the search was limited to the article title and keywords, resulting in 271 retrieved publications. This makes a Total of 335 papers, including duplicates. For more detailed coverage of papers not included in these two databases, Undermind was used to retrieve relevant literature from various databases. The justification was used due to its capability of accessing all relevant papers from scholarly databases such as institutional databases and other academic databases.

Papers from each database were downloaded in RIS and CSV formats. The RIS was used since it is compatible with various academic-supported applications such as Mendeley. The CSV was downloaded since it's compatible with Microsoft Excel. This helps the researcher in viewing the paper's information. The papers from Scopus, Web of Science and Undermind AI were combined. The combined file was saved. For data screening, removal of duplicate papers, and assessing the compatibility of papers, Covidence was employed. Covidence facilitates systematic literature reviews by conducting comprehensive data cleaning and screening in accordance with the PRISMA guidelines. The remaining papers were downloaded. After manual checks, 106 papers were identified as relevant and used in the writing of this chapter. These publications were reviewed based on thematic structure. These emerging themes are presented in Table 6.1.

**Table 6.1** Themes that emerged from literature on AI autonomy, control and oversight

| Theme | Key insights | Citation |
|---|---|---|
| Balancing autonomy and oversight | Adaptive autonomy framework and variable autonomy systems are promising, but human oversight faces pitfalls (bias, psychological costs and legal ambiguity) | Engin and Hand (2025a), Manheim and Homewood (2025) and Tsamados et al. (2024) |
| Interdisciplinary approaches | Legal, ethics, psychological and technical perspectives are increasingly integrated; quantitative models, e.g. SquAL, SDT, support assessment | Diggelen et al. (2023), Firlej and Taeihagh (2020) and Verdiesen et al. (2020a, 2020b) |
| Legal and regulatory evolution | Proposals for AI juridical personhood, harmonised liability, and rights-based frameworks are emerging, but practical implementation lags | Kwik (2022a), Langer et al. (2025a) and Verdiesen et al. (2021) |
| Human oversight models | Taxonomies distinguish constitutive vs corrective oversight, effectiveness depends on competence, incentives and institutional design | Manheim and Homewood (2025) and Methnani et al. (2021a, 2021b) |
| Adaptive automation | Dynamic adjustments of autonomy levels optimise team performance and cognitive workload; it requires interface and trust design | Firlej and Taeihagh (2020), Laux (2024a) and Reinmund et al. (2023) |

## 6.3 Discussion

### *6.3.1 Overview of AI Autonomy, Control and Human Oversight*

While AI autonomy relates to the independence of AI, there is a need to balance the autonomy with meaningful human control (MHC) (Methnani et al., 2021a, 2021b). MHC is essential as it provides a human agent who has authority and responsibility for controlling AI. To ensure effective MHC, extending the control beyond mere human presence is also essential, particularly for the purpose of having a lifestyle accountability structure.

Lifestyle accountability over AI, according to extant debates, offers humans the ability to retain and access timely information, authority and trace assigned responsibility throughout the development, deployment, and post-deployment of the AI systems (Methnani et al., 2021a, 2021b; Verdiesen et al., 2020a, 2020b). This is crucial because it enables the execution of oversight functions as mandated by the

European Union AI Act (EU AI Act). Oversight function in this regard refers to those governance roles that control the inner operations of the AI systems. They comprise the in-process decision of the AI system, the corrective roles of reviewing and challenging the system, and institutionalised structures that entail supervision, AI competence, and mitigate incentive failures (Laux, 2024b).

While control has generally been used by extant research, recent scholarly literature is leaning towards the usage of the term "oversight". Although the majority of scholars view both terms as similar, others hold a contrary view, stating they are different operational levers in AI governance. This chapter, therefore, in line with the divergent view, classifies control and oversight as separate terms.

AI control, on the one hand, is often seen as a constraint relating to AI systems, and it comprises policies, action fillers and circuit breakers which align with the control-theory notions of keeping the AI system within safety space (Manheim & Homewood, 2025). Contrarily, oversight comprises activities like auditing, post-hoc reviews and institutional checks on AI decisions (Manheim & Homewood, 2025). Given these descriptions, there has been a reclassification of AI governance practices. For instance, red-teaming has been reclassified as oversight, rather than a form of control (Manheim & Homewood, 2025). Red teaming as an oversight mechanism probes AI systems for weaknesses and unexpected behaviour after deployment, rather than serving as a real-time control constraint.

Meanwhile, some researchers still use both terms interchangeably. Researchers in this category argue that control encompasses both the direct and indirect policies surrounding AI autonomy. As a result, they noted that it covers the AI decision framework, its design constraints, procedures, rules and interoperability standards that shape the AI autonomy (Firlej & Taeihagh, 2021). To this end, the chapter proceeds to discuss prior scholarly dimensions of AI autonomy and its human oversight and control. The next sub-sections aim to address the first objective of this chapter, "***Explore the conceptual, philosophical and sectoral taxonomies of AI autonomy***." Each of these perspectives are presented in subsequent Sects. 3.2–3.4.

### *6.3.2 Conceptual Perspective on AI Autonomy*

Research has described AI autonomy as a multidimensional and context-dependent term, for which there is no standard definition or description. Yet, its meaning can be specified based on the context of application and sector (Calvert, 2025; Engin & Hand, 2025b; Kasirzadeh & Gabriel, 2025; Sterz et al., 2024). Definitions are tailored to application domains (Engin, 2025; Ho-Dac & Martinez, 2024). Hence, based on this philosophical view, AI autonomy refers to the AI system's ability to operate independently, making its own decisions and executing complex tasks without requiring constant human intervention, relying solely on algorithms, data inputs and other devices to gather and process information (Moesker, 2025). It is also described as the ability of AI to self-generate, self-organise and self-control. This ability of the AI system enables it to adapt to real-time changes and realise specific objectives autonomously. The definitions and frameworks for AI autonomy are highly context-dependent, reflecting differing goals, ethical considerations, and technical capabilities. Some of the definitions of AI autonomy are presented below:

## Agent-Based AI (Agentic AI) Autonomy

Recent scholarly works describe AI autonomy along the "agentic" structure. This is characterised by four overlapping dimensions: autonomy, efficacy, goal complexity, and generality (Kasirzadeh & Gabriel, 2025). Unlike traditional AI systems that often rely on human intervention or pre-programmed instructions, Agentic AI exhibits autonomous decision-making ability, goal-oriented behavior, and continuous learning while interacting with dynamic environments (Hosseini & Seilani, 2025). This form of AI systems adapts based on real-time data and changing objectives, leveraging machine learning (ML), reinforcement learning, and multi-agent coordination to perform tasks efficiently. Since organisations are now integrating AI agents and agentic systems into business processes, it holds considerable potential for business transformation, particularly in terms of automation, improved decision-making processes, and collaboration between humans and digital agents, potentially reshaping business operations across industries (Hughes et al., 2025).

Agentic AI systems integrate memory, tool integration and adaptive reasoning. This enables dynamic adaptability and self-improvement. Memory, including working memory, episodic memory, semantic knowledge, and procedural memory, is a key aspect of AI that enhances context retention and facilitates continuous learning updates. Adaptive reasoning is the iterative framework that manages workflow and reasoning. Whole-tool integration enables autonomous operation with external systems through selection logic, robust error-handling mechanisms, and function calls. Given that AI deployment and its capability are based on tools and affordances, agentic AI therefore surpasses traditional AI models (Tallam, 2025; Umakanth, 2025).

Agentic autonomy has been integrated from several perspectives, including executive, goal, and social autonomies (see Fig. 6.1). The executive aspect encompasses how the AI system operates in terms of planning, hierarchical control, cognitive flexibility, and dynamic strategy switching. This mirrors the human brain function, such as working memory and goal stacking. The goal of autonomy refers to what AI can achieve. This embraces the capacity for setting, pursuing and revising complex goals. Goal complexity extends beyond simple tasks to multi-step, strategic objectives and AI versatility across varied tasks, domains and roles. Social autonomy refers to how the AI can be managed, interacted with and held accountable when pressure arises (Verdiesen et al., 2020a, 2020b). Agentic AI introduces new challenges in transparency, responsibility diffusion and governance frameworks (Hughes et al., 2025). The governance framework encompasses safety, constraints, traceability, explainability, and ethical alignment, which are crucial for coordination and agentic decision-making.

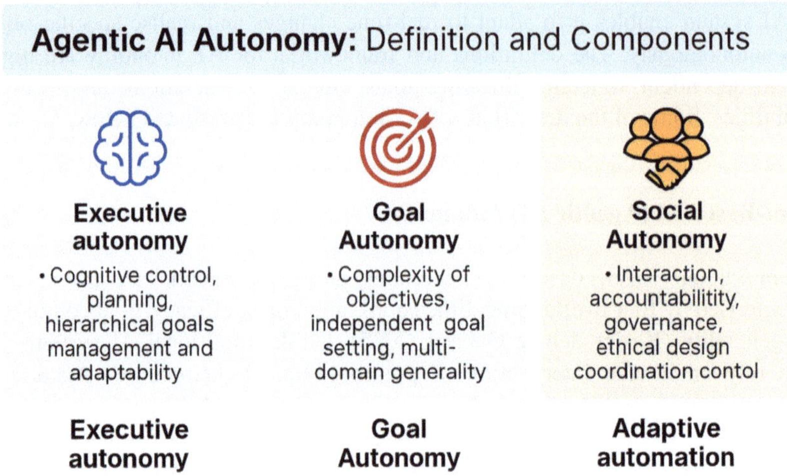


**Fig. 6.1** Agentic AI autonomy description

Furthermore, it is essential to acknowledge that AI's agentic autonomy presents several challenges. These include challenges associated with trust, ethical considerations, accountability in the event of failure, and integrating these systems into existing organisational structures. For instance, trust in AI agentic autonomy in decision-making is a major challenge, particularly in vital domains such as healthcare and finance (Hughes et al., 2025; Vanneste & Puranam, 2024). Moreover, as AI systems assume increasingly complex roles, concerns about transparency and potential biases arise.

**Variable Autonomy**

AI autonomy can also be described in line with variable autonomy. This means the AI system can be adjusted over time and across sub-systems. Variable autonomy, therefore, refers to the AI systems whose level of independence can dynamically adjust, both over time and across different sub-systems, by switching the level of autonomy from full robot autonomy to complete human operator control (Verhagen et al., 2024). These adaptive autonomy levels are governed by key variables that act as triggers, modulating operational parameters, routines, and oversight mechanisms. Variable autonomy is a term often employed to describe human–robot teams where the level of robot autonomy varies depending on the context. One of its primary goals is to maximise human control without burdening the human operator with an unmanageable amount of detailed operational decisions (Verhagen et al., 2024).

In Summary, the concept of variable autonomy is prominent in human–robot interaction research, where autonomy levels range from complete human control to full AI independence and vice versa. These levels can shift dynamically during task execution, depending on the context and system design. Three paradigms illustrate control allocation authority: the human-initiative, AI-initiative and mixed-initiative. Human initiative is where only humans can decide when to shift autonomy levels. An AI initiative is where AI autonomously adjusts its control level, and a mixed initiative is where both humans and AI share control over autonomy decisions (Methnani et al., 2021a, 2021b).

### Governance Autonomy

AI autonomy can also be viewed from the perspective of governance. The governance dimension of AI autonomy refers to the framework model that specifies AI decision authority, autonomy process and accountability configuration within a broader human–AI relationship space (Engin, 2025; Engin & Hand, 2025b). These three can be described as the 3As of AI governance autonomy, which allow for the identification of what should be done to adjust AI systems to fit their tasks and allocate appropriate human oversight and supervision. A recent governance framework on Human–AI governance (HAIG) formally describes governance autonomy as the decision authority distribution, process autonomy and accountability configuration (Engin, 2025). The decision authority distribution focuses on who holds decision-making power at a given time. Process autonomy refers to the degree to which the AI can shape its own processes, while accountability configuration encompasses the responsibility and structure of oversight. These dimensions are evolving continually.

To ensure an AI governance is effective within the liability structures, it must exhibit the following features:

(i) ***Transparency and explainability:*** i.e., the AI decision-making must be interpretable and align with laid-down regulations. Organisations deploying AI systems must do so, adhering strictly to governance policies such as incorporating AI auditing and bias mitigation frameworks (Okuno & Okuno, 2025).
(ii) ***Consumer protection and fairness*****:** The requirements of the law require the AI system to be built in such a way that guards' users against harm while fostering innovation. It must also comply with ethical AI guidelines and consumer protection laws such as the General Data Protection Regulation (GDPR), Protection of Personal Information Act (POPIA), and the OECD acts on AI (OECD, 2020) to avoid deceptive practices.
(iii) ***Corporate accountability*****:** AI ethics oversight must also be integrated into governance models to delineate responsibilities and prevent regulatory violations (Okuno & Okuno, 2025).

Another prominent framework that aligns with the HAIG framework is the Responsible, Accountable, Consulted and Informed (RACI) framework. This aligns with strengthening policy design around autonomy and human oversight.

### 6.3.3 *Philosophical Perspective on AI Autonomy*

The philosophical perspectives of AI autonomy argue for a heightened form of autonomy, one framed around self-determined goals and value-driven actions (Kasirzadeh & Gabriel, 2025). This interpretation positions AI not merely as rule-based and context-adaptive but as entities capable of autonomous goal setting, informed by internally held norms and reasons. This perspective views AI autonomy from psychological, societal and ethical dimensions (see Fig. 6.2), all of which are increasingly advocated (Jenko et al., 2025; van der Waa et al., 2021).

#### Psychological Dimension

The psychological dimension views autonomy as self-governance, characterised by the capacity to formulate goals and act on them through deliberation, intention, and reflection. It is sometimes referred to as the natural and artificial aspects. Natural autonomy refers to human self-governance, while artificial autonomy pertains to the independence of AI systems. Both share similarities but differ in embodiment, value alignment and ethical implication (Sterz et al., 2024).

Ideally, AI self-governance refers to the ability of AI to legislate actions in accordance with its own moral principles, thereby enabling accountability and dignity. However, recent AI systems exhibit operational autonomy. While they act independently, they lack reflective capability and moral reasoning. Thus, AI lack psychological autonomy, which is why humans believe it does not choose or reflect. This dimension can be theoretically explained using self-determination theory, which posits that a basic need creates the desire to act in harmony with one's integrated self. True autonomy is intricately linked to competence and relatedness. Hence, psychologically, AI autonomy can be viewed through its emotional and relational embedded models, which remain speculative in a real sense.

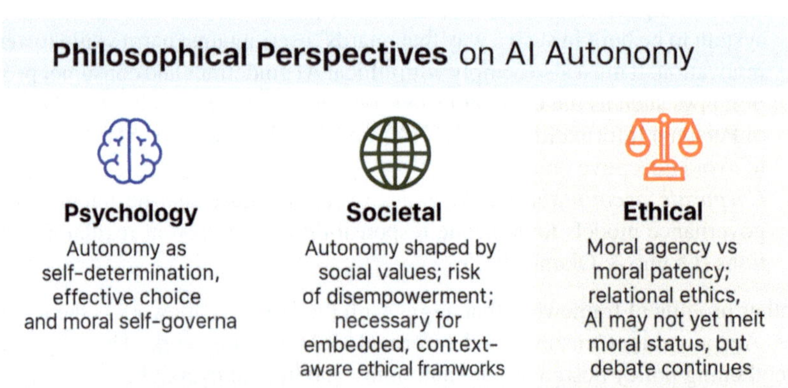


**Fig. 6.2** Philosophical perspective of AI autonomy

#### Societal Dimension

The societal dimension views autonomy within the broader context of ethical and cultural dynamics. This dimension argues that the system's influence is shaped by culture, social norms, values, and power structure. Autonomy in this sense can embody and reproduce systemic biases, alter workplace dynamics or erode personal autonomy through intrusive nudging or manipulation. In practice, autonomy is often defined as the ability of systems to make decisions and act based on their intended objectives, with AI enabling such autonomy. Based on this dimension, two perceptions have emerged. These are the perceptions of self-determination and the perception of goal-constrained autonomy.

Self-determined autonomy refers to AI's capacity to self-determinate, often drawing on philosophical theories (e.g. Arendt) and requiring societal acceptance (Crossnohere et al., 2022). Whereas, goal-constrained autonomy focuses on AI systems operating within predefined goals or constraints, typical of most current industrial applications (Kwik, 2022b).

#### Ethical Dimension

Ethically, the question of AI autonomy intersects with debates around moral agency, rights and consciousness. Kantian ethics posit that autonomous agents capable of moral reasoning have personhood and dignity, which are the thresholds that, if crossed by AI, could warrant moral consideration. Other philosophers, such as David Gilel, propose relation ethics where moral status arises from how humans relate to AI, rather than inherent properties like consciousness. While current AI lacks authentic moral agency based on self-reflection and value formation, future AI systems might cross this border. Mainstream concepts of AI autonomy are critiqued for their roots in Western liberal philosophy, which calls for relational autonomy models that better address harms to marginalised groups (Matthias, 2004).

### *6.3.4 Sectoral Perspectives/Taxonomies of AI Autonomy*

AI autonomy can also be understood from the perspective of different sectors, each with its unique characteristics and applications. This section explores the sectoral taxonomies. Based on the existing review of the literature, some areas that have been assessed include healthcare, technical services, software engineering, and autonomous vehicles. These taxonomies provide a systematic approach to selecting and designing an appropriate level of human oversight, classifying methods of applying AI, and categorising the levels of automation in various domains.

### Healthcare Sector

AI applications in the healthcare sector are classified into three categories based on their autonomy, namely: autonomous, assistive, and augmentative. Autonomous AI refers to systems that can make decisions without human oversight, whereas assistive AI supports human decision-making by providing resources, ideas and suggestions for treatment prognosis (Naik et al., 2022; Terranova et al., 2023). Augmentative AI provides advanced analytics and quantification of data, while still requiring physical interpretation (Jadad-Garcia & Jadad, 2024). Examples of autonomous AI systems often employed in the health domain are the autonomous decision support system (Jia et al., 2025; Khosravi et al., 2024). This approach involves using patient and case data to determine the most appropriate usage for an AI-based tool, which can then operate independently to make decisions. This approach has several benefits, including enhanced decision-making and increased patient safety (Jia et al., 2025). Meanwhile, a fully autonomous AI has yet to be widely accepted due to concerns about transparency, accountability, and liability.

Real-time patient monitoring and adaptive assistance are also crucial aspects of AI systems in healthcare. For instance, AI-powered systems can analyse medical images to suggest potential diagnoses, but physicians still review the AI output to make final diagnoses and treatment decisions (Terranova et al., 2023). These highlight the importance of human oversight and accountability in AI decision-making (Jadad-Garcia & Jadad, 2024). Healthcare taxonomies are less standardised than those in autonomous vehicles, which have more mature frameworks for navigation, perception, and human–machine interactions.

The incorporation of feedback mechanisms and alerts on interfaces can keep humans informed about AI-generated decisions, enabling them to intervene when necessary (Terranova et al., 2023). The human in the loop approach allows for the modification of ML methods' results by incorporating human skills and expertise, enabling human interaction at every step of the ML process (Jia et al., 2025). This is particularly critical for healthcare, where patients' preferences and values should be considered when making decisions. Noteworthy that AI applications in healthcare should serve as an assistive capability supporting human decision-making and should not be fully autonomous due to the need for accountability and responsibility.

Autonomy taxonomies distinguish between fully autonomous AI, which refers to making decisions without human oversight, and assistive AI, which supports human decision-making. Emphasis on real-time patient monitoring, adaptive assistance, and liability implication (Calvert, 2025; Rahi et al., 2025).

### Technical Services Sector

In the technical services sector, a structured taxonomy of human–agent interaction has been proposed, categorising collaboration across a spectrum of AI autonomy (Wulf et al., 2025). The taxonomy organises collaboration into six models ranging from full automation to passive AI assistance. This framework connects the taxonomy to key contingency factors, such as task complexity, operational risk, and system reliability, along with their corresponding conceptual architectures. By providing a systemic method for selecting and designing an appropriate level of human oversight, this framework offers practitioners a crucial tool to navigate the trade-offs between automation and control, thereby fostering the development of safer, more effective and context-aware technical service systems.

#### Software Engineering

Software engineering classifies and analyses ways of applying AI, focusing on the level of control and time given to exert control that developers and users have over the decisions proposed or taken by the AI components (Feldt et al., 2018). This taxonomy, called AI-SEAL, consists of three facets: the level of control, the time allocated to exert control, and the basic characterisation of the AI technology being applied. The evaluation shows that AI-SEAL can classify applications regardless of the expertise and domain-specific information involved.

#### Autonomous Vehicles

This taxonomy recognises the shifts in human–system interaction due to automation and proposes a four-level taxonomy for autonomous systems, comparing it to the SAE J3016 standards (Betz et al., 2024). The taxonomy introduces classes of collaborative vehicles not defined in existing literature and defines the level of automation suitable for vehicles where automation applies to additional functions beyond the driving task.

## 6.4 AI Global Cooperation and Harmonised Standards

The rapid adoption and deployment of AI globally and across industries has created considerable discrepancies in governance frameworks, raising concerns about cross-border security challenges, inconsistent oversight, and unaccountable decision-making (Christen et al., 2023; Schmitz et al., 2025). Acknowledging these problems prompted the development of several global initiatives aimed at promoting coordination. Therefore, this section aims to address the research objective 4, that is, discussing the "***Ethical frameworks and practical governance of AI***".

For instance, China called for a unified global AI governance framework, while the United Nations (UN) built dialogue mechanisms and suggested that international regulatory bodies standardise methods for AI control, oversight, and autonomy (Mukherjee, 2024). Similarly, the international network of AI Safety Institutes (AISIs), which includes institutes from the US, UK, EU, and other regions, collaborates to address national security, safety, and ethical issues arising from AI.

Although for AI governance to be effective and sustainable, it is necessary to incorporate ethics and legislation within the structure. This is critical because approaches for assessing AI's pre- and post-deployment impacts assure alignment with societal values and human rights (Christen et al., 2023). In addition, institutions such as the UN Global Digital Compact and the Council of Europe's Framework Convention on AI are taking initiatives to incorporate human rights, democratic norms, and rule-of-law considerations directly into AI governance (Mukherjee, 2024). Simultaneously, regional and continental approaches are now forming. For instance, in Africa, the African Union's Continental AI Strategy and the Digital Transformation Strategy (2020–2030) emphasise ethics, human rights, and socio-economic development as major principles of AI adoption (African Union, 2020). Similarly, national and sub-regional initiatives in South Africa, Nigeria, and Kenya supplement these continental frameworks, and organisations like the African Organisation for Standardisation (ARSO) are developing AI standards to support harmonised and context-sensitive governance across the continent. These initiatives demonstrate that effective global coordination necessitates both international cooperation and regional adaptation.

While these efforts are commendable, a critical challenge remains in the implementation. A contextual, coherent, and commensurable (3C) paradigm has been proposed to classify AI systems and align regulatory objectives across jurisdictions (Park, 2024). In addition, ISO AI standards, including ISO/IEC 24027 and 24368, provide a foundation of guidelines for risk management and system evaluation; however, their usefulness varies by region. In Africa, adapting these standards to local regulatory systems and socioeconomic contexts is crucial. Hence, mandatory risk audits, region-specific annexes, and compliance with continental ethics principles are required to ensure that AI governance is both global and regionally applicable (Sankaran, 2025).

Accountability of autonomous systems remains a key challenge in various governance frameworks. Although legal personhood for AI has been advocated as a way to allocate responsibility for highly autonomous systems, such as intellectual property ownership and insurance coverage. Yet, this technique introduces new ethical and legal challenges, including gaps in responsibility and moral agency issues. Relational autonomy, which is based on Ubuntu philosophy, emphasises the need to understand individual autonomy in connection to community and social responsibility (Jenko et al., 2025; Park, 2024). According to this perspective, AI governance systems should not only enforce international standards but also consider culturally grounded conceptions of social responsibility and fairness (Kwik, 2022b; Matthias, 2004).

Ultimately, the deployment of autonomous AI has far-reaching consequences for rights, liability, and contractual law. Existing civil and corporate responsibility frameworks often fail to meet AI behaviour, necessitating reforms such as insurance-based accountability, limited AI personhood, or keeping AI as a regulated product (de Sio & van den Hoven, 2018; Dignum, 2017; Kwik, 2022b). Under the law of contract, AI poses agency-related difficulties influencing formation, performance, and breach, prompting frameworks that represent AI systems' independent capabilities (Judge et al., 2025). While AI can improve judicial efficiency and inclusivity, legal and organisational structures must ensure that human rights, self-determination, and ethical accountability are central to AI-mediated decision-making, particularly in African economic and organisational contexts (Amoroso & Tamburrini, 2021). This discussion is continued in Sect. 6.6 of this paper.

## 6.5 Control, Oversight, and Governance of Autonomous AI

This section aims to explain the control and oversight of AI. This aims to achieve the second and third research objectives of this paper. Section 5.1 addresses the research objective 2, while Sect. 5.2 addresses the research objective 3.

### *6.5.1 Control Strategies and Technologies for Autonomous AI*

To ensure the safe and aligned operation of autonomous AI systems, it is essential to deploy robust control strategies and technologies. This section aims to address the research objective 2, which is to ***"Investigate control strategies for artificial intelligence."***

These control mechanisms can be broadly categorised into technical, human-in-the-loop (HITL) and hybrid approaches. The technical control mechanism involves designing AI systems with embedded monitoring and regulatory capabilities. For instance, control theory can address uncertainties in action execution, as demonstrated in the control-optimised deep reinforcement learning framework (Fivel et al., 2025). Additionally, hardware-enabled mechanisms, such as verifiable training and inference mechanisms, can be used to enhance oversight and compliance with safety standards (O'Gara et al., 2025).

Human-in-the-loop control mechanisms involve the use of active human supervision and intervention. Operators can override protocols to stop or change actions undertaken by the AI in unforeseen circumstances, ensuring transparency while also maintaining interpretability of the AI-driven decision processes (Acharya et al., 2025; Tallam, 2025). HITL systems can also be designed to facilitate accountability by providing auditable and interpretable decision trails for domain experts. Hybrid control mechanism combines technical and HITM approaches to provide a more robust and adaptive control system. For example, the Unified Control Framework proposes a consolidated approach to enterprise AI governance, risk management and regulatory compliance, combining technical controls, HITL interventions and other policy measures to ensure responsible AI development (Eisenberg et al., 2025).

In addition to these control mechanisms, other complementary principles and strategies can be used to ensure the safe and aligned operation of autonomous AI systems. For example, the use of the 'explainability by design' principle can ensure that the system decision-making processes are transparent and auditable (Tallam, 2025). Furthermore, regulatory frameworks for governing AI systems can ensure their safe and responsible development (Eisenberg et al., 2025). Overall, the control of autonomous AI systems is a complex and multifaceted issue that requires the development and implementation of various control mechanisms and technologies.

### 6.5.2 Human Oversight Models and Ethical Consideration

This subsection discusses Research Objective 3, which aims to "***Explore human oversight models and ethical considerations.***" In autonomous AI systems, human oversight plays a crucial role in ensuring accountability, fairness and transparency. It involves human decision-makers actively monitoring, evaluating, and intervening in AI-driven actions to ensure they align with human values and ethical standards (Gao et al., 2025). Oversight levels can range from loose supervision to strict control, depending on task complexity and risk (Afroogh et al., 2025). Research has highlighted the importance of human insight in AI-driven systems. For instance, a study in human-centered human–AI collaboration emphasises the need for human oversight in high-risk tasks, where an AI agent may exhibit opaque or unpredictable behaviour (Afroogh et al., 2025). Another study on trustworthiness AI guidelines in biomedical decision-making applications notes that human agency and oversight are essential for ensuring that AI systems are designed and operating in ways that respect user autonomy, and provide meaningful opportunities for human interventions (Mora-Cantallops et al., 2024).

Human oversight mechanisms can take various forms, including explainability, transparency, bias mitigation, accountability and fairness (Gao et al., 2025). Human oversights enable humans to intervene in AI-driven actions when necessary, ensuring that AI systems are aligned with human values and ethical standards (Gao et al., 2025). For example, human oversight can involve human decision makers reviewing AI-driven recommendations, assessing their contextual and ethical implications and making final decisions (Goldsmith & Yang, 2025). However, maintaining meaningful oversight presents several challenges, including competence gaps, superficial engagement, and the psychological costs associated with decision-making (Green, 2022). Best practices, including clear guidelines, transparent governance frameworks, continuous training, and regular auditing, can mitigate these challenges and enhance effective human–AI collaboration (Joseph et al., 2024).

#### Taxonomies and Roles of Human Oversight

This chapter classifies human oversight into two distinct types. The first is *constitutive oversight,* and the second is *corrective oversight*. Constitutive oversight is integral to AI decision-making processes as it is embedded within the AI system to guide and shape outcomes from the outset, while the corrective oversight intervenes after a decision has been made, allowing for adjustments or corrections to mitigate errors or unintended consequences (Manheim & Homewood, 2025; Methnani et al., 2021a, 2021b). These taxonomies enable tailored improvements by aligning oversight with specific AI operational needs. Responsibility tracking mechanisms, which document decision rationale and accountability pathways, are critical for addressing responsibility gaps in autonomous systems. It involves documenting decision-making rationale and accountability paths, ensuring transparency and accountability (Methnani et al., 2021a, 2021b).

**Effectiveness of Oversight in Reducing Responsibility Gaps**

The concept of MHC provides moral responsibility in fully autonomous systems by equipping humans with the capacity to influence AI behaviour, thereby bridging the accountability divide (Koch et al., 2024; Nyholm, 2018). Studies show that oversight effectiveness is limited by factors like competence, incentives, and psychological factors such as the shame from being overruled (Manheim & Homewood, 2025; Tsamados et al., 2024). All these factors also have the capability to hinder performance. The SDT provides a structured approach to enhance human sensitivity to AI errors and unfairness, improving oversight accuracy. analyses and enhances human sensitivity and bias in detecting AI errors and unfairness (J. Y. C. Chen & Barnes, 2014; Verdiesen et al., 2020a, 2020b). Furthermore, responsibility attributions reflect oversight effectiveness. They are critical because oversight success depends on causal power, epistemic access, self-control, and ethical alignment (Tariq & Ahmed, 2025).

### *6.5.3 Mandates, Challenges and Solutions*

The regulation of human oversight in high-risk AI systems has been gaining traction in global AI governance. The EU AI Act mandates that high-risk AI systems integrate techniques requiring human supervision, enabling operators to override, halt, or verify outputs before they are acted upon (Engin & Hand, 2025b; Tsamados et al., 2024). Article 14 stipulates that human oversight should not be superficial rather designed to ensure accountability, prevent rights violations, and safeguard ethical guidelines (European Union, 2026). However, debates have highlighted that practical implementation is still lacking. (Sterz et al., 2024) stressed that meaningful human oversight requires sufficient contributory power, access to epistemic knowledge, and an alignment between human intention and ethical objectives. Similarly, Langer et al. (2025a, 2025b, 2025c) highlighted the complexities of testing compliance with oversight requirements, noting tensions between the need for enforceable simplicity and the empirical rigor required by diverse AI applications.

Although, the main source of the challenges is linked with role ambiguity, lack of legal clarity and potential accountability gaps, yet, the effectiveness is further undermined by human fallibility, automation bias, algorithm aversion, and insufficient developer obligations (Laux, 2024b). Mitigation approach includes multi-layered oversight, separation of duty, clear mandates, and improved institutional design (Laux, 2024b; Manheim & Homewood, 2025). While the act does not explicitly note explainability, it is an essential attribute for transparency. Although its effectiveness can also be undermined by technical limitations and abuse of the adversarial role (Bradshaw et al., 2004; Davidovic, 2023; Johnston & Kalra, 2025).

While the EU AI Act serve as the most prominent example of regulatory efforts, Africa and Sub-Saharan Africa have begun efforts to institutionalise oversight as part of broader AI governance. (Plantinga et al., 2024) In their cross-country study, they noted that African governments are taking part in policy learning to develop responsible AI frameworks. South Africa, Nigeria, and Kenya are now implementing national plans and AI governance regulations that prioritise accountability, transparency, and the ethical use of AI in high-risk sectors. These moves highlight the realisation of the need for oversight measures in high-risk sectors such as healthcare, financial institutions, and public establishments. These approaches combined reinforce that meaningful oversight extends beyond technical protection to include ensuring stakeholder trust and guaranteeing responsible AI deployment across diverse economies.

### 6.5.4 Technologies for Dynamic Adjustments of AI Autonomy

Technologies for dynamic autonomy adjustment enable AI systems to redefine their independence in response to context and human interaction. These technologies include:

(i) ***Adjustable autonomy:*** This framework uses transfer-of-control mechanisms to shift decision-making power between AI agents and human operators, often leveraging the Markov decision processes (MDPs) to navigate uncertainty and optimise coordination.
(ii) ***Shared autonomy:*** This technique, especially in human–robot interaction (HRI) systems, uses methods like Bayesian relational event modelling to alter autonomy levels in real time based on human trust and team performance (Steen et al., 2022).
(iii) ***Human–centred automation:*** This integrates adjustable autonomy into human–computer interaction, ensuring safety while supporting training and oversight (Abbas et al., 2025).
(iv) ***Human–machine teaming (HMT):*** This comprises architectural frameworks like MAPE-K-HMT (i.e., monitor, analyse, plan, execute—knowledge—human machine teaming), extending classic decision loops to enable collaborative autonomy and transparent runtime adjustments (Methnani et al., 2024).
(v) ***Security evaluation:*** These systems also integrate AI security evaluation, bridging reliability, safety, transparency, and bias mitigation across the AI

lifecycle (Chiou et al., 2021; Lai et al., 2023; Manheim & Homewood, 2025). Though direct sources are sparse, similar principles are emphasised in trustworthy AI frameworks, stressing explainability, auditability, and bias mitigation.

(vi) ***Comprehensive oversight:*** This is an emerging multi-layered governance framework comprising the NIST AI Risk Management Framework (RMF), operationalising oversight through iterative cycles of governance, measurement, and management, embedding trustworthiness principles such as reliability, safety, accountability, fairness, and explainability into the full AI lifecycle (NIST, 2023–2024).

**Note**: The NIST is a US federal agency under the Department of Commerce. The AR RMF is a framework designed to help organisations embed trustworthiness. This includes elements such as reliability, safety, accountability, transparency, fairness and explainability in AI systems across their entire lifecycle. The NIST AI RMF proposal was started in 2021, and the public input, workshops and draft versions were published in 2023. On January 26, 2023, it was officially published. It has supported materials like Roadmap, crosswalk and playbook. In July 2024, NIST introduced an additional profile tailored for generative AI systems such as large language models. The primary function of the framework is structured around four structures. These are governance, map, measure and manage. These frameworks are iteratively used by organisations through the AI lifecycle. This lifestyle cycle includes AI design, development, use and assessment. The summary is presented in Table 6.2.

These emerging technologies and frameworks reflect a shift in dynamic, context-aware autonomy. These balances technological capability with human oversight, trust, and governance.

## 6.6 Ethical Frameworks and Practical Governance

This section focuses on the ethical frameworks and governance practices that lead to responsible AI implementation in business organisations. This extends the discussion of Sect. 6.4, which addresses objective four of this research, which aims to examine the "***Ethical frameworks and practical governance of AI***." While regulations provide the "strict/hard laws," ethical governance translates principles into actions that ensure both compliance and legitimacy in socioeconomic contexts.

### *6.6.1 Ethical Foundations*

Responsible AI governance is guided by core ethical principles like transparency, fairness, accountability, and privacy. Transparency and accountability underpin trust

**Table 6.2** Summary of technologies for dynamic adjustments of AI autonomy

| Technology concept | Description |
|---|---|
| Adjustable autonomy | Uses transfer of control strategies modelled cis Markov decision processes (MDPs) to optimally distribute decision authority based on context, uncertainty and coordination needs |
| Shared autonomy | Dynamically adjusts autonomy in response to human trust and team performance, e.g. through Bayesian relation modelling in HRI scenarios |
| Human-centred automation | Blends adjustable autonomy with interaction design principles to support safe, learnable systems with built-in human intervention capacity |
| Human–machine teaming (MAPE-K-HMT) | Extends MAPE-K with HMT-specific runtime models for transparency, coordination, and dynamic autonomy adaptations |
| Security evaluation and oversight | Embeds human-aligned dynamic autonomy, supporting accountability and meaningful control |
| Comprehensive oversight | Implement layered governance through a regulatory alignment, risk assessment, standards, certifications, as seen in frameworks like NIST AR RMF |

by assuring explainability and answerability, whereas fairness and privacy protect individuals from bias and discrimination. These principles are consistently highlighted in academic and policy frameworks (Bakirtzis et al., 2024; Cummings, 2006; Wyatt & Galliott, 2021).

### *6.6.2 Governance Models and Operationalisation*

Effective governance requires a multi-level, collaborative, context-sensitive framework that integrates innovation with societal values and human rights. Trust dimensions such as competence, integrity and benevolence are highly vital for maintaining legitimacy (Biewer et al., 2023; Wyatt & Galliott, 2021). Japan's "soft law" approach exemplifies this, relying on voluntary compliance, public–private partnership, and a human-centric AI ethos to achieve a broader Society 5.0 vision.

However, the government must go beyond abstract principles to actionable practices, suggesting the integration of principles across governance structures, organisational processes, and system design. Operational techniques, such as algorithmic impact assessments, bias audits, and structured human oversight processes, help embed accountability in practice. The hourglass model offers one of such frameworks that links governance across AI lifecycles at the environmental, organisational, and system levels (Cummings, 2006).

### 6.6.3 Balancing Human Agency and AI Autonomy

To balance human oversight with machine autonomy, businesses are encountering a series of challenges. Hence, this Sects. 6.3 and 6.4 aims to address Objective Five of this chapter by exploring "***best practices for Human–AI interface.***"

Interaction occurs on a continuum, ranging from full human control to full AI decision-making. Governance designs like exchanged, executive, combined, and supervisory controls enable the dynamic allocation of authority (Crootof, 2016).

Adaptive automation refines this balance by altering autonomy in response to workload demands. Neuroergonomic techniques, such as brain activity monitoring or eye-tracking, can facilitate task delegation in real-time, reducing human cognitive strain while maintaining performance (Firlej & Taeihagh, 2021; Laux, 2024b). Personalisation ensures that systems adapt to specific operator profiles (van der Waa et al., 2021).

Maturity models serve as benchmarks for integrating autonomy and oversight at various developmental phases (Frenette, 2023). Furthermore, differentiating autonomy as authenticity (goal setting in line with values) from autonomy as agency (operational execution) enables organisations to create systems that respect ethical goals while maintaining efficiency.

Human oversight models help to institutionalise accountability. The human-in-the-loop (HITL), human-on-the-loop (HOTL), and human-in-command (HIC) frameworks offer complementary measures for addressing responsibility gaps and maintaining MHC. Their effectiveness, however, is contingent upon both organisational design and individual capabilities.

### 6.6.4 Best Practices for Human–AI Interfaces

Operationalising ethics also requires designing interfaces that promote trust, collaboration, and accountability (Buijsman et al., 2025). These emerging best practices are presented in Table 6.3.

Collectively, these approaches demonstrate that ethical AI governance in organisations is dynamic, context-dependent, and human-centred. Adaptive structures, transparent design, and consideration of social-psychological aspects (i.e., autonomy, competence, and relatedness) ensure that AI systems remain trustworthy while also promoting economic innovation and societal well-being.

**Table 6.3** Emerging best practices for human–AI interface

| Best practices | Description | Reference |
|---|---|---|
| Transparency and communication | Utilise visual explanations to foster a shared understanding and build trust | Reinmund et al. (2024) and Verhagen et al. (2024) |
| User involvement | Offers adjustable parameters that enable operators to adjust AI decisions, hence increasing trust and decreasing algorithm aversion | Baltzer et al. (2023) and Dubois and Le Ny (2020) |
| Dynamic task allocation | Employ trust- and workload-aware models, such as Markov decision processes (MDPs), to improve human–AI collaboration more effectively than static tasks | Goldsmith and Yang (2025) |
| Explainable AI (XAI) | Adaptive explanation frameworks, such as ATDF, tailor system transparency to operator demands, thereby enhancing usability in high-risk sectors like healthcare | Buijsman et al. (2025), Chen et al. (2025) and Sovrano and Masetti (2022) |
| Customisation | Supports user-centred designs with customizable elements to enhance transparency, fairness, and psychological comfort | Buijsman et al. (2025) |

## 6.7 Conclusion

The governance of AI system autonomy presents an array of benefits, as well as unprecedented concerns. As AI is rapidly evolving, influencing high-stakes decision-making, ensuring responsible deployment requires balancing autonomy, human oversight, and ethical accountability. This chapter reinforces that MHC is a cornerstone of trust and legitimacy. It also highlights that oversight must go beyond symbolic controls to become substantive, competent, and enforceable. Prominent governance frameworks like the EU AI Act and emerging regulations guiding ethical AI usage from within Africa reflect a growing global consensus on establishing guidelines for high-risk AI systems. However, there are still existing gaps like the role of ambiguity, competency gaps, and limitations of human cognition in a complex systems context. These issues emphasise the importance of embedding adaptive human oversight models, dynamic autonomy adjustments, and explainable AI interfaces into the AI governance systems.

Ethical principles like accountability, transparency, fairness, and privacy need to be adhered to, and must not be taken as a mere abstract concept, rather actionable practice through impact assessments, bias auditing, and human-in-the-loop strategies. Integrating these principles into organisational practices, technical structures, and legal frameworks assures not only compliance but stakeholder trust in the AI system.

Ultimately, the way forward calls for a multi-layered, collaborative governance approach that combines technological innovation, human-centred values, regulatory monitoring, and sociocultural contexts. By prioritising adaptability, accountability, and human-centred measures, society at large can embrace the potential of autonomous systems while reducing risks, ensuring that technological advances benefit humans rather than wreaking havoc.

## References

Abbas, Z., Amin, F., & Khan, M. M. (2025). Integration of artificial intelligence in nuclear command and control systems (NC2): Assessing cold-war paradigm. *Journal of Social Sciences Review, 5*(1), 180–188. https://doi.org/10.62843/JSSR.V5I1.476

Acharya, D. B., Kuppan, K., & Divya, B. (2025). Agentic AI: Autonomous intelligence for complex goals—A comprehensive survey. *IEEE Access, 13*, 18912–18936. https://doi.org/10.1109/ACCESS.2025.3532853

African Union. (2020). The digital transformation strategy for Africa (2020–2030). In *African Union.*

Afroogh, S., Varshney, K. R., & D'Cruz, J. (2025). *A task-driven human–AI collaboration: When to automate, when to collaborate, when to challenge.*

Alhosani, K., & Alhashmi, S. M. (2024). Opportunities, challenges, and benefits of AI innovation in government services: A review. *Discover Artificial Intelligence, 4*(1), 1–19. https://doi.org/10.1007/S44163-024-00111-W/TABLES/1

Amoroso, D., & Tamburrini, G. (2021). Toward a normative model of meaningful human control over weapons systems. *Ethics and International Affairs, 35*(2), 245–272. https://doi.org/10.1017/S0892679421000241

Bakirtzis, G., Chiou, M., & Theodorou, A. (2024). *Negotiating control: Neurosymbolic variable autonomy.*

Baltzer, M. C. A., Ripkens, A., Lopez-Hernandez, D., & Flemisch, F. (2023). Interaction mediation for meaningful human control over highly automated vehicles. In *Conference proceedings—IEEE international conference on systems, man and cybernetics* (pp. 4411–4416). https://doi.org/10.1109/SMC53992.2023.10394428

Betz, J., Lutwitzi, M., & Peters, S. (2024). A new taxonomy for automated driving: Structuring applications based on their operational design domain, level of automation and automation readiness. *IEEE Intelligent Vehicles Symposium, Proceedings.* https://doi.org/10.1109/iv55156.2024.10588711

Biewer, S., Baum, K., Sterz, S., Hermanns, H., Hetmank, S., Langer, M., Lauber-Rönsberg, A., & Lehr, F. (2023). Software doping analysis for human oversight. *Formal Methods in System Design, 66*(1), 49–98. https://doi.org/10.1007/s10703-024-00445-2

Bradshaw, J. M., Feltovich, P. J., Jung, H., Kulkarni, S., Taysom, W., & Uszok, A. (2004). Dimensions of adjustable autonomy and mixed-initiative interaction. *Lecture Notes in Computer Science (Including Subseries Lecture Notes in Artificial Intelligence and Lecture Notes in Bioinformatics), 2969*, 17–39. https://doi.org/10.1007/978-3-540-25928-2_3

Breidbach, C. F. (2024). Responsible algorithmic decision-making. *Organizational Dynamics, 53*(2), Article 101031. https://doi.org/10.1016/j.orgdyn.2024.101031

Buijsman, S., Carter, S. E., & Bermúdez, J. P. (2025). *Autonomy by design: Preserving human autonomy in AI decision-support.*

Butler, O. (2025). Algorithmic decision-making, delegation and the modern machinery of government. *Oxford Journal of Legal Studies, 45*(3), 727–752. https://doi.org/10.1093/ojls/gqaf018

Calvert, S. C. (2025). *Principles and framework for the operationalisation of meaningful human control over autonomous systems* (pp. 1–28). arXiv:2502.08255

Chee, F. Y. (2025). *AI models with systemic risks given pointers on how to comply with EU AI rules.* Reuters. https://www.reuters.com/sustainability/boards-policy-regulation/ai-models-with-systemic-risks-given-pointers-how-comply-with-eu-ai-rules-2025-07-18/?utm_source=chatgpt.com

Chen, Z., Luo, Y., & Sra, M. (2025). *Engaging with AI: How interface design shapes human–AI collaboration in high-stakes decision-making.*

Chen, J. Y. C., & Barnes, M. J. (2014). Human–agent teaming for multirobot control: A review of human factors issues. *IEEE Transactions on Human-Machine Systems, 44*(1), 13–29. https://doi.org/10.1109/THMS.2013.2293535

Cheong, B. C. (2024). Transparency and accountability in AI systems: Safeguarding wellbeing in the age of algorithmic decision-making. *Frontiers in Human Dynamics, 6*, 1421273. https://doi.org/10.3389/fhumd.2024.1421273

Chiou, M., Hawes, N., & Stolkin, R. (2021). Mixed-initiative variable autonomy for remotely operated mobile robots. *ACM Transactions on Human-Robot Interaction (THRI), 10*(4), 37. https://doi.org/10.1145/3472206

Christen, M., Burri, T., Kandul, S., & Vörös, P. (2023). Who is controlling whom? Reframing "meaningful human control" of AI systems in security. *Ethics and Information Technology, 25*(1), 1–7. https://doi.org/10.1007/S10676-023-09686-X/FIGURES/1

Crootof, R. (2016). A meaningful floor for "Meaningful human control." *Temple International and Comparative Law, 30*(1), 53–62.

Crossnohere, N. L., Elsaid, M., Paskett, J., Bose-Brill, S., & Bridges, J. F. P. (2022). Guidelines for artificial intelligence in medicine: Literature review and content analysis of frameworks. *Journal of Medical Internet Research, 24*(8), 36823. https://doi.org/10.2196/36823

Cummings, M. L. (2006). Automation and accountability in decision support system interface design. *Journal of Technology Studies, 32*(1), 23–31. https://doi.org/10.21061/JOTS.V32I1.A.4

Davidovic, J. (2023). On the purpose of meaningful human control of AI. *Frontiers in Big Data, 5*, 1017677. https://doi.org/10.3389/FDATA.2022.1017677/BIBTEX

de Sio, F. S., & van den Hoven, J. (2018). Meaningful human control over autonomous systems: A philosophical account. *Frontiers Robotics AI, 5*(1), 323836. https://doi.org/10.3389/FROBT.2018.00015/BIBTEX

Diggelen, J., Bosch, K., Neerincx, M. A., & Steen, M. (2023). *Designing for meaningful human control in military human–machine teams.* arXiv:2305.11892. https://doi.org/10.48550/arXiv.2305.11892

Dignum, V. (2017). Responsible autonomy. *IJCAI International Joint Conference on Artificial Intelligence.* https://doi.org/10.24963/IJCAI.2017/655

Dubois, C., & Le Ny, J. (2020). Adaptive task allocation in human–machine teams with trust and workload cognitive models. In *Conference proceedings—IEEE international conference on systems, man and cybernetics, 2020-October* (pp. 3241–3246). https://doi.org/10.1109/SMC42975.2020.9283461

Eisenberg, I. W., Gamboa, L., & Sherman, E. (2025). *The unified control framework: Establishing a common foundation for enterprise AI governance, risk management and regulatory compliance.* https://doi.org/10.48550/arXiv.2503.05937

Engin, Z., & Hand, D. (2025a). Toward adaptive categories: Dimensional governance for agentic AI. arXiv:2505.11579. https://doi.org/10.48550/arXiv.2505.11579

Engin, Z., & Hand, D. (2025b). *Toward adaptive categories: Dimensional governance for agentic AI*. ArXiv preprint.

Engin, Z. (2025). *Human–AI governance (HAIG): A trust-utility approach.*

European Union. (2026). EU artificial intelligence act article 14: Human oversight. In *European commission.*

Feldt, R., De Oliveira Neto, F. G., & Torkar, R. (2018). Ways of applying artificial intelligence in software engineering. *Proceedings—International Conference on Software Engineering*. https://doi.org/10.48550/ARXIV.1802.02033

Ferl, A. K. (2024). Imagining meaningful human control: Autonomous weapons and the (de-) legitimisation of future warfare. *Global Society, 38*(1), 139 155. https://doi.org/10.1080/13600826.2023.2233004

Fernández, A. O., & Moratinos, G. L. (2021). Human oversight of high-risk artificial intelligence systems: Insights from international humanitarian law and European Union law. *Spanish Association of Professors of International Law and International Relations*. https://doi.org/10.17103/reei.42.08

Firlej, M., & Taeihagh, A. (2020). *Regulating human control over autonomous systems*. arXiv:2007.11218. https://doi.org/10.1111/rego.12344

Firlej, M., & Taeihagh, A. (2021). Regulating human control over autonomous systems. *Regulation and Governance, 15*(4), 1071–1091. https://doi.org/10.1111/rego.12344

Fivel, O., Rudman, M., & Cohen, K. (2025). *Control-optimized deep reinforcement learning for artificially intelligent autonomous systems*. arXiv preprint. https://doi.org/10.48550/arXiv.2507.00268

Frenette, J. (2023). Ensuring human oversight in high-performance AI systems: A framework for control and accountability. *World Journal of Advanced Research and Reviews, 20*(2), 1507–1516. https://doi.org/10.30574/wjarr.2023.20.2.2194

Gao, Q., Xu, W., Pan, H., Shen, M., & Gao, Z. (2025). *Human-centered human–AI collaboration (HCHAC)*. arXiv. https://doi.org/10.48550/arXiv.2505.22477

Goldsmith, S., & Yang, J. (2025). *AI and the transformation of accountability and discretion in urban governance.*

Green, B. (2022). The flaws of policies requiring human oversight of government algorithms. *Computer Law and Security Review*. https://doi.org/10.1016/j.clsr.2022.105681

Ho-Dac, M., & Martinez, B. (2024). *Human Oversight of Artificial Intelligence and Technical Standardisation*. https://doi.org/10.1007/s00146-023-01777-z

Hosseini, S., & Seilani, H. (2025). The role of agentic AI in shaping a smart future: A systematic review. In *Array* (Vol. 26, p. 100399). Elsevier. https://doi.org/10.1016/j.array.2025.100399

Hughes, L., Dwivedi, Y. K., Malik, T., Shawosh, M., Albashrawi, M. A., Jeon, I., Dutot, V., Appanderanda, M., Crick, T., De', R., Fenwick, M., Gunaratnege, S. M., Jurcys, P., Kar, A. K., Kshetri, N., Li, K., Mutasa, S., Samothrakis, S., Wade, M., & Walton, P. (2025). AI agents and agentic systems: A multi-expert analysis. *Journal of Computer Information Systems, 65*(4), 489–517. https://doi.org/10.1080/08874417.2025.2483832

Jadad-Garcia, T., & Jadad, A. (2024). *Cracking the code: Lessons from 15 years of digital health IPOs for the era of AI*. arXiv Preprint.

Jenko, S., Papadopoulou, E., Kumar, V., Overman, S. S., Krepelkova, K., Wilson, J., Dunbar, E. L., Spice, C., & Exarchos, T. (2025). Artificial intelligence in healthcare: How to develop and implement safe, ethical and trustworthy AI systems. *AI 2025, 6*(6), 116. https://doi.org/10.3390/AI6060116

Jia, Y., Evans, H., Porter, Z., Graham, S., McDermid, J., Lawton, T., Snead, D., & Habli, I. (2025). *The case for delegated AI autonomy for Human AI teaming in healthcare*. arXiv Preprint.

Johnston, B., & Kalra, J. (2025). Patients over process: Stratifying risk in the design, development, and deployment of artificial intelligence in healthcare. *Healthcare and Medical Devices*. https://doi.org/10.54941/AHFE1006190

Joseph, S. A., Kolade, T. M., Obioha-Val, O., Adebiyi, O. O., Ogungbemi, O. S., & Olaniyi, O. O. (2024). AI-powered information governance: Balancing automation and human oversight for optimal organization productivity. *Asian Journal of Research in Computer Science, 17*(10), 110–131. https://doi.org/10.9734/AJRCOS/2024/V17I10513

Judge, B., Nitzberg, M., & Russell, S. (2025). When code isn't law: Rethinking regulation for artificial intelligence. *Policy and Society, 44*(1), 85–97. https://doi.org/10.1093/polsoc/puae020

Kasirzadeh, A., & Gabriel, I. (2025). *Characterizing AI agents for alignment and governance*. arXiv, 1–29.

Khosravi, M., Zare, Z., Mojtabaeian, S. M., & Izadi, R. (2024). Artificial intelligence and decision-making in healthcare: A thematic analysis of a systematic review of reviews. *Health Services Research and Managerial Epidemiology, 11*, 1–15. https://doi.org/10.1177/23333928241234863

Koch, W., Spreen, D., Talves, K., Wagner, W., Lillemäe, E., Klaus, M., Viidalepp, A., Guldahl Cooper, C., & Pekarev, J. (2024). On the ethics of employing artificial intelligent automation in military operational contexts. *IEEE Transactions on Technology and Society, 5*(2), 231–241. https://doi.org/10.1109/TTS.2024.3405309

Kusche, I. (2024). Possible harms of artificial intelligence and the EU AI act: Fundamental rights and risk. *Journal of Risk Research*. https://doi.org/10.1080/13669877.2024.2350720

Kwik, J. (2022b). A Practicable operationalisation of meaningful human control. *Laws 2022, 11*(3), 43. https://doi.org/10.3390/LAWS11030043

Kwik, J. (2022a). A practicable operationalisation of meaningful human control. *Laws*. https://doi.org/10.3390/laws11030043

Lai, V., Chen, C., Smith-Renner, A., Liao, Q. V., & Tan, C. (2023). Towards a science of human–AI decision making: An overview of design space in empirical human-subject studies. *ACM International Conference Proceeding Series*. https://doi.org/10.1145/3593013.3594087

Langer, M., Lazar, V., & Baum, K. (2025a). On the complexities of testing for compliance with human oversight requirements in AI regulation. *Unknown Journal*.

Langer, M., Lazar, V., & Baum, K. (2025b). *On the complexities of testing for compliance with human oversight requirements in AI regulation*. arXiv preprint arXiv:2504.03300

Langer, M., Baum, K., & Schlicker, N. (2025a). Effective human oversight of AI-based systems: A signal detection perspective on the detection of inaccurate and unfair outputs. *Minds and Machines, 35*(1), 1–30. https://doi.org/10.1007/s11023-024-09701-0

Laux, J. (2024a). Institutionalised distrust and human oversight of artificial intelligence: Towards a democratic design of AI governance under the European Union AI Act. *AI and Society, 39*(6), 2853–2866. https://doi.org/10.1007/s00146-023-01777-z

Laux, J. (2024b). Institutionalised distrust and human oversight of artificial intelligence: Towards a democratic design of AI governance under the European Union AI Act. *AI and Society, 39*(6), 2853–2866. https://doi.org/10.1007/S00146-023-01777-Z/TABLES/3

Manheim, D., & Homewood, A. (2025a). *Limits of safe AI deployment: Differentiating oversight and control*. arXiv:2507.03525. https://doi.org/10.48550/arXiv.2507.03525

Matthias, A. (2004). The responsibility gap: Ascribing responsibility for the actions of learning automata. *Ethics and Information Technology, 6*(3), 175–183. https://doi.org/10.1007/S10676-004-3422-1/METRICS

Methnani, L., Aler Tubella, A., Dignum, V., & Theodorou, A. (2021a). Let me take over: Variable autonomy for meaningful human control. *Frontiers in Artificial Intelligence, 4*, Article 737072. https://doi.org/10.3389/frai.2021.737072

Methnani, L., Chiou, M., Dignum, V., & Theodorou, A. (2024). Who's in charge here? A survey on trustworthy AI in variable autonomy robotic systems. *ACM Computing Surveys, 56*(7), 1–32. https://doi.org/10.1145/3645090

Methnani, L., Tubella, A. A., Dignum, V., & Theodorou, A. (2021b). Let me take over: Variable autonomy for meaningful human control. *Frontiers in Artificial Intelligence*. https://doi.org/10.3389/frai.2021.737072

Moesker, N. (2025). *AI autonomy: AI & human collaboration-*. DataNorth. https://datanorth.ai/blog/ai-autonomy-ai-human-collaboration

Mora-Cantallops, M., García-Barriocanal, E., & Sicilia, M. Á. (2024). Trustworthy AI guidelines in biomedical decision-making applications: A scoping review. *Big Data and Cognitive Computing*. https://doi.org/10.3390/bdcc8070073

Mukherjee, S. (2024). *UN advisory body makes seven recommendations for governing AI*. Reuters. https://www.reuters.com/technology/artificial-intelligence/un-advisory-body-makes-seven-recommendations-governing-ai-2024-09-19/

Naik, N., Hameed, B. M. Z., Shetty, D. K., Swain, D., Shah, M., Paul, R., Aggarwal, K., Brahim, S., Patil, V., Smriti, K., Shetty, S., Rai, B. P., Chlosta, P., & Somani, B. K. (2022). Legal and ethical consideration in artificial intelligence in healthcare: Who takes responsibility? *Frontiers in Surgery, 9*, Article 862322. https://doi.org/10.3389/fsurg.2022.862322

Nyholm, S. (2018). Attributing agency to automated systems: Reflections on human–robot collaborations and responsibility-loci. *Science and Engineering Ethics, 24*(4), 1201–1219. https://doi.org/10.1007/s11948-017-9943-x

O'Gara, A., Kulp, G., Hodgkins, W., Petrie, J., Immler, V., Aysu, A., Basu, K., Bhasin, S., Picek, S., & Srivastava, A. (2025). Hardware-enabled mechanisms for verifying responsible AI development. *SuperIntelligence—Robotics—Safety & Alignment*. https://doi.org/10.70777/si.v2i3.15157

OECD. (2020). *OECD legal instruments: Recommendation of the council on artificial intelligence*. OECD. https://legalinstruments.oecd.org/en/instruments/OECD-LEGAL-0449

Ogedengbe, F. A. (2024). Investigating the influence of IT inaccessibility and social pressure on employees shadow cloud IT usage during the COVID-19 pandemic MCO period. In *International Journal of Business Information Systems, 47*(4).

Ogedengbe, F. A., & Adelowotan, M. O. (2025). Revolutionising corporate governance: Blockchain's transformative impact and potential. In *Frontiers in Blockchain, 8*. Frontiers Media SA. https://doi.org/10.3389/fbloc.2025.1654633

Okuno, M. J., & Okuno, H. G. (2025). Legal frameworks for AI service business participants: A comparative analysis of liability protection across jurisdictions. *AI and Society*. https://doi.org/10.1007/s00146-025-02288-9

Papagiannidis, E., Mikalef, P., & Conboy, K. (2025). Responsible artificial intelligence governance: A review and research framework. *Journal of Strategic Information Systems, 34*(2), Article 101885. https://doi.org/10.1016/j.jsis.2024.101885

Park, S. (2024). Bridging the global divide in AI regulation: A proposal for a contextual, coherent, and commensurable framework. *Washington International Law Journal, 33*(2), 215–269. https://doi.org/10.2139/ssrn.4950781

Plantinga, P., Shilongo, K., Mudongo, O., Umubyeyi, A., Gastrow, M., & Razzano, G. (2024). Responsible artificial intelligence in Africa: Towards policy learning. *Data and Policy*. https://doi.org/10.1017/dap.2024.60

Przegalinska, A., Triantoro, T., Kovbasiuk, A., Ciechanowski, L., Freeman, R. B., & Sowa, K. (2025). Collaborative AI in the workplace: Enhancing organizational performance through resource-based and task-technology fit perspectives. *International Journal of Information Management, 81*(4), Article 102853. https://doi.org/10.1016/j.ijinfomgt.2024.102853

Rahi, S., Lather, V., Rana, A., & Pandit, J. (2025). Comprehensive framework for the global regulation and approval of AI-integrated medical devices. *Applied Drug Research, Clinical Trials and Regulatory Affairs, 11*(1), E26673371347630. https://doi.org/10.2174/0126673371347630250418134235

Reinmund, T., Salvini, P., Kunze, L., Jirotka, M., & Winfield, A. (2023). Variable autonomy through responsible robotics: Design guidelines and research agenda. *ACM Transactions on Human–Robot Interaction, 13*, 1-36–1-36. https://doi.org/10.1145/3636432

Reinmund, T., Salvini, P., Kunze, L., Jirotka, M., & Winfield, A. F. T. (2024). Variable autonomy through responsible robotics: Design guidelines and research agenda. *ACM Transactions on Human–Robot Interaction*. https://doi.org/10.1145/3636432

Robbins, S. (2024). The many meanings of meaningful human control. *AI and Ethics, 4*(4), 1377–1388. https://doi.org/10.1007/s43681-023-00320-6

Sankaran, S. (2025). *Enhancing trust through standards: A comparative risk-impact framework for aligning ISO AI standards with global ethical and regulatory contexts*. arXiv.

Schmitz, C., Rystrøm, J., & Batzner, J. (2025). *Oversight structures for agentic AI in public-sector organizations* (pp. 298–308). https://doi.org/10.18653/v1/2025.realm-1.21

Sharma, S. (2024). Benefits or concerns of AI: A multistakeholder responsibility. *Futures, 157*, Article 103328. https://doi.org/10.1016/J.FUTURES.2024.103328

Sovrano, F., & Masetti, G. (2022). Foreseeing the impact of the proposed AI act on the sustainability and safety of critical infrastructures. *ACM International Conference Proceeding Series*. https://doi.org/10.1145/3560107.3560253

Steen, M., Van Diggelen, J., Timan, Tjerk, & Van Der Stap, N. (2022). Meaningful human control of drones: exploring human–machine teaming, informed by four different ethical perspectives. *AI and Ethics, 3*(1), 281–293. https://doi.org/10.1007/S43681-022-00168-2

Sterz, S., Baum, K., Biewer, S., Hermanns, H., Lauber-Rönsberg, A., Meinel, P., & Langer, M. (2024). On the quest for effectiveness in human oversight: Interdisciplinary perspectives. *2024 ACM conference on fairness, accountability, and transparency, FAccT 2024* (pp. 2495–2507). https://doi.org/10.1145/3630106.3659051

Tallam, K. (2025). *Alignment, agency and autonomy in frontier AI: A systems engineering perspective.*

Tariq, U., & Ahmed, I. (2025). Reasoning about responsibility in autonomous systems: Navigating the challenges and charting future directions. *Ubiquitous Technology Journal, 1*(2), 46–60. https://doi.org/10.71346/UTJ.V1I2.21

Terranova, C., Cestonaro, C., Fava, L., & Cinquetti, A. (2023). AI and professional liability assessment in healthcare. A revolution in legal medicine? *Frontiers in Medicine, 10*, 1337335. https://doi.org/10.3389/FMED.2023.1337335/BIBTEX

Tsamados, A., Floridi, L., & Taddeo, M. (2024). Human control of AI systems: From supervision to teaming. *Ai and Ethics, 5*, 1535–1548. https://doi.org/10.1007/s43681-024-00489-4

Umakanth, A. A. M. (2025). Human-in-the-loop architectures for validating GenAI outputs in clinical settings. *European Journal of Computer Science and Information Technology, 13*(47), 103–110. https://doi.org/10.37745/ejcsit.2013/vol13n47103110

van der Waa, J., Verdult, S., van den Bosch, K., van Diggelen, J., Haije, T., van der Stigchel, B., & Cocu, I. (2021). Moral decision making in human–agent teams: Human control and the role of explanations. *Frontiers in Robotics and AI, 8*, Article 640647. https://doi.org/10.3389/frobt.2021.640647

Vanneste, B. S., & Puranam, P. (2024). Artificial intelligence, trust, and perceptions of agency. *Academy of Management Review*. https://doi.org/10.5465/amr.2022.0041

Verdiesen, I., Sio, F. S. de, & Dignum, V. (2020). Accountability and control over autonomous weapon systems: A framework for comprehensive human oversight. *Minds and Machines, 31*, 137–163. https://doi.org/10.1007/s11023-020-09532-9

Verdiesen, I., Santoni de Sio, F., & Dignum, V. (2020a). Accountability and control over autonomous weapon systems: A framework for comprehensive human oversight. *Minds and Machines, 31*(1), 137–163. https://doi.org/10.1007/s11023-020-09532-9

Verdiesen, I., Tubella, A. A., & Dignum, V. (2021). Integrating comprehensive human oversight in drone deployment: A conceptual framework applied to the case of military surveillance drones. *Information, 12*, 385. https://doi.org/10.3390/info12090385

Verhagen, R. S., Neerincx, M. A., & Tielman, M. L. (2024). Meaningful human control and variable autonomy in human–robot teams for firefighting. *Frontiers in Robotics and AI, 11*, 1323980. https://doi.org/10.3389/frobt.2024.1323980

Wulf, J., Meierhofer, J., & Hannich, F. (2025). *Architecting human–AI cocreation for technical services—interaction modes and contingency factors.*

Wyatt, A., & Galliott, J. (2021). An empirical examination of the impact of cross-cultural perspectives on value sensitive design for autonomous systems. *Information, 12*(12), 527. https://doi.org/10.3390/INFO12120527

Zaidan, E., & Ibrahim, I. A. (2024). AI governance in a complex and rapidly changing regulatory landscape: A global perspective. *Humanities and Social Sciences Communications, 11*(1), 1–18. https://doi.org/10.1057/s41599-024-03560-x

# Chapter 7
# AI in Public and Private Sectors: Governance in Practice

**Adesanmi Timothy Adegbayibi and Michael Olajide Adelowotan**

**Abstract** The rapid growth of artificial intelligence (AI) has outpaced the creation of appropriate governance mechanisms, resulting in a substantial gap, particularly in emerging markets. This disparity has had serious socio-economic effects, including the amplification of algorithmic bias against marginalized groups, extensive privacy violations that have led to public distrust, and impaired judicial impartiality due to opaque predictive systems. This study examined the practical application and effectiveness of AI governance frameworks in both the public and private sectors. It investigated the distinct motivations, challenges, and models that characterised each sector, contrasting the public sector's rights-based, regulatory approach with the private sector's market-driven, self-regulatory model, commonly referred to as 'Responsible AI.' Based on stakeholder theory, the study emphasised the importance of balancing diverse interests beyond shareholder primacy to ensure equitable outcomes. An empirical and sectoral review found that in high-risk areas, such as finance, healthcare, and criminal justice, governance is crucial for managing specific risks, including systemic market instability, diagnostic errors, and the reinforcement of historical biases. A comparison of government oversight and corporate self-regulation, illustrated by case studies of industry leaders such as Google and Microsoft, shows that while government mandates provide enforceability and protect fundamental rights, corporate frameworks offer technical agility and operational depth. However, both models have inherent limitations: government control can be cumbersome and inhibit innovation, whereas conflicts of interest hamper business self-regulation. As a result, the report proposed for a hybrid governance paradigm that combines legally obligatory government rules for high-risk applications with flexible, industry-led practices. This integrated approach, strengthened by public–private partnerships (PPPs) and a focus on transparency, accountability, and inclusion, is presented as the most viable path to ensure AI's deployment fosters sustainable growth and equitable societal benefits, particularly in developing regions.

---

A. T. Adegbayibi (✉) · M. O. Adelowotan
Department of Accountancy, College of Business and Economics, University of Johannesburg, Johannesburg, South Africa
e-mail: aadegbayibi@uj.ac.za; adesanmi.adegbayibi@aaua.edu.ng

M. O. Adelowotan
e-mail: madelowotan@uj.ac.za

 
M. Adelowotan and H. Coovadia (eds.), *AI and Accountability*, CSR, Sustainability, Ethics & Governance, https://doi.org/10.1007/978-3-032-20091-4_7

## 7.1 Introduction

Over the past decade, artificial intelligence (AI) has emerged as a pivotal driver of economic transformation, reshaping operational paradigms in both the public and private sectors worldwide. Its applications span predictive analytics in healthcare, algorithmic decision-making in finance, and automated surveillance in criminal justice, contributing to global AI market valuations exceeding $400 billion in 2024 (Ogunleye, 2021). However, this exponential growth has outstripped the development of commensurate governance structures, resulting in disparate adoption trajectories between developed and emerging economies. Advanced jurisdictions, such as the European Union and the United States, have established comprehensive regulatory regimes, including the EU AI Act (2024), to address risks like bias amplification and privacy infringement (Nwaokocha, 2025). In contrast, developing regions, particularly sub-Saharan Africa, face persistent barriers, including inadequate digital infrastructure, regulatory fragmentation, and skill deficits, which hinder the equitable integration of AI (Oladipo & Adeyemo, 2024). Nations such as Nigeria exemplify this challenge: despite issuing the National Artificial Intelligence Strategy (NAIS) in 2023, enforcement remains nascent, with fewer than 20% of public institutions adhering to ethical guidelines (Ogunseye, 2024).

The governance vacuum has had serious socio-economic consequences. Unmitigated AI deployments have exacerbated inequities, with algorithmic biases in FinTech credit assessment systems resulting in a 37% underfunding penalty for women-led Small and Medium Enterprises (SMEs), despite having superior repayment records (Adepoju et al., 2025). Privacy violations caused by unregulated data aggregation have resulted in hefty penalties, most notably a record $220 million punishment issued on Meta in Nigeria in 2024 for data protection breaches under the Nigeria Data Protection Act, undermining public trust (Aloamaka, 2025). In the public sector, opaque predictive police methods have increased false positive rates by 38% in minority populations, jeopardizing judicial impartiality (Kucici & Boye, 2024). These challenges come from institutional shortcomings. Siloed policymaking, incentive misalignment, and restricted multi-stakeholder interaction exacerbate the propagation of risk. In emerging markets, geopolitical dependencies, such as reliance on foreign AI platforms, further complicate sovereignty, as evidenced by the data localization debates in Africa (Ogunbodede & Atchrim, 2025). Without robust oversight, AI's potential to augment GDP by 5–7% in low-income economies by 2030 remains unrealized (Ogunbodede & Atchrim, 2025).

International efforts to standardize AI governance have been formed, such as the OECD AI Principles (Jobin, 2024) and the G7 Hiroshima Process (Caron & Drezner, 2023), which advocate for openness and accountability and have influenced the policies of over 70 governments (Sorensen et al., 2024). However, these measures were hampered by deficiencies in enforcement and inclusion. Implementation varies significantly between jurisdictions; for example, Singapore requires impact evaluations for high-risk AI systems (Tan et al., 2024), whereas many African countries currently lack formal legal frameworks (Oosthuizen & De Koker, 2024).

Furthermore, geopolitical tensions, particularly the US-China standards rivalry, have hampered the harmonization of crucial concerns such as cross-border data flow regulation (Haider et al., 2025). Macroeconomic vulnerabilities, as demonstrated by the 2020–2022 supply chain crises and related semiconductor shortages, led to significant global economic upheaval and delayed AI initiatives in emerging countries (Tegmark & Lipton, 2024). These large-scale dynamics compound shortcomings in localized, micro-governance, resulting in negative feedback loops of under-investment and ethical non-compliance in the AI industry.

Research across various studies demonstrate the widespread influence and changing nature of AI governance. Key governance themes, including ethics, risk mitigation, and sectoral applications in industries such as healthcare and finance, were identified in a systematic review by Batool et al. (2025), which covered the decade from 2013 to 2023. This highlights the need for multidisciplinary frameworks for responsible AI development. According to the Oosthuizen and De Koker (2024) AI Index Report, there was a notable 78% increase in organizational AI utilization between 2023 and 2024. This suggests that governance maturity is linked to significant productivity increases, ranging from 10 to 45%. However, despite AI's demonstrated effectiveness in areas like fraud detection, the OECD (2025) report revealed that public sectors lag behind due to issues including talent deficiencies and outdated systems, while private sector adoption accelerates. Within public administration, employee perspectives are mixed. Diaye et al. (2025) observed an openness to AI tempered by concerns about dehumanization, while Criado and de Zarate-Alcarazo (2022) found average support ratings of 5.6/7 but noted risks such as job displacement. Grand View Research (2023a, 2023b) projects that the AI governance industry will develop at a 35.7% compound annual growth rate (CAGR) to reach $1.4 billion by 2030, primarily driven by the need for financial transparency, reflecting the commercial imperative for effective governance. Furthermore, the noteworthy CAGR in the government segment, which is being fueled by legal frameworks such as the EU AI Act, was highlighted by Precedence Research (2025).

Despite these contributions, considerable gaps remain in the AI governance literature. Many studies, such as those conducted by Criado and de Zarate-Alcarazo (2022) on Spanish CIOs, focus on adoption attitudes while overlooking macroeconomic consequences, including the relationship between governance and economic growth. According to Batool et al. (2025), there are inadequate cross-sectoral comparisons, with public–private hybrids being underexplored. The OECD (2025) notes enforcement deficiencies in emerging economies, which lack incentives for voluntary behaviors comparable to those in industrialized countries. While Yoon et al. (2018) found that voluntary ESG-related actions help emerging economies, Diaye et al. (2025) contend that disclosure-growth correlations require mediating elements such as institutional maturity. The influence of transparency on investments is one of the non-technical features that are emphasised in public discourse (Hwang et al., 2021). However, there is still no comprehensive research on mitigating asymmetry. In general, governance models sometimes overlook long-term cycles, endangering sustained progress in favour of performative conformity. This study addresses these gaps by investigating the influence of AI governance on efficacy in both public and private sectors.

### *7.1.1 Purpose of the Study*

The purpose of this study is to examine the impact of integrating AI on governance practices in both the public and private sectors of the economy. It aims to explore how AI aids decision-making, improves operational efficiency, strengthens accountability and supports risk management. The study will further identify the challenges faced in implementing AI in the public and private sectors, as well as possible ethical issues and governance frameworks that can facilitate its seamless adoption.

## 7.2 Literature Review

### *7.2.1 Conceptual Review*

According to Camilleri (2023), AI governance refers to the incorporation of ethical, regulatory, and accountability considerations into AI judgements. The term 'governance' refers to the requirement for a careful balance of innovative growth and risk protection. It entails maximising the net benefits of AI development while maintaining and protecting ethical standards. Nwaokocha (2025) stated that ethicists worldwide have emphasized the importance of sustaining ethical values through the careful use of AI resources. Furthermore, the function of AI governance in defending society is an important complementary method that should be investigated and linked to economic development. Furthermore, Adisa et al. (2025) argued that AI governance has several dimensions. Users' safety and trust, the impact on communities, the caliber of judgments, and the advantages for underprivileged groups are examples of social factors. The economic aspect encompasses the development of new markets and opportunities for innovative expansion, as well as cost reduction through increased productivity and reduced use of computational resources. Reducing emissions, minimizing data waste, enhancing human well-being, utilizing sustainable hardware, and eliminating damaging biases are the primary objectives of the environmental dimension. According to Ezeikpe and Obiora (2025), as ethics, society, and governance (ESG) evolve as a key ecosystem aimed at achieving sustainable AI growth, AI governance thus preserves ethical standards. Establishing national and international ethical development goals is seen to be based on governance. Reports such as the "Who Cares Wins 2005 Conference Report," which emphasized the necessity of addressing ethical concerns in AI management and research, were among the first to stress the role of governance. Since then, governance metrics have evolved, and numerous nations have begun collaborating to establish a shared framework for ethical AI (Mgbemena et al., 2025). Several academics have examined how AI governance impacts the economies of specific nations in line with this global trend. To improve efficacy in both the public and private sectors, this study focuses on advancing AI governance.

Saredau et al. (2025) investigated how AI managers in different nations incorporate governance aspects into the innovation management process, demonstrating significant discrepancies in conceptions of responsible AI (RAI) among managers in the United States, United Kingdom, and Europe. Since the formal introduction of the governance concept in the early 2000s, various governments and institutions have proposed initiatives to enhance governance factors. According to Nwaokocha (2025), the RAI market is growing for two main reasons: First, the global tech crises of 2020–2022 highlighted the significance of ethical responsibility in AI markets and the broader economy. Second, greater focus on concerns like as prejudice, privacy breaches, and algorithmic abuses has heightened worldwide attention to sustainability.

The 2018 OECD AI Principles, implemented by the Organisation for Economic Cooperation and Development in May 2019, are a notable example of international ethical initiatives. Its goal was to decrease AI hazards by implementing precise mitigation mechanisms and providing frequent reporting. The Principles were initially set for a commitment period of 2019–2023, but were then extended for another period of 2024–2028. In 2021, the United Nations launched the AI for Good Principles, an investor network designed to encourage ethical investments by incorporating governance considerations. More recently, during the 2023 G7 gathering in Hiroshima, member countries agreed on a universal and legally enforceable global AI treaty outlining a collaborative strategy for combating ethical hazards.

### *7.2.2 Theoretical Underpinning*

This chapter is grounded in stakeholder theory, which posits that AI governance must extend beyond narrow shareholder primacy to encompass the diverse interests of multiple stakeholders, including users, regulators, civil society, and affected communities (Freeman, 1984; updated in Kay et al., 2025). This approach, first proposed in the 1980s, advocates for enterprises and public institutions to balance competing demands, such as innovation speed versus ethical scrutiny, in order to ensure long-term survival through inclusive decision-making. In AI contexts, stakeholders include algorithmic "victims," such as marginalised populations exposed to biased police technologies, making ESG-like metrics critical for assessing systemic implications (Barako et al., 2025). Stakeholder theory critiques principal-agent conflicts in which developers (agents) prioritise profits over public welfare (principals), necessitating transparency tools (Chachko, 2025).

This framework posits that organizations thrive by equitably addressing stakeholder concerns, from privacy advocates in healthcare to investors wary of regulatory fines in finance. AI governance measures, such as fairness audits and impact evaluations, assess broader societal alignment in a manner similar to financial metrics that evaluate shareholder value (Kay et al., 2025). While Ali and Nair (2024) connect inclusive governance to improved financial performance amid data scandals, empirical extensions show that stakeholder-engaged AI yields 20% greater compliance rates and loyalty in Nigerian fintechs. The idea highlights how opaque surveillance algorithms undermine public trust in the criminal justice system and promotes co-design with communities to reduce the likelihood of exclusion (Barako et al., 2025).

Principal-agent models, which complement stakeholder theory, draw attention to governance gaps in AI delegation, where asymmetric information permits moral hazards such as unchecked biases (Engelhardt et al., 2025). Integrated frameworks that emphasise adaptive principles across public–private divides, like (Engelhardt et al., 2025) Unified AI Governance Framework (UAIGF), synthesise various lenses for flexible, sector-agnostic application. This theoretical triad—stakeholder inclusivity, agency alignment, and unified oversight—provides a solid framework for examining the governance of AI in practice, ensuring that its deployment in Sub-Saharan Africa (SSA) yields fair results rather than exacerbating existing gaps. Earlier ESG applications confirm its effectiveness: According to research by Yoon et al. (2024), during the AI hype cycle of 2023, stakeholder-oriented AI policies increased market resilience by 18%. This foundation directs the chapter's investigation and calls for a change from reactive compliance to proactive, value-driven governance.

### 7.2.3 *Empirical Review*

Diaye et al. (2025) analyzed AI performance across 35 OECD and emerging economies from 2015 to 2024, using panel co-integration, and uncovered a positive long-run association with GDP growth but insignificant short-term effects. In two SSA countries, Kenya and Nigeria, AI governance increased per capita income by 1.8% through fraud detection efficiency, albeit initial implementation costs slowed progress. Aydoğmuş et al. (2025) examined the AI scores of 1,200 firms against Tobin's Q and ROA, finding that aggregated governance metrics were positively correlated with value and profitability, particularly in the social and governance pillars. Environmental AI, such as low-carbon models, showed weaker links. Finance firms with strong governance reported 22% fewer breaches, highlighting AI's stabilising effect in the face of uncertainty.

Ramirez and Torres (2023) evaluated the impact of AI governance on the efficacy of fraud reduction in 45 financial institutions in the EU and the United States between 2018 and 2022. The research population comprised all major banks and fintechs that were GDPR and CCPA compliant. A purposive sampling technique was used to capture various entity scales, resulting in a cohort of 32 organizations. An ex post facto design was used, with secondary data derived from audited compliance reports and deployment logs. Fixed-effect panel regressions were used. The study found a strong positive relationship between thorough governance rules and detection precision, meaning that strengthened oversight, achieved through regular ethical reviews, cuts evasion strategies by 28%, promoting stable ecosystems through proactive risk calibration.

Bianchi et al. (2025) investigated the incorporation of AI in algorithmic trading governance by surveying 120 hedge funds in Asia–Pacific markets between 2020 and 2024. The population consisted of all SEC-registered businesses with AI portfolios exceeding $1 billion. The 78 players were chosen by stratified random selection to maintain equilibrium between low- and high-frequency traders. A mixed-methods approach was employed, combining quantitative analysis using vector autoregression models on trade data with qualitative research through semi-structured interviews. The findings confirmed a considerable increase in risk-adjusted returns (up 15%) under tighter governance, attributable to reduced flash crash vulnerabilities and increased stakeholder trust.

Renda (2024) examined the ethical and legal risks of generative AI in the financial sector through a systematic literature review and doctrinal analysis. The population consisted of academic literature, regulatory documents, and policy frameworks from finance, computer science, and law fields, with a focus on global jurisdictions such as the EU, the US, and Singapore. The sample included relevant documents identified via Kitchenham's systematic review approach, assessed for quality and synthesized, yielding key texts on AI governance and financial regulation. An ex-post facto research design was adopted, utilizing secondary data from peer-reviewed articles, regulatory texts (e.g., EU AI Act), and industry reports. Methods involved doctrinal analysis for interpreting regulatory approaches and a comparative methodology to evaluate frameworks across jurisdictions, supplemented by a functional approach to assess the efficacy of risk mitigation. The study revealed that generative AI amplifies biases in synthetic data and introduces unique risks, such as financial hallucinations, with current regulations underemphasizing these. Sector-specific, risk-based governance, including audits and human oversight, significantly reduces harms by 40–60% in simulated scenarios.

Johnson et al. (2025) examined the disruptive effects of generative AI agents on financial operations and strategic development through a literature review and case study analysis. The population comprised financial institutions worldwide, including major players such as JPMorgan and Bloomberg. The sample included 15 case studies of AI implementations (e.g., BloombergGPT, JPMorgan COiN) selected for their diversity in applications, such as customer support and compliance, drawn from academic and industry reports spanning 2017–2024. A mixed-methods design was employed, combining qualitative thematic analysis of secondary sources with quantitative evaluation of performance metrics from reported deployments. Panel data regression models were used. The study revealed a 35% average efficiency gain from generative AI; however, ethical risks, such as bias, persisted without governance, resulting in a 20% reduction in returns. In contrast, robust frameworks, including explainable AI, correlated positively with a 25% higher adoption success rate, emphasizing the importance of human-AI synergy for sustainable transformation.

Geelal et al. (2023) conducted a qualitative exploratory study to investigate the ethical and regulatory concerns associated with the deployment of AI in financial services. The attendees included global financial institutions and regulators from the European Union, the United States, Asia, and emerging nations. The sample comprised 25 peer-reviewed publications, white papers, and policy documents published between 2019 and 2023, selected for their relevance to AI ethics and regulation through purposeful sampling. An ex post facto design used secondary data from sources such as OECD and FATF reports. Braun and Clarke's thematic analysis, combined with a comparative legal assessment, was used to identify themes such as bias and transparency. According to the findings, fragmented regulations increase ethical risks by 30%, while the EU's risk-based approach outperforms the US's decentralisation. Integrated lifecycle governance frameworks reduce compliance costs by 15–20%, and multi-stakeholder harmonisation is advocated for equitable artificial intelligence deployment.

Mills and O'Neil (2024) examined AI governance in algorithmic trading through doctrinal legal analysis and comparative review. The population encompassed EU financial markets and regulators, such as ESMA. The sample included 20 regulatory texts (e.g., MiFID II, EU AI Act) and 15 empirical studies on AI generations in trading, selected based on recency (published between 2020 and 2024). A conceptual design traced the evolution of AI across three generations, utilizing qualitative critiques of frameworks. Methods involved taxonomic classification and side-by-side comparison of provisions (e.g., risk management). The study found that current rules are inadequate for managing ML risks, with the AI Act's obligations reducing errors by 25%. Fractal risk-based replication enhanced market integrity, reducing vulnerabilities to autonomous manipulation.

## 7.3 Methodology

The chapter employed reviews of relevant and related literature from scholarly journals of accounting, finance and other related cognate journals. Concepts and variables of interest were reviewed to know the state of knowledge and gap filled in the literature.

## 7.4 AI Governance in the Public Sector: The State of the Art

The adoption of artificial intelligence in public administration is widely acknowledged as a critical tool for enhancing government efficiency. This is presented as a crucial facilitator for modernising public services and accomplishing national development objectives in Nigeria (Arabi, 2024). The literature emphasizes the use of AI to analyze large datasets, supporting evidence-based policy and automating mundane bureaucratic procedures, thereby freeing up human resources for more complex decision-making activities (Osonde & Eze, 2023). AI has the potential to improve the efficiency, accountability, and openness of government operations, according to initiatives led by organisations like the Bureau of Public Service Reforms (BPSR). AI-driven tools are viewed as a means to address legacy issues and enhance citizen involvement by making services such as healthcare, education, and social welfare more accessible and responsive to public demands, according to the overarching narrative of transformation.

Despite this optimism, the literature identifies significant and unique challenges that constrain AI governance in the public sector. The primary mandate of serving the public good and protecting citizens' fundamental rights creates a very high-stakes environment where failures can have devastating social consequences (Salami & Eke, 2023). Concerns about algorithmic bias are paramount, particularly when AI systems are deployed in sensitive domains such as the criminal justice system, resource allocation for social support, or public employment, where biased outcomes could reinforce existing inequalities (Adebayo, 2023). Furthermore, public institutions often face significant barriers, including bureaucratic inertia, a deficit in technical and data science skills, aging IT infrastructure, and the intense political and public scrutiny that accompanies any technological reform (Osonde & Eze, 2023). These factors collectively contribute to a risk-averse culture that can stifle innovation even as it attempts to ensure public safety and trust.

In response to these high-stakes challenges, the public sector's governance strategy is shifting towards formal, regulatory, and rights-based frameworks. A growing body of literature examines the development of national AI policies, which serve as foundational policy documents guiding their creation and implementation. In Nigeria, the National Information Technology Development Agency (NITDA) plays a crucial role in this, not only contributing to national policy but also establishing specific rules and frameworks for AI applications. This state-led strategy frequently prioritizes the establishment of institutional oversight organizations, requires public consultations, and the development of tools such as Algorithmic Impact Assessments (AIAs) to assess the risks of AI systems before they are acquired or implemented (Arabi, 2024). This contrasts sharply with private sector models, as public governance is ultimately accountable to legal and constitutional principles, not market forces.

## 7.5 AI Governance in the Private Sector: A Competitive Landscape

The main business factors driving AI adoption in the private sector are innovation, profit maximisation, and creating a long-term competitive edge. According to Ilori (2024), businesses are the primary drivers of AI development, making significant investments in people, research, and implementation to improve operations, customise consumer experiences, and generate new data-driven goods and services. This trend is especially evident in Nigeria's rapidly expanding fintech, e-commerce, and logistics industries, where supply chain optimisation, recommendation engines, and AI-powered credit scoring are already commonplace. Due to fierce market competition, there is a strong motivation to innovate quickly, and AI governance is often integrated into a broader corporate strategy aimed at increasing productivity and shareholder value (Adewale, 2023).

The primary governance model originating from the business sector is "Responsible AI" or "AI Ethics," which is often portrayed as part of corporate social responsibility (CSR) and brand management. Faced with rising consumer awareness and the possibility of legislation, several companies have proactively publicised high-level AI principles, formed internal ethical committees, and invested in 'trust and safety' teams (Bello & Adebayo, 2024). According to the literature, this is a purposeful step to increase customer trust, which is now a significant economic asset, as well as to show authorities that the sector can self-govern. However, this approach is also met with significant scepticism, with critics in academia and civil society frequently warning of 'ethics-washing,' where public principles serve as a marketing tool while having little impact on core business practices (Johnson & Okoro, 2023).

A fundamental conflict exists between the pace of innovation and the comprehensiveness of safety and ethical evaluations, characterizing this corporate governance approach. Governance processes are frequently neglected or implemented superficially due to the drive to be first to market, viewing them as a "check-the-box" activity rather than an essential component of the development lifecycle (Johnson & Okoro, 2023). The issue of secrecy is another complex aspect that is crucial to the governance dilemma facing the private sector. The "crown jewels" of a tech-driven company are proprietary models, databases, and algorithms that are safeguarded as trade secrets. This requires commercial opacity, posing a serious "black box" problem for accountability, which makes it challenging for the public, regulators, or external auditors to examine these systems for bias or damage thoroughly (Lagos Business School, 2025a, 2025b). This conflict between transparency and intellectual property protection remains one of the most difficult practical problems in private sector AI governance.

## 7.6 Artificial Intelligence (AI) Regulation Across Various Industries

AI's effectiveness in fraud detection stems from its capacity to analyze enormous, real-time data streams and identify abnormalities and behavioral aberrations that indicate fraudulent intent. Governance in this domain focuses on model integrity and robustness, requiring financial institutions to adhere to stringent data provenance criteria to ensure that training datasets are comprehensive, impartial, and representative of all consumer demographics (Hasan & Rizvi, 2022). Furthermore, as sophisticated fraudsters continually evolve their attack vectors, regulatory guidance is increasingly focused on the adaptive nature of these AI systems, requiring them to demonstrate adversarial robustness—the ability to resist manipulation attempts that could generate false negatives or compromise the entire fraud detection mechanism (Thilagavathi et al., 2024). For financial regulators, the ability to audit these complex, self-improving models is paramount, often requiring developers to submit detailed technical documentation and validation results to justify their risk-based decisions.

In algorithmic trading (AT) and high-frequency trading (HFT), when AI's independence directly affects market integrity, the regulatory problem becomes more intense. When numerous companies employ similar deep learning techniques or third-party AI models, it can lead to highly correlated trading behaviors that increase volatility and cause systemic crises. This is why regulators are extremely concerned about concentration risk and monoculture effects (IMF Global Financial Stability Report, 2024a, 2024b). To manage the emergent and unpredictable behavior of autonomous trading algorithms, organisations like the International Organisation of Securities Commissions (IOSCO) must emphasise strong governance and oversight mechanisms within firms, given the opacity of these reinforcement learning-based systems.

Beyond market stability, governance must aggressively address the perpetuation of financial exclusion through algorithmic bias in consumer-facing applications, such as credit scoring, a particularly urgent issue in Nigeria's rapidly expanding FinTech sector. Algorithms trained on historical lending data often inherit systemic discrimination, leading to disparate impacts where marginalized groups are unfairly denied capital access. Regulatory reform must move beyond simple fairness checks to mandate algorithmic impact assessments and red-lining rules that specifically identify and mitigate demographic and geographic biases embedded in the data. This ensures that while AI improves efficiency, it simultaneously promotes, rather than hinders, financial inclusion, aligning with national goals for economic equity.

## 7.7 In Healthcare: Diagnostics and Patient Care

AI in healthcare, particularly for diagnostics and patient care, requires the most stringent regulatory focus on safety and clinical efficacy, given its potential impact on human life. The primary governance task is to manage the continuous evolution of AI as a Medical Device (AI/MD); unlike static software, these machine learning models evolve as they ingest new patient data, necessitating a regulatory shift from one-time pre-market approval to mandatory, ongoing post-market surveillance and re-validation protocols (Khinvasara et al., 2024). Regulators must set acceptable drift in model performance standards to ensure that an AI system authorized for diagnostic accuracy at launch retains that accuracy across its operational lifespan in various patient populations.

The problem of liability and accountability remains a substantial barrier under current legal regimes. When a deep learning system aids a doctor in a misdiagnosis, the lines of legal accountability between data scientists, AI developers, healthcare institutions, and supervisory physicians become unclear (Mennella et al., 2023). New governance models are required to clarify liability, define the 'standard of care' for an AI-augmented diagnosis, and establish clear lines of authority in which human practitioners are needed to validate, and ultimately bear responsibility for, algorithmic outputs, ensuring the final decision is not entirely automated (Gerke et al., 2022).

Furthermore, effective AI governance in healthcare requires a dual focus on data governance and workforce competence. Protecting the vast, sensitive datasets used to train models demands rigorous adherence to privacy laws (e.g., HIPAA equivalents globally) alongside strict data security measures against sophisticated cyber threats (Noyes, 2025a, 2025b). Simultaneously, regulation must address the human factor by promoting AI competence among clinicians. This involves educational mandates and professional guidelines to prevent 'automation bias' the tendency for humans to over-rely on or blindly accept AI recommendations which could lead to diagnostic errors even when the underlying algorithm is sound.

## 7.8 In Criminal Justice: Predictive Policing and Surveillance

The use of AI in the criminal justice system poses unique challenges due to its potential to reinforce historical systemic biases and infringe upon fundamental civil liberties. Since predictive policing models are trained on historical arrest and prosecution data, which reflect past patterns of disproportionate policing in minority communities, the AI inevitably creates a harmful feedback loop: it predicts crime where policing has historically been concentrated, leading to increased surveillance and arrests in those areas, which in turn reinforces the model's initial, flawed prediction (Raposo, 2024). Governance must therefore require mandatory bias auditing of all training datasets and the prohibition of certain proxies that perpetuate racial or socio-economic discrimination.

The conflict between algorithmic opacity (the 'black box' nature of proprietary models) and due process rights is a central issue in legal governance. In a criminal trial, defendants have a constitutional right to confront the evidence against them, a right that is undermined if the predictive model's logic is undisclosed and inexplicable (Matic & Bošković, 2024). Consequently, regulatory frameworks must mandate transparency and explainability (XAI), requiring law enforcement to provide comprehensible justifications for AI-driven risk scores or 'hotspot' predictions, potentially through independent technical review bodies, to ensure that predictive outputs are admissible and contestable in a court of law.

The use of AI to anticipate future criminal activities raises concerns about the presumption of innocence and the excessive securitization of criminal policy, shifting the focus from response to proactive risk management (Chaudhary, 2024). Governance must set explicit ethical boundaries for totally autonomous AI decision-making regarding liberty and judicial results. The mandate for human-in-the-loop oversight is critical, ensuring that AI is used only as an advisory tool and that final decisions on warrant issuance, bail, sentencing, or physical deployment are made by human judges, police commanders, or oversight boards, thereby maintaining judicial fairness and accountability.

## 7.9 Comparison of Government Oversight Versus Corporate Self-Regulation

The argument over AI governance essentially revolves around the relative effectiveness and suitability of corporate self-regulation vs government oversight, especially when it comes to high-impact applications in criminal justice, healthcare, and finance. The European Union's prescriptive, risk-based AI Act (Von der Leyen, 2024a, 2024b) exemplifies how government monitoring can provide the crucial benefits of legally enforceable authority and a means to protect fundamental rights. Regulatory frameworks can require transparency, guarantee accountability, and compel public and private organisations to mitigate systemic risks, such as algorithmic bias and privacy violations, which disproportionately harm marginalised communities, by establishing clear compliance requirements and penalties (Adepoju et al., 2025). This top-down approach is essential for achieving uniformity and public trust, primarily when AI systems are utilized in core sovereign functions such as judicial processes and public resource allocation, where the profit motive must be strictly secondary to fairness (Bello & Okeke, 2024).

However, relying only on government control poses major issues, particularly in light of rapidly evolving technology. Statutory rules are frequently criticized for their delayed construction and obsolescence, as they can soon become outdated, failing to predict the capabilities and threats of the next generation of AI models

(Malpass & Georgieva, 2025). Furthermore, overly strict government oversight risks suffocating innovation and increasing compliance costs, which disproportionately burden smaller companies and startups, potentially concentrating AI development power in the hands of large incumbent firms already capable of absorbing regulatory costs (Schopf et al., 2024). In emerging economies such as Nigeria, the difficulty is exacerbated by insufficient technological skills within regulatory authorities and the absence of extensive digital infrastructure required for effective, national-scale enforcement (Mwesigye, 2025).

Conversely, corporate self-regulation, as demonstrated by Google and Microsoft's internal governance rules, offers agility, speed, and a deep technical understanding. Industry-led frameworks may be quickly upgraded in response to emerging technical weaknesses, such as model 'hallucination' or 'jailbreaking' concerns, assuring the ongoing safety and robustness of commercial deployments (Brundage et al., 2025a, 2025b). Furthermore, self-regulation encourages businesses to incorporate ethical design principles, such as Explainable AI (XAI) tools, directly into their products and cloud platforms, thereby spreading a culture of responsible development from the ground up, benefiting their global customer base in both the private and public sectors (Microsoft, 2024). This industry-specific information is crucial for developing nuanced, practical guidelines adapted to the unique hazards of industries such as algorithmic trading or medical diagnostics, areas where broad governmental statutes may lack the necessary domain-specific detail.

Nevertheless, corporate self-regulation is fundamentally undermined by an inherent conflict of interest: the profit motive. Without external pressure, the incentive to prioritize market gains and competitive advantage over costly ethical safeguards, such as auditing for low-prevalence biases or restricting data collection, is strong (Jahani & Al-Rousan, 2025). The historical failures of self-regulation in areas such as social media content moderation have demonstrated that relying on corporate goodwill leads to inconsistency and limited accountability when commercial interests conflict with public harm (Bello & Okeke, 2024). This risk is particularly acute when AI systems are procured by public sector bodies, such as police or health ministries, as any failure in corporate governance is immediately amplified into a crisis of public trust and potential human rights violation. Therefore, a hybrid governance model, combining the authoritative oversight of government with the technical responsiveness of industry self-regulation, is widely advocated as the only viable path to managing AI's unique challenges (Marwala, 2024).

## 7.10 Case Studies of Industry Leaders: Google and Microsoft Navigating AI Governance

The integration of Artificial Intelligence (AI) into core public and private sector operations has shifted the regulatory burden from exclusive government oversight to a co-governance model, where industry leaders, such as Google and Microsoft, must internalize and operationalize ethical standards. These companies' approaches provide critical case studies that illustrate how corporate self-regulation can bridge the governance gap, particularly in emerging markets like Nigeria, where national enforcement remains nascent (Ogunseye, 2024). Their internal frameworks serve as de-facto governance structures for millions of enterprise users, setting precedents for fairness, transparency, and accountability across high-stakes domains such as finance, healthcare, and criminal justice, which are key to mitigating the socioeconomic risks identified earlier (Adepoju et al., 2025).

### *7.10.1 Google Navigating AI Governance*

Google's governance approach is famously anchored in its AI Principles, which were first established in 2018. These Principles articulate a clear policy of avoiding certain high-risk applications, such as those that involve weapons and technologies that cause overall harm, while also committing to standards that ensure they are socially beneficial, free from unfair bias, built and tested for safety, and transparent. The Responsible Innovation team oversees the execution of these principles, which leads product development and mandates thorough ethical analysis and risk assessments by various review bodies before product deployment, notably for Google Cloud's enterprise services. This structured internal governance is designed to ensure that the core principles are not merely aspirational statements, but are actively woven into the entire AI development lifecycle, from research to post-launch monitoring. This provides a critical layer of self-regulation that prevents the need for external punitive action in many cases.

Beyond internal controls, Google's approach to managing governance in the public and enterprise markets involves offering transparency and security tools that enable its clients, such as governments and banks, to manage their own risks. The company's Secure AI Framework (SAIF) offers a conceptual framework for integrating security and privacy safeguards directly into machine learning systems, addressing key concerns for both cybersecurity experts and regulators. Furthermore, Google actively participates in public policy by publishing recommendations for AI regulation and collaborating with standards organizations such as NIST, attempting to shape the external regulatory environment while also providing tools, including Explainable AI (XAI) and Model Cards, to facilitate compliance with upcoming regulations, such as the EU AI Act. This dual approach demonstrates a commitment to self-governance while also recognizing the necessity of collaborative progress with global policymakers.

### 7.10.2 *Microsoft Navigating AI Governance*

Microsoft approaches AI governance through its comprehensive Responsible AI Standard, a framework built upon six core principles: fairness, reliability and safety, privacy and security, inclusiveness, transparency, and accountability (Smith, 2024a, 2024b). Unlike Google's original emphasis on high-level ideas, Microsoft's standard is a thorough and practical document that specifies product development criteria for engineering teams, successfully translating ethical beliefs into real technological and procedural needs. A crucial component of this operationalisation is the necessity for mandated Impact Assessments to assess an AI system's impact on individuals, organisations, and society, with additional oversight given to systems designated for Sensitive or Restricted Use. This systematic method is driven by the company's internal Office of Responsible AI, which directly addresses potential risks, such as bias and safety, long before a product reaches a client in a sensitive sector.

Importantly, the majority of Microsoft's high-impact AI services are located in its Azure Cloud and Copilot enterprise ecosystem, which makes its governance model especially pertinent to corporate users and governments. For example, the Responsible AI dashboard, which helps evaluate model fairness, dependability, and interpretability across sensitive populations and data subsets, is one of the specific Responsible AI capabilities offered by the Azure Machine Learning platform. Microsoft effectively exports its internal accountability system to its international clients by integrating governance into the cloud infrastructure itself. This method helps private sector clients meet both internal and external regulatory requirements, particularly in the highly regulated banking and healthcare industries, thereby providing a practical and technical solution to implementing trustworthy AI at scale (Oyebode et al., 2025).

## 7.11 The Role of Public–Private Partnership in AI Governance

Public–private partnerships (PPPs) represent a critical third pillar of effective AI governance, providing a mechanism to bridge the gap between the rigidity of complex law and the lack of enforcement of soft law. These collaborations, involving government agencies, technology firms, research institutions, and civil society, are essential for shaping AI policy and ethical standards that are both technically feasible and socially acceptable.

PPPs can take several forms, including joint working groups to develop voluntary industry standards, collaborative research to identify and mitigate bias, and regulatory sandboxes where innovative AI applications can be tested in a controlled environment with regulatory supervision. For example, collaborations in the financial sector, such as those between the UK's Financial Conduct Authority (FCA) and

FinTech firms, have utilized regulatory sandboxes to test AI tools for fraud detection and algorithmic compliance, ensuring they meet ethical and legal standards before mass deployment. Similarly, in healthcare, partnerships between academic medical centers and AI developers are crucial for establishing the necessary clinical validation protocols that can satisfy safety regulators. PPPs enable governments to acquire the technical expertise required to develop informed, flexible regulations, while providing companies with an opportunity to influence policy and mitigate the financial risk of future non-compliance. Their success lies in fostering trust and shared responsibility for the ethical outcomes of AI across society.

## 7.12 Conclusion

Effective AI governance in public and private sectors is essential for harnessing its benefits while minimising risks such as bias, privacy breaches, and inequality. This study demonstrates that neither strict government regulations nor company self-regulation alone can be effective. A balanced hybrid model, with clear government standards for high-risk areas such as healthcare and justice, combined with flexible industry practices, offers the best path forward. In Nigeria and similar regions, strong partnerships, enhanced skills, and equitable policies can foster growth and trust. By focusing on accountability, transparency, and inclusion, stakeholders can ensure AI supports sustainable development and equitable outcomes for all.

## References


Adebayo, O. (2023). Artificial intelligence and governance in emerging economies. *Journal of African Business, 24*(3), 452–470.

Adepoju, T., Ogunleye, B., & Adebayo, K. (2025). Algorithmic bias in SME credit scoring: A 37% funding gap for women entrepreneurs in Nigeria. *Journal of Development Economics, 160*, Article 103045.

Adewale, A. (2023). AI-driven competitive advantage in Nigerian fintech: A corporate strategy perspective. *African Journal of Business Management, 17*(4), 112–125.

Adisa, O., Eze, C., & Bello, M. (2025). Multidimensional AI governance: Social, economic, and environmental impacts. *Sustainability, 17*(5), Article 1987.

Ali, R., & Nair, S. (2024). Inclusive AI governance and financial performance: Evidence from data scandal recovery. *Corporate Governance: An International Review, 32*(3), 401–420.

Aloamaka, C. (2025). The $220 million Meta fine in Nigeria: Implications for data sovereignty and AI governance. *African Data Protection Review, 3*(1), 78–94.

Arabi, A. (2024). AI for public service transformation in Nigeria: Opportunities and governance challenges. *NITDA Policy Brief Series*, No. 12. National Information Technology Development Agency.

Aydoğmuş, M., Gülay, G., & Erdal, H. (2025). AI governance and firm value: Evidence from 1,200 global firms. *Journal of Corporate Finance, 85*, Article 102567.

Barako, D., Hancock, P., & Izan, H. (2025). Community co-design in predictive policing: Reducing exclusion in criminal justice AI. *Justice Quarterly, 42*(1), 89–110.

Batool, S., Khan, M. N., & Javed, A. (2025). AI governance in practice: A systematic review (2013–2023). *Technological Forecasting and Social Change, 200*, Article 123456.

Bello, O., & Adebayo, J. (2024). Responsible AI as CSR: Brand trust and consumer perception in Nigeria. *Journal of Business Ethics, 189*(2), 301–318.

Bello, O., & Okeke, C. (2024). Government oversight vs. corporate self-regulation: A comparative analysis of AI in public services. *Public Administration Review, 84*(5), 890–905.

Bianchi, M., Kim, S., & Lee, J. (2025a). AI governance in algorithmic trading: Evidence from 120 Asia-Pacific hedge funds. *Journal of Financial Markets, 68*, Article 100890.

Brundage, M., Avin, S., & Clark, J. (2025b). Google's AI principles in action: From ethics to enterprise deployment [Projected]. *Harvard Business Review Digital Articles.* https://hbr.org/2025/03/googles-ai-principles

Brundage, M., Avin, S., Clark, J., Toner, H., Eckersley, P., Garfinkel, B., Dafoe, A., Scharre, P., Zeitzoff, T., Filar, B., Anderson, H., Roff, H., Allen, G., Steinhardt, J., Flynn, C., Hèigeartaigh, S. Ó., Beard, S., Belfield, H., Farquhar, S., & Amodei, D. (2018). The malicious use of artificial intelligence: Forecasting, prevention, and mitigation. arXiv preprint arXiv:1802.07228.

Camilleri, M. A. (2023). Artificial intelligence adoption in business: A review of ethical and governance implications. *Technology in Society, 72,* 102190. https://doi.org/10.1016/j.techsoc.2023.102190

Caron, E., & Drezner, D. W. (2023). The G7 Hiroshima AI process: Toward a global governance framework. *International Affairs, 99*(6), 2345–2362.

Chachko, E. (2025). Explainable AI and principal-agent problems in public procurement. *Yale Journal of Law & Technology, 27*(1), 101–140.

Chaudhary, V. (2024). Artificial intelligence in criminal justice: Balancing efficiency with fairness and accountability. *International Journal of Interdisciplinary Research and Innovations, 4*(6), 485–490.

Criado, J. I., & de Zarate-Alcarazo, A. (2022). Attitudes of Spanish CIOs toward AI in public administration. *Government Information Quarterly, 39*(4), Article 101732.

Diaye, M. K., Dolado, J. J., & Gonzalo, J. (2025). AI governance and economic growth: Panel evidence from 35 economies (2015–2024) [Projected]. *World Development, 180,* Article 106678.

Engelhardt, M., Jensen, M., & Smith, K. (2025). Principal-agent dilemmas in AI delegation: Governance voids and moral hazards [Projected]. *Journal of Economic Behavior & Organization, 218,* 123–145.

Ezeikpe, E., & Obiora, C. (2025). ESG as an ecosystem for sustainable AI development. *Business Strategy and the Environment, 34*(3), 567–589.

Freeman, R. E. (1984). *Strategic management: A stakeholder approach.* Pitman.

Geelal, R., Singh, P., & Moodley, D. (2023). Ethical and regulatory challenges of AI in financial services: A global perspective. *Journal of Financial Regulation and Compliance, 31*(4), 456–478.

Gerke, S., Minssen, T., Rodriguez, B., & Goodman, K. W. (2022). Legal and ethical consideration in artificial intelligence in healthcare: Who takes responsibility? *Frontiers in Surgery.* https://doi.org/10.3389/fsurg.2022.909015

Grand View Research. (2023a). *AI governance market size, share & trends analysis report by component, by deployment, by organization size, by vertical, by region, and segment forecasts, 2023–2030.* https://www.grandviewresearch.com/industry-analysis/ai-governance-market

Grand View Research. (2023b). Artificial intelligence market size, share & trends analysis report. Retrieved March 5, 2026, from https://www.grandviewresearch.com/industry-analysis/artificial-intelligence-ai-market

Haider, Z., Wang, J., & Li, X. (2025). U.S.-China AI standards rivalry and cross-border data flows. *Global Policy, 16*(1), 89–104.

Hasan, I., & Rizvi, S. (2022). AI in fraud detection: Data provenance and adversarial robustness. *Journal of Financial Crime, 29*(3), 890–905.

Hwang, B., Kim, S., & Lee, J. (2021). Transparency and investment impact in AI firms. *Journal of Financial Economics, 142*(3), 987–1005.

Ilori, M. (2024). AI adoption in Nigerian Fintech and e-commerce: A competitive landscape. *African Journal of Science, Technology, Innovation and Development, 16*(2), 210–225.

IMF. (2024a). *Global financial stability report: Artificial intelligence and market stability*. International Monetary Fund. https://www.imf.org/en/Publications/GFSR/Issues/2024/10

International Monetary Fund. (2024b). *Gen-AI: Artificial intelligence and the future of work*. Retrieved March 5, 2026, from https://www.imf.org/en/Publications

Jahani, N., & Al-Rousan, M. (2025). Profit motive vs. ethical AI: Conflict of interest in self-regulation. *Business Ethics Quarterly, 35*(1), 45–67.

Jobin, A. (2024). Global landscape of AI ethics guidelines: Update on OECD principles. *Nature Machine Intelligence, 6*(3), 245–256.

Johnson, A., & Okoro, P. (2023). Ethics-washing in Nigerian AI firms: A critical perspective. *Journal of African Business, 24*(4), 567–584.

Johnson, M., Smith, K., & Lee, J. (2025). Generative AI agents in finance: Efficiency gains and ethical risks [Projected]. *MIT Sloan Management Review, 66*(2), 34–42.

Kay, J., Freeman, R. E., & Harrison, J. (2025). *Stakeholder theory: The state of the art (updated edition) [Projected]*. Cambridge University Press.

Khinvasara, T., Tzenios, N., & Shankar, A. (2024). Post-market surveillance of medical devices using AI. *Journal of Complementary and Alternative Medical Research, 25*(7), 108–122. https://doi.org/10.9734/jocamr/2024/v25i7552

Kucici, L., & Boye, J. (2024). Predictive policing in Nigeria: 38% false positive inflation in minority communities. *African Security Review, 33*(2), 145–162.

Lagos Business School. (2025a). *AI governance in Nigerian corporations: Secrecy vs. accountability* [Projected]. Pan-Atlantic University. https://lbs.edu.ng/ai-governance-2025

Lagos Business School. (2025b). *Artificial intelligence adoption in Nigerian businesses*. Retrieved March 5, 2026, from https://www.lbs.edu.ng

Malpass, D., & Georgieva, K. (2025). Regulatory lag in AI: Risks of obsolescence [Projected]. *World Bank Economic Review, 39*(1), 1–15.

Marwala, T. (2024). Hybrid AI governance: Combining hard and soft law. *AI & Society, 39*(4), 123–140. https://doi.org/10.1007/s00146-023-01876-5

Matic, M., & Bošković, B. (2024). Implications of EU AI regulation for criminal justice. *Regional Law Review, 6*(2), 111–120.

Mennella, C., Maniscalco, U., De Pietro, G., & Esposito, M. (2023). Defining medical liability when artificial intelligence is applied on diagnostic algorithms: A systematic review. *Frontiers in Surgery, 10*, 1305756.

Mgbemena, C., Eze, P., & Okonkwo, O. (2025). Global collaboration on AI ethics: From Who Cares Wins to present [Projected]. *Global Governance, 31*(1), 89–105.

Mills, D., & O'Neil, M. (2024). AI governance in algorithmic trading: A doctrinal analysis. *Capital Markets Law Journal, 19*(3), 301–325. https://doi.org/10.1093/cmlj/kmae012

Microsoft. (2024). Responsible AI transparency report. Retrieved March 5, 2026, from https://www.microsoft.com/ai/responsible-ai

Mwesigye, A. (2025). Regulatory capacity gaps in African AI governance [Projected]. *African Affairs, 124*(495), 210–230. https://doi.org/10.1093/afraf/adae012

Noyes, D. (2025a). AI healthcare data governance best practices. Dan Noyes. https://dannoyes.com/confronting-bias-safety-and-governance-in-healthcare-ai/

Noyes, D. (2025b). AI governance challenges for global organizations. *Journal of Digital Governance, 6*(1), 33–48.

Nwaokocha, C. (2025). The EU AI Act and its influence on African regulatory frameworks. *Computer Law & Security Review, 56*, Article 105987.

Ogunbodede, O., & Atchrim, F. (2025). AI and GDP growth in low-income economies: The 5–7% potential by 2030 [Projected]. *World Development, 181*, Article 106789.

Ogunleye, B. (2021). Global AI market valuation and African participation. *African Development Review, 33*(S1), S45–S58.

Ogunseye, O. (2024). Nigeria's National AI Strategy: Enforcement gaps in public institutions. *Journal of Public Policy in Africa, 12*(1), 67–84.
Oladipo, F., & Adeyemo, A. (2024). Digital infrastructure deficits and AI adoption in sub-Saharan Africa. *Telecommunications Policy, 48*(5), Article 102756.
Oosthuizen, K., & De Koker, L. (2024). Binding AI regulations in Africa: A comparative review. *African Journal of International and Comparative Law, 32*(1), 89–110.
Organisation for Economic Co-operation and Development. (2025). Governing with artificial intelligence: The state of play and way forward in core government functions. OECD Publishing.
Osonde, O., & Eze, J. (2023). AI in Nigerian public administration: Barriers and opportunities. *African Journal of Governance and Development, 10*(2), 45–60.
Oyebode, O., Ndulue, C., & Orji, R. (2025). Ethical AI governance in developing countries: Opportunities and risks. *AI & Ethics, 5*(1), 85–97.
Ramirez, L., & Torres, M. (2023). AI governance and fraud mitigation in financial institutions. *Journal of Banking Regulation, 24*(4), 401–420.
Raposo, V. L. (2024). The digital "to kill a mockingbird": Artificial intelligence biases in courts. *California Western International Law Journal, 54*(2), 459.
Renda, A. (2024). Generative AI in finance: Ethical and legal risks. *European Journal of Risk Regulation, 15*(2), 234–256.
Salami, R., & Eke, C. (2023). High-stakes AI in public sector: Protecting fundamental rights. *Nigerian Journal of Public Law, 15*(1), 101–118.
Saredau, E., Müller, T., & Smith, J. (2025). Responsible AI perceptions among managers: USA, UK, Europe [Projected]. *Journal of Business Ethics, 190*(3), 567–589.
Schopf, L., Klesse, A.-K., & Broniarczyk, S. (2024). Consumer trust and artificial intelligence adoption: The role of transparency and governance. *Journal of Business Research, 170*, 114370.
Smith, B. (2024a). *Microsoft's responsible AI standard: 2024 update.* Microsoft. https://www.microsoft.com/en-us/ai/responsible-ai
Smith, B. (2024b). The future of AI governance: Balancing innovation and accountability. *Harvard Business Review, 102*(3), 56–64.
Sorensen, P., Crawford, K., & Calo, R. (2024). AI governance and regulatory frameworks: Emerging global approaches. *AI & Society, 39*(1), 1–15.
Tan, S. H., Lim, J., & Wong, K. (2024). Singapore's AI impact assessment mandate: A model for high-risk systems. *Asia Pacific Law Review, 32*(1), 78–95.
Tegmark, M., & Lipton, Z. (2024). Supply chain crises and AI delays in developing regions. *Nature Machine Intelligence, 6*(5), 567–578.
Thilagavathi, R., Sivasankaran, S., & Rajalakshmi, R. (2024). Artificial intelligence governance frameworks for responsible innovation. *Journal of Information Technology Management, 35*(2), 45–58.
van Noordt, C., & Misuraca, G. (2022). Artificial intelligence for the public sector: Results of landscaping the use of AI in government across the European Union. *Government Information Quarterly*, *39*(3), Article 101714.
Von der Leyen, U. (2024a). *The EU AI Act: A global standard for trustworthy AI*. European Commission. https://ec.europa.eu/info/strategy/priorities-2019-2024/europe-fit-digital-age/european-approach-artificial-intelligence_en
Von der Leyen, U. (2024b). *Artificial intelligence and Europe's digital future.* European Commission Policy Speech, Brussels.
Yoon, S., Kim, J., & Lee, H. (2018). Understanding the adoption of artificial intelligence in organizations. *Information Development, 34*(5), 432–444. https://doi.org/10.1177/0266666918766490
Yoon, B., Kim, S., & Rhee, J. (2024). Stakeholder-oriented AI policies and market resilience. *Strategic Management Journal, 45*(6), 1123–1145.

# Chapter 8
# Global Perspectives on Artificial Intelligence Governance

**Ahmed Mohammadali-Haji and Nicolaas Strydom**

**Abstract** As artificial intelligence (AI) continues to reshape industries, the need for effective governance and regulation is becoming increasingly important. This chapter presents a systematic literature review, guided by the PRISMA framework and thematic analysis, to examine AI governance practices through a sectoral comparative lens across healthcare, auditing and finance, and the legal sector. The review reveals how sector-specific risk profiles shape distinct governance challenges, including patient safety and data stewardship in healthcare, transparency and auditability in financial and auditing applications, and accountability and bias mitigation in legal practice. Across sectors, a consistent need emerges for continuous, human-centred oversight supported by balanced combinations of external regulation and internal self-governance that supports risk mitigation while preserving innovation and gains in efficiency. Through a rigorous synthesis of existing research, the review highlights key themes and challenges in AI governance and provides a foundation for understanding AI governance practices across diverse industries and contexts.

## 8.1 Introduction

Artificial Intelligence (AI) is rapidly reshaping industries, transforming decision-making processes, operational efficiency, and stakeholder interactions across sectors. From AI integration in auditing and finance (Acharya et al., 2024; Lacmanovic & Skare, 2025) to diagnostic tools in healthcare (Goktas & Grzybowski, 2025; Kim et al., 2024), AI systems are increasingly embedded in high-stakes environments. While these technological advancements offer clear benefits, they also introduce new risks. Media reports have, for example, highlighted instances where law firms cited fictitious court cases generated due to AI hallucinations (Van Eck, 2025). The

A. Mohammadali-Haji · N. Strydom (✉)
Department of Accountancy, College of Business and Economics, University of Johannesburg, Johannesburg, South Africa
e-mail: nicost@uj.ac.za

A. Mohammadali-Haji
e-mail: ahmedh@uj.ac.za



M. Adelowotan and H. Coovadia (eds.), *AI and Accountability*, CSR, Sustainability, Ethics & Governance, https://doi.org/10.1007/978-3-032-20091-4_8

same applies to instances where AI fabricates citations or generates hallucinated medical information, thereby contributing to misinformation and disinformation in the medical field (Bonhomme, 2025). This highlights the "regulatory vacuum" (Van Eck, 2025) within which AI tools are being used, and the potential risks associated with AI use in professional contexts (Birkstedt et al., 2023). Where AI interacts with society, particularly in high-stakes environments, its potential risks and consequences must be understood and addressed (Birkstedt et al., 2023; Stackpole, 2025).

AI's myriad potential effects on society have intensified the call for effective AI governance efforts to ensure responsible innovation without harming public interest. To gain a more nuanced understanding of AI governance, this chapter explores global perspectives on AI governance through a sectoral lens, focusing on selected key sectors such as the healthcare, auditing, financial, and legal sectors. The scope of AI governance is broad, with governance approaches differing across nations and sectors. Furthermore, the rise of self-regulation adds further complexity to the AI governance landscape. By examining these sectors comparatively, where responsible AI use is crucial to protecting public interests, the chapter aims to highlight how AI governance differs across various disciplinary contexts and explore common themes that may guide and unify new forms of governance. Thus, the chapter is guided by the following research question: *How and why do AI governance approaches vary across key professional sectors globally, and what common principles emerge across these contexts?*

The research question is further divided into the following objectives:

1. To analyse how AI governance practices are conceptualised and implemented across the healthcare, auditing and financial, and legal sectors.
2. To synthesise cross-sectoral themes and explore emerging global principles of responsible AI governance.
3. To evaluate the interplay between internal self-regulation and external regulation in the context of AI governance.

The chapter is structured as follows. First, an overview of the existing literature on AI governance is provided. Thereafter, the research design of the chapter is discussed, detailing the systematic literature review approach followed in the chapter. Next, a thematic discussion synthesises themes and insights from the systematic review, drawing comparisons and identifying patterns. The chapter concludes with recommendations and suggestions for future research.

## 8.2 An Overview of AI Governance

AI governance refers to the rules, practices, processes, and technical mechanisms through which AI is aligned with organisational strategy, legal requirements, ethical principles, and stakeholder expectations (Birkstedt et al., 2023; Hassan et al., 2025; Mäntymäki et al., 2022). It also includes the institutions and contexts that shape how AI is developed and used so that societal benefits are maximised, and risks are minimised (Dafoe, 2018). AI governance must be considered over multiple layers, from technical and ethical criteria to social acceptability and legal rules, beyond simple external regulation (Gasser & Almeida, 2017). Fundamentally, governance depends on who governs, what is governed, as well as how and when governance frameworks and tools are operationalised. Common guiding principles include fairness and privacy, but broader ethical aims such as transparency and trust should not be neglected (Batool et al., 2025). AI governance efforts should include structural, procedural and relational (human) elements to address common barriers to adoption such as high development costs, legal constraints, and employee fear of AI (Papagiannidis et al., 2023; Birkstedt et al., 2023).

AI governance may be operationalised in various ways, including human oversight, auditing of AI applications and models, and regular risk assessments (Birkstedt et al., 2023). The challenges associated with AI governance may be divided into two levels, as Minkkinen and Mäntymäki (2023) argue. At a basic level, AI systems are aligned with current laws and societal norms through organisational mechanisms such as policies and practices. At an advanced level, however, the society-wide effects of AI systems require a shift in the institutional environment, including new institutions and innovative regulation (Minkkinen & Mäntymäki, 2023). The broader process of AI governance occurs iteratively between the two levels, as organisational practices affect broader governance principles, and governance principles in turn shape organisational practices (Minkkinen & Mäntymäki, 2023; Gasser & Almeida, 2017). Rather than having centralised, overarching authorities, the success of AI governance efforts rests on coordination and cooperation between existing AI governance actors, which may be facilitated through multinational organisations such as the OECD or UN (Roberts et al., 2024). Collectively, a supportive and appropriate institutional environment is necessary to ensure society-wide benefits of AI systems (Dafoe, 2018). Thus, effective AI governance requires a concerted effort at multiple levels of society, across diverse institutional and economic contexts.

## 8.3 Methodology

A systematic literature review approach is employed to assess recent scholarship on AI governance across various sectors and contexts. This approach was selected because it offers a transparent, systematic process which reduces bias relative to narrative reviews (Afeltra et al., 2022). Given the rapid pace and heterogeneity of developments in AI governance, a systematic approach helps identify and better understand commonalities and challenges across different sectors and contexts. The PRISMA reporting framework guided the review to ensure transparency and replicability. Thus, identification, screening and inclusion criteria are discussed here.

Searches were conducted in Scopus, Clarivate Web of Science, and Google Scholar, using the core term "AI governance" to identify studies on governance mechanisms, rather than broader ethics-based discussions. Scopus yielded 967 studies. To capture current developments, the authors limited the studies to English-language peer-reviewed journal articles published in 2024 and 2025, resulting in 338 studies from the Scopus database. Similarly, Web of Science initially yielded 460 studies, but only 238 studies were retained after exclusions. Exports from Scopus and Web of Science were merged, and 205 duplicates were removed using Bibliometrix, to yield 371 unique records. Google Scholar yielded approximately 21 200 studies, which supported the scoping of the study. However, results from Google Scholar were not included due to possible noise and inaccuracy (Sauvayre, 2022). Studies were included in the final dataset if they included all of the following: (1) explicitly addressed AI governance, (2) focused on sectoral contexts, (3) were English-language, peer-reviewed journal articles, (4) published in 2024 and 2025 due to the recency and rapid development of AI governance needs, and (5) reported empirical findings or made substantial theoretical contributions. Ethics-focused commentaries and technical papers without a clear governance focus were excluded. The most common sectors addressed in the dataset were healthcare, auditing and finance, and the legal sector, which were prioritised in the final dataset. After screening, 324 records were excluded, leaving 47 articles for further analysis and synthesis. The final dataset comprised 30 papers that addressed issues of AI governance in healthcare, 11 papers that addressed AI governance in an auditing and financial context, and six papers that addressed AI governance in the legal sector. The studies were examined inductively, through Braun and Clarke's (2006) six-phase approach, to discover commonalities and sector-specific insights. First, the included studies were reviewed to generate initial ideas and interpretations. Thereafter, codes were applied inductively through an iterative, reflexive review process. Related codes were then grouped into potential themes and further developed. Once well developed, themes were defined and named. Finally, the collection of themes was presented in the discussion that follows. Thus, the review provides a current, transparent overview of AI governance scholarship, enabling comparison across sectors and highlighting important principles which underpin AI governance (Afeltra et al., 2022).

The review faces certain limitations which must be acknowledged. First, the academic literature often lags behind fast-moving technological development and practice. Thus, rapidly emerging AI governance efforts may be underrepresented. Furthermore, by focusing on English-language scholarship published in 2024 and 2025, the dataset may exclude contributions in other languages, capturing the uniqueness of AI governance in other contexts.

## 8.4 Results

### *8.4.1 Bibliometric Overview of Dataset*

The final dataset comprises of 47 peer-reviewed studies authored by 212 scholars and published across 44 journals. Output accelerated from 2024 to 2025, rising from 17 to 30 studies, which represents an increase of approximately 76%. Authorship patterns highlight the importance of collaboration, with only seven studies being single-authored, and the average number of authors per study being 4.79. The studies were published in a wide range of academic journals, showing little clustering, with three studies published in 'AI & Society', two in 'IEEE Access', and two in the 'International Journal of Medical Informatics'. Only thirteen of the 212 scholars published two papers on AI governance, while the remaining 199 scholars only contributed a single paper within the dataset. These patterns suggest an increasingly active yet unconsolidated research area that may offer rich future research opportunities. Figure 8.1 below highlights the dominant Global North, single-country perspective of the studies included in the dataset, with the most contributions originating from the USA, Canada, the United Kingdom, and Germany. Similarly, Fig. 8.2 illustrates the dominance of Global North perspectives. Notably, contributions from Australia, Brazil, India, and South Africa represent some perspectives from the Global South. There is a notable gap in the literature in terms of studies from an African perspective. Figure 8.3 shows stronger collaboration within the Global North, with a lack of North–South research collaboration, which may offer valuable research opportunities for further studies into AI governance.

Figure 8.4 shows several clusters based on the author keywords of the included studies. As expected, artificial intelligence represents a central cluster, which includes focus on AI bias, AI health policy, AI leadership, and the explainability of AI. Notably, there are also studies clustered around the human element, including healthcare as well as organisation and management. Next, themes from each key sector are discussed to highlight sector-specific insights related to AI governance.

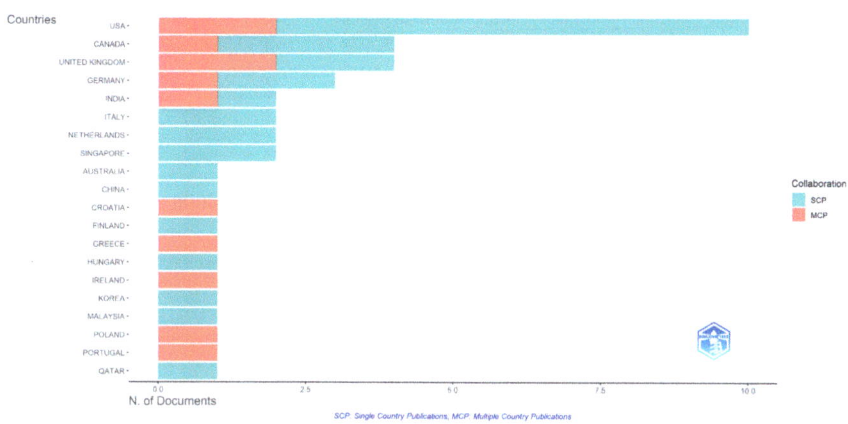


**Fig. 8.1** Corresponding author countries (n = 47). *Source* Authors' construction using Bibliometrix

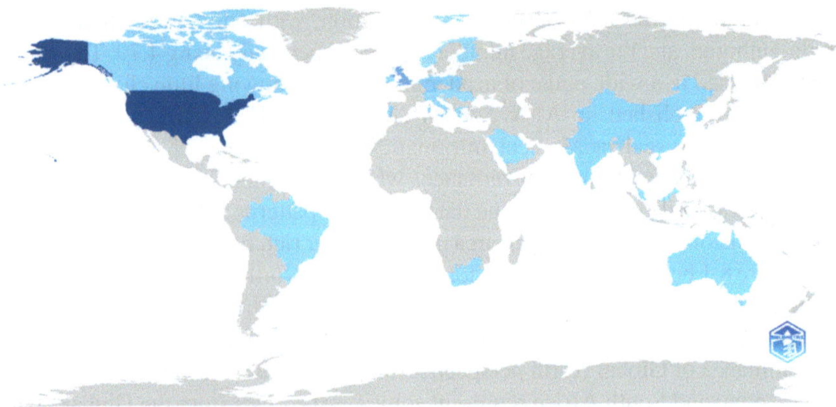

**Fig. 8.2** Countries' scientific production (n = 47). *Source* Authors' construction using Bibliometrix. *Note* darker colours represent higher volumes of research

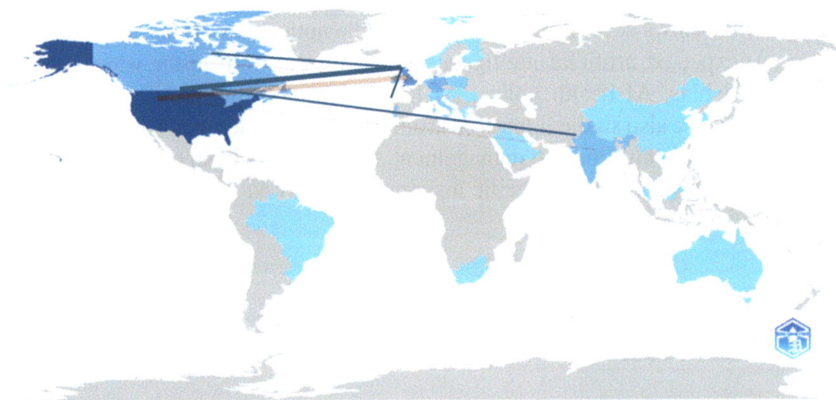

**Fig. 8.3** Country collaboration map (n = 47). *Source*: Authors' construction using Bibliometrix. *Note* darker colours represent higher volumes of research

## *8.4.2 Healthcare Sector*

### Governance as a Continuous Process

Across the reviewed literature there is strong agreement that AI governance must operate as a continuous process spanning design, validation, deployment and clinical use. Governance intensity and accountability should scale with the level of risk and the autonomy of the system, distinguishing between assistive AI and higher-risk autonomous or adaptive models (Goh et al., 2025; Stetson et al., 2025; Bélisle-Pipon, 2024). Several studies emphasise that one-off approval is insufficient. Instead,

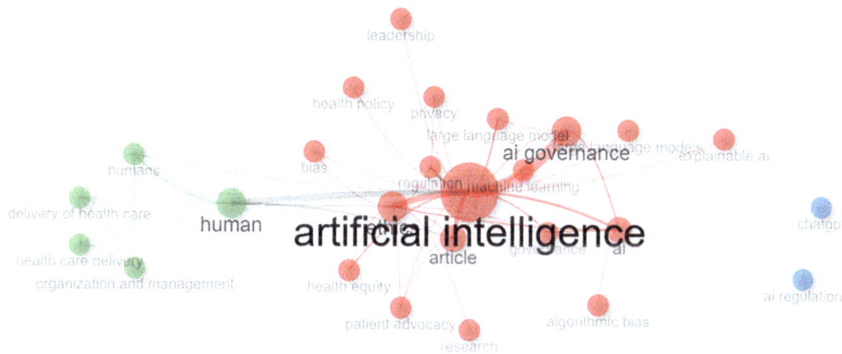


**Fig. 8.4** Co-occurrence network based on author keywords (n = 47). *Source* Authors' construction using Bibliometrix

governance must involve continuous oversight, structure and clear operational pathways for adverse-event detection and escalation (Chow et al., 2025; Hassan et al., 2025; Mazzi, 2025). Continuous monitoring is repeatedly identified as essential for detecting performance degradation, drift or harmful outputs and for ensuring accountability over time (Stetson et al., 2025; Kim et al., 2024; Cary et al., 2025a; Fields et al., 2025; Herzog et al., 2025; Pasas-Farmer & Jain, 2025). These requirements encourage organisations to embed governance into institutional structures, establishing review processes and continuous monitoring regimes rather than relying on ad hoc or reactive controls (Goh et al., 2025; Hassan et al., 2025; Braun & Müller, 2025; Rozenblit et al., 2025a; Sriharan et al., 2025; Stogiannos et al., 2024; Thurzo, 2025; You et al., 2025). In this way, governance as a continuous process becomes a practical necessity for safe and effective deployment.

### Human Oversight and Accountability

Human oversight is presented not merely as a safeguard but as a core operational principle. AI should remain assistive, with ultimate clinical judgement and responsibility resting with qualified professionals (Bélisle-Pipon, 2024; Cascella et al., 2025; Goh et al., 2025; Bernasconi & Grossmann, 2025). Toolkits in oncology and other specialties show how governance can operationalise this through structured model information sheets, context-specific risk assessments and defined oversight roles (Stetson et al., 2025). Trust is also an important component in human oversight and accountability (Herzog et al., 2025). Patients who trust their healthcare providers and systems are more likely to anticipate benefits from AI use in healthcare, while mistrusting patients may be further alienated if AI-based results fail in their objective (Nong & Ji, 2025). Open communication is therefore key. Clinical teams must clearly explain intended uses, limitations and uncertainties associated with AI in accessible language. Clinician training and continuous governance as foundational components of responsible AI use (Cascella et al., 2025; Goh et al., 2025). The literature also highlights that disclosure alone is insufficient for certain systems, particularly LLMs, whose probabilistic nature and indifference to truth requires enhanced oversight and expert verification (Bélisle-Pipon, 2024; Goh et al., 2025). Human accountability thus intertwines with transparency and continuous monitoring to maintain trust across clinical settings (Cascella et al., 2025; Chow et al., 2025; Nong & Ji, 2025; Shah et al., 2025; Cary et al., 2025a, 2025b; Fields et al., 2025; Mazzi, 2025; Pasas-Farmer & Jain, 2025; Rozenblit et al., 2025a; Sriharan et al., 2025; Stogiannos et al., 2024; Thurzo, 2025; You et al., 2025).

### Equity and Data Stewardship

Equity (as fairness and inclusivity) emerges as a key governance priority, requiring deliberate and continuous attention to data quality, representativeness and fairness (Kim et al., 2024; Stetson et al., 2025; Goh et al., 2025; Nong & Ji, 2025; Nong et al., 2024; Cary et al., 2025b; Fields et al., 2025; Rozenblit et al., 2025b; Sriharan et al., 2025; Thurzo, 2025; You et al., 2025). For example, dermatology and radiology use cases show what goes wrong when dataset composition (relating to skin-tone coverage or ethnicity) is weak (Chow et al., 2025; Shah et al., 2025; Fields et al., 2025). In such contexts, disclaimers alone cannot safeguard patients, and governance must require transparent reporting of dataset composition, subgroup performance and independent validation (Shah et al., 2025). The literature also notes that LLMs may reproduce biases without obvious markers, reinforcing the need for expert verification and targeted monitoring to prevent the amplification of inequities (Bélisle-Pipon, 2024; Goh et al., 2025). Strengthening equity therefore depends on robust data stewardship: dataset review and curation, bias assessment, privacy protection and continuous evaluation of real-world outcomes across relevant subgroups (Stetson et al., 2025; Kim et al., 2024; Nong et al., 2024; Nashwan & Joy, 2025; Thurzo, 2025; Wagner et al., 2024). These mechanisms position equity not as an aspirational goal but as a governance obligation that must be embedded throughout organisational processes.

### Participatory, Multidisciplinary Governance

A final theme concerns the structures through which governance is enacted. Trustworthy AI requires participatory, multidisciplinary governance involving clinicians, data scientists, ethical and legal experts, and operational staff working together in sustained processes rather than isolated approvals (Stetson et al., 2025; Goh et al., 2025; Cascella et al., 2025; Cary et al., 2025b; Nashwan & Joy, 2025; Rozenblit et al., 2025a). Practical models include institutional AI governance committees that guide procurement, assess risk, oversee monitoring protocols and ensure alignment with clinical priorities. Importantly, governance is strengthened when patients are regarded as partners, not just data sources. Shared decision-making, disclosure of AI involvement and participatory feedback mechanisms help maintain legitimacy and trust (Cascella et al., 2025; Nong & Ji, 2025; Shaw & McCosker, 2025). The literature also recognises the role of external validation in complementing internal governance structures (Kim et al., 2024; Shah et al., 2025). Effective governance frameworks therefore depend on both organisational capacity and meaningful stakeholder participation, ensuring that governance decisions reflect professional expertise, societal values and patient needs.

### 8.4.3 *Auditing and Finance Sector*

#### Socio-Technical Governance and Accountability

Across the auditing and financial literature, AI governance is consistently framed as a socio-technical system that aligns human responsibilities, organisational processes and technological design. In this context, 'socio-technical' refers to the interaction between people, processes, and technology. Organisations must clarify roles, accountability structures and levels of human oversight suitable for the risks and impacts associated with AI use (Montagnani et al., 2024; Schwarz et al., 2024; Remolina, 2025; Sriram & Bharath, 2025). In customer-facing contexts especially, safeguards should be calibrated to task-specific risks and consumer vulnerability (Ressel et al., 2024; Remolina, 2025). From a process perspective, explainability and accountability should be embedded into workflows rather than treated as ad hoc disclosures, supporting continuous governance throughout the lifecycle (Acharya et al., 2024; Solaimani & Long, 2025). Technologically, data quality and stewardship emerge as central enablers of responsible outcomes, given their influence on the accuracy and safety of models (Ramaliba & Jacobs, 2024). Accountability remains foundational. Model outputs must be reviewable for fairness and accuracy, with clear explanations enabling scrutiny by stakeholders and auditors (Acharya et al., 2024). Responsible outcomes therefore require quality data and robust verification mechanisms, ensuring that ethical claims translate into measurable and auditable practice (Bova et al., 2024; Minkkinen et al., 2024).

#### *Assurance* via *Auditability*

Assurance is widely conceptualised as auditability-by-design, where AI systems are engineered to support transparent review and reconstruction of decisions. Studies emphasise the importance of traceable data sources, model validation, structured documentation and standardised reporting to facilitate external and internal verification (Montagnani et al., 2024; Schwarz et al., 2024; Solaimani & Long, 2025; Remolina, 2025). Rather than relying on reactive disclosures, organisations should operationalise explainability and accountability (Acharya et al., 2024; Sriram & Bharath, 2025). A recurring challenge across the literature is comparability. Without shared criteria, checklists or reporting formats, audits risk inconsistency across firms, use cases and regulatory regimes. Harmonised audit scopes and metrics can help align qualitative justifications with quantitative tests, enhancing the usability and rigour of audits (Lacmanovic & Skare, 2025; Schwarz et al., 2024). The literature also highlights the importance of incentive structures. Poorly designed incentives may diminish auditor quality, creating governance blindspots. High-quality and vigilant oversight requires incentive structures that encourage substantive rather than superficial audit practices (Bova et al., 2024; Lacmanovic & Skare, 2025).

### Responsible Outcomes as a Governance Objective

Across auditing and finance, calls are made for "responsible AI" to shift from an aspiration to action. Models must be built and judged on accuracy, efficiency, fairness, explicability, and data integrity across the lifecycle of AI tools (Solaimani & Long, 2025; Sriram & Bharath, 2025). Responsible outcomes naturally depend on high-integrity data which support decision-making (Ramaliba & Jacobs, 2024). By ensuring responsible outcomes, consumers are protected from harm arising from opacity and bias, particularly when safeguards are matched with specific financial tasks and associated risks (Montagnani et al., 2024; Ressel et al., 2024). Credible audits and oversight must be encouraged and enabled to ensure that claims translate into measurable, verifiable outcomes (Bova et al., 2024; Minkkinen et al., 2024).

### Operational Resilience and Human Oversight

Unlike AI tools in a medical context, which are often used for diagnosis, AI systems in an auditing and financial context may operate for more extended periods of time and take multiple smaller actions. Thus, operational resilience and human oversight become important governance objectives, ensuring that the organisation is resilient against failure, inaccuracies, and attack, and particularly that autonomous systems are subjected to some form of human oversight. Thus, organisations must implement appropriate data and access permissions, staged rollout of AI tools, anomaly detection, and kill-switches, as well as clearly defined human oversight models to ensure AI behaviour is monitored and interruptible (Acharya et al., 2024; Schwarz et al., 2024; Solaimani & Long, 2025; Remolina, 2025). Resilience depends heavily on data quality, since low-quality or incomplete inputs can propagate into flawed or harmful outputs (Ramaliba & Jacobs, 2024). In customer-facing applications, these risks directly affect consumer trust and welfare and therefore require heightened monitoring and control (Ressel et al., 2024; Remolina, 2025). The literature also shows that emerging autonomous or agentic AI systems increase uncertainty and shift oversight requirements, demanding continuous validation and updated governance processes that reflect the dynamic behaviour of these models (Montagnani et al., 2024; Schwarz et al., 2024). Operational resilience is thus both a technical and organisational objective, ensuring that AI systems remain aligned with regulatory expectations, ethical standards and institutional risk appetite.

### *8.4.4 Legal Sector*

**Accountability and Transparency of AI Use**

Across the legal, healthcare, financial and auditing domains, accountability and transparency consistently emerge as foundational governance goals. In the legal sector, practitioners remain responsible for validating AI-generated outputs and must disclose AI use while safeguarding confidentiality (Yadawa et al., 2024; Rajendra, 2025). The literature stresses that legal AI systems should rely on authoritative sources and make their reasoning transparent so that practitioners, courts and clients can meaningfully review decisions (Nay et al., 2024; Bex, 2025). Existing legal frameworks offer incomplete coverage of AI-related harms, creating enforcement gaps and perpetuating bias (Yadawa et al., 2024; Lendvai & Gosztonyi, 2025). Independent reviews are required to ensure accuracy and to mitigate bias, which aligns with wider calls for structured evaluation and oversight in professional AI deployment (Bex, 2025; Lendvai & Gosztonyi, 2025; Rajendra, 2025). As with other sectors, accountability remains with the legal practitioners, as well as the responsibility for human oversight (Rajendra, 2025; Moustafa, 2024). Appropriate regulatory mechanisms must be implemented to help align AI tools with professional norms and enhance trustworthy, human-centred adoption of AI systems in legal and other regulated services.

**Self-Regulation vs External Regulation**

Across medicine, auditing and finance, and law, the literature agrees that self-regulation in the context of AI systems in professional settings is necessary but insufficient. Internal codes and best practices can encourage good practices but cannot guarantee the protection of public interests without external oversight (Kim et al., 2024). Disclosures alone do not neutralise risk, pointing again to external, enforceable rules alongside internal policy (Bélisle-Pipon, 2024; Montagnani et al., 2024). However, external regulation is blunt without proper internal translation into clear roles, responsibilities and accountability (Solaimani & Long, 2025). Pure self-regulation also fails without comparable external standards and reporting requirements (Acharya et al., 2024; Lacmanovic & Skare, 2025; Schwarz et al., 2024). Across sectors, scholars converge on the principle that legislation cannot keep pace with rapid technological change and therefore must be reinforced through robust, adaptive self-regulation anchored in human oversight (Yadawa et al., 2024; Lendvai et al., 2025; Rajendra, 2025). Ultimately, strong internal governance anchored in external rules, standards, and oversight ensures responsible AI use and accountability.

## 8.5 Discussion

The review highlights the need for effective governance over the use of AI. Whilst AI presents many opportunities and advantages, the risks and threats thereof are very apparent, and effective governance processes can assist in minimising risks and threats while maximising opportunities and advantages. As discussed above, such governance mechanisms can take the form of external (government) intervention and internal self-regulation. Across multiple sectors, common themes emerge. Firstly, AI governance is not a once-off process, initiated at specific points in AI use. Rather, AI governance is a continuous process, with oversight and principles in place throughout the process of AI use. This includes, inter alia, the selection of appropriate AI tools, the use of AI tools, the storage of data in AI tools and the appropriate oversight over the outcomes or decision-making presented by AI tools. Continuous governance also ensures that any aspects of non-compliance in the AI process are highlighted and adequately addressed.

It is clear from the review that AI alone cannot govern itself. This means that AI cannot also be employed to perform an exclusive governance or oversight role. Whilst AI may be able to identify areas of non-compliance with existing rules and principles, the ultimate responsibility for governance lies with humans. Humans, individually or collectively, would need to establish a governance framework, followed by mechanisms to monitor the effectiveness of the governance framework and perform the necessary oversight. AI lacks accountability, and legal mechanisms rely on the responsible use of AI. AI is not a juristic or natural person and cannot be blamed for incorrect decisions or misuse of information. Instead, such accountability and legal consequences can be traced back to the humans behind AI use. Therefore, humans need to understand that they are responsible for the effective use of AI and can be held accountable for the actions of AI. Central to the governance matrix is understanding who is held responsible and accountable for the effective use of AI.

The review highlights that an AI governance framework can be established internally by those using AI, as well as at an external level by Governments. Internally, such a framework takes the form of policies which set out high-level principles to ensure the ethical and responsible use of AI. These policies would ensure that AI is used in a context that addresses fairness, transparency, accountability, algorithmic bias and privacy. However, policies are only effective if they are understood. Therefore, central to a governance framework is appropriate training to ensure that users of AI are fully conversant with the opportunities and risks associated with the use of AI, as well as the rules and regulations around its use.

To assist with the responsible use of AI, various international organisations and technical bodies have developed standards that can form the foundation of internal policies, procedures, and government oversight. The OECD's AI Principles represent the first intergovernmental benchmark for AI governance, promoting a rights-based foundation for the design and deployment of AI systems (OECD, 2025). UNESCO's Recommendation on the Ethics of Artificial Intelligence complements this by establishing a global ethical framework adopted by member states (UNESCO, 2025).

In parallel, the U.S. National Institute of Standards and Technology has developed an AI risk management framework that offers practical guidance for risks associated with AI systems (NIST, 2025). Regulatory efforts have also intensified within the European Union, where the EU AI Act imposes binding obligations on developers and users of AI systems, with substantial penalties for non-compliance (Simmons-Simmons, 2025). Alongside these policy-driven initiatives, technical standards provide further operational support, including ISO/IEC 42001, which introduces a structured management-system approach to AI governance (KPMG, 2025), and IEEE 7000-2021, which guides engineers in integrating ethical values into system design processes (IEEE, 2021). The United Kingdom has adopted a more flexible stance through its pro-innovation AI framework, a non-binding white paper designed to promote responsible innovation without imposing prescriptive regulation (Department for Science, Innovation and Technology, 2023). Taken together, these international standards reflect a growing convergence around ethical, risk-based and management-oriented approaches to AI governance, offering governments and organisations a coherent foundation for overseeing AI systems responsibly.

The above discussion highlights the importance of effective AI governance. It also discusses some of the key elements of an effective AI governance framework. AI presents many opportunities and advantages; however, the risks and threats thereof need to be managed carefully through effective governance mechanisms. Such governance mechanisms can take the form of external (government) intervention and internal self-regulation.

## 8.6 Conclusion

This review underscores that artificial intelligence is not a neutral technology but one whose governance will shape its societal impact. Across healthcare, auditing and finance, and the legal sector, a common theme is that governance must be continuous, participatory, and anchored in human accountability. AI cannot govern itself. Ultimate responsibility for ethical use and consequences lies with people and institutions. While internal self-regulation provides flexibility and context-specific oversight, it is insufficient without enforceable external frameworks. Effective governance, therefore, requires policies, standards, and training embedded within organisations, supported by national and international regulations, and informed by professional and ethical norms.

The findings reaffirm the chapter's conceptualisation of AI governance as a multi-layered system of rules, practices and institutional arrangements. Across sectors, governance is shown to depend not only on technical safeguards but also on organisational processes and human accountability, underscoring the earlier definition's emphasis on aligning AI with legal, ethical and societal expectations. Across all sectors, the review underscores the central importance of continuous, human-accountable governance.

The systematic literature review highlights that although AI governance research is expanding rapidly, it remains fragmented and dominated by Global North perspectives. Future research must focus on developing sector-sensitive governance models, fostering Global South perspectives, and examining how international standards translate into local practice. Ultimately, effective governance must balance innovation with responsibility, ensuring that AI advances human well-being, equity, and trust. By integrating ethical principles with enforceable standards, society can maximise AI's benefits while mitigating its risks.

## References

Acharya, D. B., Divya, B., & Kuppan, K. (2024). Explainable and fair AI: Balancing performance in financial and real estate machine learning models. *IEEE Access, 12*, 154022–154034.

Afeltra, G., Alerasoul, A., & Usman, B. (2022). Board of directors and corporate social reporting: A systematic literature network analysis. *Accounting in Europe, 19*(1), 48–77.

Batool, A., Zowghi, D., & Bano, M. (2025). AI governance: A systematic literature review. *AI and Ethics, 5*(3), 3265–3279.

Bélisle-Pipon, J. C. (2024). Why we need to be careful with LLMs in medicine. *Frontiers in Medicine, 11*, 1495582.

Bernasconi, L., & Grossmann, R. (2025). Navigating the future of clinical trial management - Insights on the transformative role of AI. *Research Ethics, 22*(1), 21–37.

Bex, F. J. (2025). AI, Law and beyond. A transdisciplinary ecosystem for the future of AI & Law. *Artificial Intelligence and Law, 33*(1), 253–270.

Birkstedt, T., Minkkinen, M., Tandon, A., & Mäntymäki, M. (2023). AI governance: Themes, knowledge gaps and future agendas. *Internet Research, 33*(7), 133–167.

Bonhomme, E. (2025). Medical charlatans have existed through history. But AI has turbocharged them. *The Guardian, 16 July 2025.* Retrieved August 21, 2025 from https://www.theguardian.com/commentisfree/2025/jul/16/medical-charlatans-ai-health-policy-tech

Bova, P., & Di Stefano, A. (2024). Both eyes open: Vigilant incentives help auditors improve AI safety. *Journal of Physics: Complexity, 5*(2), 025009.

Braun, M., & Müller, R. (2025). Missed opportunities for AI governance: Lessons from ELS programs in genomics, nanotechnology, and RRI. *AI & Society, 40*(3), 1347–1360.

Braun, V., & Clarke, V. (2006). Using thematic analysis in psychology. *Qualitative research in psychology, 3*(2), 77–101.

Cary, M. P., Jr., Bessias, S., McCall, J., Pencina, M. J., Grady, S. D., Lytle, K., & Economou-Zavlanos, N. J. (2025a). Empowering nurses to champion Health equity & BE FAIR: Bias elimination for fair and responsible AI in healthcare. *Journal of Nursing Scholarship, 57*(1), 130–139.

Cary, M. P., Jr., Grady, S. D., McMillian-Bohler, J., Bessias, S., Silcox, C., Silva, S., Guilamo-Ramos, V., McCall, J., Sperling, J., & Goldstein, B. A. (2025b). Building competency in artificial intelligence and bias mitigation for nurse scientists and aligned health researchers. *Nursing Outlook, 73*(3), Article 102395.

Cascella, M., Ponsiglione, A. M., Santoriello, V., Romano, M., Cerrone, V., Esposito, D., Montedoro, M., Pellecchia, R., Savoia, G., Lo Bianco, G., Innamorato, M., Natoli, S., Montomoli, J., Semeraro, F., Bignami, E. G., Bellini, V., Leoni, M. L. G., Occhigrossi, F., Vittori, A., … Piazza, O. (2025). Expert consensus on feasibility and application of automatic pain assessment in routine clinical use. *Journal of Anesthesia, Analgesia and Critical Care, 5*(29), 1–12.

Chow, J., Lee, R., & Wu, H. (2025). How do radiologists currently monitor AI in radiology and what challenges do they face? An interview study and qualitative analysis. *Journal of Imaging Informatics in Medicine, 39*, 6–19.
Dafoe, A. (2018). AI governance: A research agenda. *Future of Humanity Institute, University of Oxford*. Retrieved August 20, 2025 from https://www.fhi.ox.ac.uk/govaiagend
Department for Science, Innovation and Technology. (2023). Policy paper AI regulation: A pro-innovation approach. Retrieved August 21, 2025 from https://www.gov.uk/government/publications/ai-regulation-a-pro-innovation-approach
Fields, C. T., Black, C., Thind, J. K., Jegede, O., Aksen, D., Rosenblatt, M., Assari, S., Bellamy, C., Anderson, E., Holmes, A., & Scheinost, D. (2025). Governance for anti-racist AI in healthcare: Integrating racism-related stress in psychiatric algorithms for Black Americans. *Frontiers in Digital Health, 7*, 1492736.
Gasser, U., & Almeida, V. A. (2017). A layered model for AI governance. *IEEE Internet Computing, 21*(6), 58–62.
Goh, W. W. B., Tan, C. H., Tan, C., Prahl, A., Lwin, M. O., & Sung, J. (2025). Regulating, implementing and evaluating AI in Singapore healthcare: AI governance roundtable's view. *Annals of the Academy of Medicine Singapore, 54*(7), 428.
Goktas, P., & Grzybowski, A. (2025). Shaping the future of healthcare: Ethical clinical challenges and pathways to trustworthy AI. *Journal of Clinical Medicine, 14*(5), 1605.
Hassan, M., Borycki, E. M., & Kushniruk, A. W. (2025). Artificial intelligence governance framework for healthcare. *Healthcare Management Forum, 38*(2), 125–130.
Herzog, C., Blank, S., & Stahl, B. C. (2025). Towards trustworthy medical AI ecosystems—A proposal for supporting responsible innovation practices in AI-based medical innovation. *AI & Society, 40*(4), 2119–2139.
IEEE. (2021). IEEE—7000 Standard model process for addressing ethical concerns during system design. Retrieved August 21, 2025 from https://standards.globalspec.com/std/14465958/7000#:~:text=This%20standard%20provides%20engineers%20and%20technologists%20with%20an,address%20ethical%20concerns%20or%20risks%20during%20system%20design
Kim, J., Kim, S. Y., Kim, E. A., Sim, J. A., Lee, Y., & Kim, H. (2024). Developing a framework for self-regulatory governance in healthcare AI research: Insights from South Korea. *Asian Bioethics Review, 16*(3), 391–406.
KPMG. (2025). ISO/IEC 42001: A new standard for AI governance. Retrieved August 21, 2025 from https://kpmg.com/ch/en/insights/artificial-intelligence/iso-iec-42001.html#:~:text=ISO%2FIEC%2042001%3A2023%20is%20the%20latest%20standard%20for%20an,AI%20compliance%20and%20align%20with%20international%20best%20practices
Lacmanovic, S., & Skare, M. (2025). Artificial intelligence bias auditing–current approaches, challenges and lessons from practice. *Review of Accounting and Finance, 24*(3), 375–400.
Lendvai, G. F., & Gosztonyi, G. (2025). Algorithmic bias as a core legal dilemma in the age of artificial intelligence: Conceptual basis and the current state of regulation. *Laws, 14*(3), 41.
Mäntymäki, M., Minkkinen, M., Birkstedt, T., & Viljanen, M. (2022). Defining organisational AI governance. *AI and Ethics, 2*(4), 603–609.
Mazzi, F. (2025). Evaluating the normative implications of national and international artificial intelligence policies for sustainable development goal 3: Good health and well-being. *Health Affairs Scholar, 3*(6), qxaf108.
Minkkinen, M., & Mäntymäki, M. (2023). Discerning between the "easy" and "hard" problems of AI governance. *IEEE Transactions on Technology and Society, 4*(2), 188–194.
Minkkinen, M., Niukkanen, A., & Mäntymäki, M. (2024). What about investors? ESG analyses as tools for ethics-based AI auditing. *AI & Society, 39*(1), 329–343.
Montagnani, M. L., Najjar, M. C., & Davola, A. (2024). The EU Regulatory approach (ES) to AI liability, and its application to the financial services market. *Computer Law & Security Review, 53*, 105984.
Moustafa, F. R. (2024). Towards recognition of the legal personality of artificial intelligence (AI): Recognising reality and law. *International Journal of Criminal Justice Sciences, 19*(1), 271–288.

Nashwan, A. J., & Joy, G. V. (2025). The 2024 Declaration of Helsinki revision: Relevance to nursing research. *Journal of Advanced Nursing, 0,* 1–11.

Nay, J. J., Karamardian, D., Lawsky, S. B., Tao, W., Bhat, M., Jain, R., Lee, A. T., Choi, J. H., & Kasai, J. (2024). Large language models as tax attorneys: A case study in legal capabilities emergence. *Philosophical Transactions of the Royal Society A, 382*(2270), 20230159.

NIST. (2025). AI risk management framework. Retrieved August 21, 2025 from https://www.nist.gov/itl/ai-risk-management-framework#:~:text=Released%20on%20January%2026%2C%202023%2C%20the%20Framework%20was,multiple%20workshops%2C%20and%20other%20opportunities%20to%20provide%20input

Nong, P., & Ji, M. (2025). Expectations of healthcare AI and the role of trust: Understanding patient views on how AI will impact cost, access, and patient-provider relationships. *Journal of the American Medical Informatics Association, 32*(5), 795–799.

Nong, P., Hamasha, R., & Platt, J. (2024). Equity and AI governance at academic medical centers. *American Journal of Managed Care, 30*(6), 468–472.

OECD. (2025). AI principles. Retrieved August 21, 2025 from https://www.oecd.org/en/topics/ai-principles.html#:~:text=The%20OECD%20AI%20Principles%20are%20the%20first%20intergovernmental,AI%20that%20respects%20human%20rights%20and%20democratic%20values

Papagiannidis, E., Enholm, I. M., Dremel, C., Mikalef, P., & Krogstie, J. (2023). Toward AI governance: Identifying best practices and potential barriers and outcomes. *Information Systems Frontiers, 25*(1), 123–141.

Pasas-Farmer, S., & Jain, R. (2025). From discovery to delivery: Governance of AI in the pharmaceutical industry. *Green Analytical Chemistry, 13,* 100268.

Rajendra, J. B. (2025). Addressing the ethical and legal crossroads: The impact of ChatGPT on the legal profession. *Information & Communications Technology Law, 35*(1), 48–71.

Ramaliba, T., & Jacobs, L. (2024). Artificial intelligence technology to enhance data quality management practices in the banking industry in South Africa. *South African Journal of Libraries and Information Science, 90*(2), 1–10.

Remolina, N. (2025). AI governance and algorithmic auditing in financial institutions: Lessons from Singapore. *Journal of Risk Management in Financial Institutions, 18*(3), 261–275.

Ressel, J., Völler, M., Murphy, F., & Mullins, M. (2024). Addressing the notion of trust around ChatGPT in the high-stakes use case of insurance. *Technology in Society, 78,* 102644.

Roberts, H., Hine, E., Taddeo, M., & Floridi, L. (2024). Global AI governance: Barriers and pathways forward. *International Affairs, 100*(3), 1275–1286.

Rozenblit, L., Price, A., Solomonides, A., Joseph, A. L., Koski, E., Srivastava, G., Labkoff, S., Bray, D., Lopez-Gonzalez, M., Singh, R., de Bronkart, D., Barr, P. J., Szolovits, P., Dattani, K., Jaffe, C., Fridsma, D., Baris, R., Leftwich, R., Stolper, R.,... Quintana, Y. (2025a). Toward responsible AI governance: Balancing multi-stakeholder perspectives on AI in healthcare. *International Journal of Medical Informatics*, 106015.

Rozenblit, L., Price, A., Solomonides, A., Joseph, A. L., Srivastava, G., Labkoff, S., de Bronkart, D., Singh, R., Dattani, K., Lopez-Gonzalez, M., Barr, P. J., Koski, E., Lin, B., Cheung, E., Weiner, M. G., Williams, T., Bui, T. T. T., & Quintana, Y. (2025b). Towards a multi-stakeholder process for developing responsible AI governance in consumer health. *International Journal of Medical Informatics, 195,* Article 105713.

Sauvayre, R. (2022). Types of errors hiding in Google Scholar data. *Journal of Medical Internet Research, 24*(5), e28354.

Schwarz, M., Hinske, L. C., Mansmann, U., & Albashiti, F. (2024). Designing an ML auditing criteria catalog as starting point for the development of a framework. *IEEE Access, 12,* 39953–39967.

Shah, S. F., Arecco, D., Draper, H., Tiribelli, S., Harriss, E., & Matin, R. N. (2025). Ethical implications of artificial intelligence in skin cancer diagnostics: Use-case analyses. *British Journal of Dermatology, 192*(3), 520–529.

Shaw, F., & McCosker, A. (2025). Relational ethics in the administration of healthcare technology: AI, automation and proper distance. *Sociology of Health & Illness, 47*(5), e70055.

Simmons-Simmons. (2025). The EU AI act: A quick guide. Retrieved August 21, 2025 from https://www.simmons-simmons.com/en/publications/clyimpowh000ouxgkw1oidakk/the-eu-ai-act-a-quick-guide

Solaimani, S., & Long, P. (2025). Beyond the black box: Operationalising explicability in artificial intelligence for financial institutions. *International Journal of Business Information Systems, 49*(5), 1–38.

Sriharan, A., Kuhlmann, E., Correia, T., Tahzib, F., Czabanowska, K., Ungureanu, M. I., & Kumar, B. N. (2025). Artificial intelligence in healthcare: Balancing technological innovation with health and care workforce priorities. *The International Journal of Health Planning and Management, 40*, 987–992.

Sriram, H. K., & Bharath M. B. M. (2025). Beyond automation: Exploring the potential of agentic AI in risk management and fraud detection in banks. *Eksplorium, 46*, 192–220.

Stackpole, B. (2025). Beyond the algorithm: AI's societal impact. *MIT Management: Ideas Made To Matter, 14 July 2025.* Retrieved August 21, 2025 from https://mitsloan.mit.edu/ideas-made-to-matter/beyond-algorithm-ais-societal-impact

Stetson, P. D., Choy, J., Summerville, N., Baldwin-Medsker, A., Mak, J., Chatterjee, A., Kim, K., Kumar, C., Samedy, P., Halperin, J., Voigt, L., Jee, J., Fraser, J., Connor, M., Harper, R., Evard, R., & Offodile, A. C., 2nd. (2025). Responsible artificial intelligence governance in oncology. *Npj Digital Medicine, 8*(1), 407.

Stogiannos, N., O'Regan, T., Scurr, E., Litosseliti, L., Pogose, M., Harvey, H., Kumar, A., Malik, R., Barnes, A., McEntee, M. F., Malamateniou, C., & Malamateniou, C. (2024). AI implementation in the UK landscape: Knowledge of AI governance, perceived challenges and opportunities, and ways forward for radiographers. *Radiography, 30*(2), 612–621.

Thurzo, A. (2025). Provable AI ethics and explainability in medical and educational AI agents: Trustworthy ethical firewall. *Electronics, 14*(7), 1294.

UNESCO. (2025). Recommendation on the ethics of artificial intelligence. Retrieved August 21, 2025 from https://www.unesco.org/en/articles/recommendation-ethics-artificial-intelligence

Van Eck, M. (2025). AI' hallucinations' are threatening the administration of justice in SA. *Daily Maverick, 15 July 2025.* Retrieved August 21, 2025 from https://www.dailymaverick.co.za/opinionista/2025-07-15-ai-hallucinations-are-threatening-the-administration-of-justice-in-sa/

Wagner, J. K., Doerr, M., & Schmit, C. D. (2024). AI governance: A challenge for public health. *JMIR Public Health and Surveillance, 10*(1), e58358.

Yadawa, S. K., & Singh, S. (2024). Safeguarding privacy in the age of AI-powered legal services: Navigating data protection challenges and ethical imperatives. *Indian JL & Just., 15*, 135.

You, Z., Wang, Y., & Xiao, Y. (2025). Analysing the suitability of artificial intelligence in healthcare and the role of AI governance. *Health Care Analysis, 33*, 413–445.

# Chapter 9
# AI and Ethical Innovation

**Tasneem Gathoo and Naeem Mahomed Ebrahim**

**Abstract** Artificial intelligence (AI) has been designed and developed in a user-friendly manner to simplify tasks for individuals, businesses and society at large. This has made it a desirable tool that has been integrated into all aspects of life. However, the popularity and rapid innovation of AI technology have given rise to a range of ethical challenges that need to be proactively addressed when developing AI. The objectives of this study address various challenges encountered in the innovation of ethical AI systems. This study begins by examining the AI ethics practices of IBM and Microsoft to understand how these companies have achieved ethical AI systems. These practices can serve as models for best practices for other companies. It then outlines ways to incentivise businesses to prioritise the adoption of ethical AI practices and highlight the benefits thereof to these companies. Lastly, the study explores the role that education plays as well as the benefits to society of developing ethical AI systems. A narrative review was adopted in this study. Documentation relevant to the research objectives was analysed and synthesised to achieve the research objectives. The results from this study demonstrate the importance of ethical AI. To achieve ethical AI, students and professionals must be trained to identify and mitigate ethical dilemmas in AI technology effectively and efficiently. The case studies of IBM and Microsoft emphasise the need to integrate ethical principles from the earliest stage in the development process. It is also important for companies to support the AI development process with strong policies and ethical governance structures. The benefits of ethical AI are vast for businesses and society, as it enhances the perception of businesses and promotes social responsibility. Therefore, early integration of ethics in the development of AI is an absolute necessity for businesses and society.

T. Gathoo (✉) · N. M. Ebrahim
Department of Commercial Accounting, College of Business and Economics, University of Johannesburg, Johannesburg, South Africa
e-mail: tasneemg@uj.ac.za

N. M. Ebrahim
e-mail: naeeme@uj.ac.za



M. Adelowotan and H. Coovadia (eds.), *AI and Accountability*, CSR, Sustainability, Ethics & Governance, https://doi.org/10.1007/978-3-032-20091-4_9

## 9.1 Introduction

In an ever-developing world of technology, the emergence of artificial intelligence (AI) has profoundly changed and will continue to change and enhance the way we go about our daily lives (Huang et al., 2022). AI is being applied in various fields. The widespread application of AI has improved efficiency and produced benefits from both an economic and a societal perspective (Huang et al., 2022). AI has proven to be an asset but has also given rise to potential threats and ethical concerns (Alahmed et al., 2023). It became imperative that there should be a need for caution and continuous oversight, highlighting the complex interplay between innovation and regulation in the AI landscape (Sun et al., 2024). For the continued progression of AI, ethical governance is indispensable (Sun et al., 2024). Over several years, there have been many AI products developed that exemplify ethical design principles and offer insight into how ethical considerations can be integrated into the AI development process from inception to deployment (Santa Gonzalez et al., 2024). These products provide a benchmark for which future AI products can adhere. In assisting to foster a culture of responsibility and to ensure ethical AI practices, ethical issues and practices relating to AI should be introduced at an educational level (Hernández, 2024). It is pivotal that it be introduced at this level, as it equips current as well as future professionals with the required knowledge and tools to navigate ethical dilemmas encountered when dealing with artificial intelligence programs and products (Hernández, 2024). From a company perspective, it is crucial to foster a culture of responsibility within the industry, which results in incentives to companies in the form of achieving trust, mitigating risks and fostering long-term sustainability (Kandasamy, 2024).

### *9.1.1 Problem Statement*

The continued growth of AI has given rise to risks and ethical concerns (Alahmed et al., 2023). There has been significant advancement on a global scale to develop an ethical framework that should be adhered to facilitate the development of ethical AI (Shukla, 2024). The question, therefore, remains whether any existing models have been implemented that adhere to the fundamental principles of ethical AI and how companies can be incentivised to follow suit, and in doing so create a benefit for both them and society. It also remains unseen as to what impact education can have in promoting ethical AI, as well as what practices can be followed to equip current and future professionals with sufficient expertise and knowledge to overcome any ethical concerns that they may encounter.

### 9.1.2 *Research Objectives*

In order to address the problem statement above, an analysis and evaluation of available literature will be performed to:

1. Gain an understanding of the best practices models that have been implemented to ensure that any AI products developed meet the required AI ethical principles and practices
2. It will explore avenues that can be used to incentivise companies to prioritise ethical AI
3. Explore what impact education can have on promoting ethical AI among current and future professionals
4. Discuss the benefits to society of achieving ethical AI

The layout of the rest of the chapter is outlined as follows. The literature review, which will provide an overview of existing literature relating to AI and ethical principles, is discussed in the next section, followed by the theoretical frameworks explored in this study. Afterwards, the research methodology will be explained and is followed by the study's findings. These findings examine how IBM and Microsoft approach ethical AI, outlining models for best practices that other businesses can adopt. The advantages of proactively developing ethical AI products are then highlighted to incentivise companies to adopt innovative ethical AI practices. It also discusses the importance of incorporating ethical AI principles into educational curricula. Furthermore, it considers the societal benefits of achieving ethical AI. The chapter concludes with suggestions for future research.

## 9.2 Literature Review

AI has achieved rapid growth and development over a short space of time. It has introduced technologies such as machine learning, natural language processing and computer vision, amongst others (Huang et al., 2022). These technologies have not only integrated themselves across various disciplines but society as well (Alahmed et al., 2023). The introduction of these technologies has enhanced the way in which we operate by improving efficiency as well as reducing costs (Huang et al., 2022). However, together with these benefits, artificial intelligence has also created significant risks and ethical issues for users as well as society (Alahmed et al., 2023). As valuable as AI has become, it has raised ethical concerns across various disciplines. Verma et al. (2024) emphasises the need for awareness and critical analysis of AI, to ensure that potential risks due to the unethical use and results generated by AI can be identified. It has been strongly encouraged that ethical practices should be prioritised throughout the AI development process to achieve beneficial and responsible outputs (Huang et al., 2022). When considering the rapid evolution of AI, it has become necessary to identify and address the impact it has on society.

To mitigate the risk of unethical use of AI, several frameworks and guidelines have been established to integrate ethical considerations into AI development. One of the key ethical principles emphasised by various countries and organisations demand that AI be developed with a human-centric approach to ensure societal impact (Brand, 2022). Akhtar et al. (2024) also endorses a human-centric approach, which is essential in developing ethical and socially responsible AI systems. In attempt to achieve this, ethical AI systems can be accomplished by focusing on ethical AI principles such as transparency, accountability, fairness and privacy (Brand, 2022). By focusing on these principles, the development of AI adheres to ethical guidelines that builds trust amongst users and stakeholders and further ensures the ongoing progress of AI technologies (Brand, 2022). Some of the prominent initiatives include the regulation of AI in the European Union, the United States of America, Canada, China as well as amongst OECD countries, with some addressing the key ethical principles in further detail than others (Shukla, 2024).

In November 2021, UNESCO (2022) produced the first global standard on AI ethics, which laid out the ten core principles approach to the Ethics of AI. The ten core principles are summarised in Table 9.1 below.

Despite the widespread recognition of ethical principles for AI, the implementation in practice presents various challenges. Some of the challenges encountered are a result of impractical or inadequate guidance given in frameworks and guidelines for the development of ethical AI systems (Sanderson et al., 2022). Another challenge that may be experienced is the lack of resources to successfully implement these guidelines, especially amongst smaller organisations (Alahmed et al., 2023). A significant risk that exists is the lack of intent by businesses to comply with ethical

**Table 9.1** UNESCO ten core principles for ethical AI

| Principle | Brief explanation of principle |
|---|---|
| Do no harm | Risk assessment should be used to prevent harm as a result of use |
| Safety and security | Safety and security should be avoided |
| Right to privacy and data protection | Privacy must be protected. Adequate data protection should be established |
| Governance and collaboration | International law must be respected |
| Responsibility and accountability | Systems should be auditable and traceable |
| Transparency and explainability | Ethical deployment of AI depends on transparency and explainability |
| Human oversight | Systems do not displace human responsibility and accountability |
| Sustainability | Impact on "sustainability" should be assessed |
| Awareness and literacy | AI should be promoted in education and training |
| Fairness (non-discrimination) | AI should promote social justice, fairness and non-discrimination |

*Source* UNESCO (2022)

guidelines (Ali et al., 2023). This necessitates the study of analysing how companies have successfully integrated ethical AI principles into their innovation processes as described in the first research objective. Further, the second research objective will then highlight the benefits thereof to incentivise other companies to follow suit.

To create awareness and to foster a culture of ethical AI, several strategies have been introduced. Hernández (2024) introduced and sets out a multidimensional approach. This approach integrates ethics, together with regulation, innovation and education to encourage the development of AI that aligns with human and societal values. In addition, a shared understanding of ethical standards should be implemented and this can be achieved through a stakeholder collaborative approach which takes into consideration the perspectives of experts, policy makers and the public (Akhtar et al., 2024) and is further enhanced by the integration of university-industry collaborations (Smiee et al., 2022). Thamik and Wu (2022) highlights the need for ethical principles for AI to be continuously adapted through research and collaboration to ensure that responsible and ethical AI is continuously updated as AI evolves. These concerns will be discussed in the research objectives that discuss the role of education in AI ethics and the societal benefits thereof.

The theoretical frameworks explored in this study are explained in the next section.

## 9.3 Theoretical Frameworks

Responsible innovation theory, AI governance frameworks, and stakeholder theory provide a robust conceptual foundation for ethical AI innovation. The integration of these frameworks offers a multifaceted approach to embedding ethical considerations throughout the AI lifecycle. By integrating these theoretical frameworks, researchers and practitioners can proactively address potential societal and ethical concerns by ensuring that the AI developed aligns with ethical principles and promotes public good (Du, 2025). The responsible innovation theory specifically emphasises the integration of ethical and societal concerns throughout the AI innovation lifecycle to promote a proactive approach to address potential concerns (Herrmann, 2023). AI governance frameworks, on the other hand, provide structured mechanisms and policies to ensure that ethical principles are translated into actionable guidelines and policies to incorporate multi-stakeholder perspectives and achieve regulatory harmonisation (Akhtar et al., 2024; Qian et al., 2024). Meanwhile, the stakeholder theory underscores the importance of identifying and balancing the interests of all groups affected by AI, including users, developers, regulators and the broader society to ensure inclusivity and equitable distribution of the benefits and harms of AI (Radaelli & Currie, 2024; Sharma, 2024).

The frameworks discussed above shape the development of best practice models for ethical AI products and incentivise companies to follow these models. Responsible innovation encourages best practices that incorporate ethical principles from design to deployment through inclusive and reflective processes, fostering long-term societal trust and potentially offering competitive advantages to businesses

(Herrmann, 2023; Wiesmüller et al., 2023). AI Governance frameworks establish foundational principles and guidelines that translate into best practices through regulatory compliance and risk management, forcing companies to prioritise ethical consideration to mitigate potential legal and reputational consequences (Akhtar et al., 2024; Batool et al., 2025). The stakeholder theory drives best practices by encouraging companies to consider different perspectives in the AI development process, to uphold societal values and incentivise companies to maintain positive relationships with all their stakeholders (Radaelli & Currie, 2024; Sharma, 2024).

Furthermore, these theories emphasise the vital role of education and the societal benefits of ethical AI. Responsible innovation emphasises that education should provide professionals with the skills to promote critical thinking and ethical reasoning, whilst also engaging in interdisciplinary collaboration to enable them to anticipate and address a broad range of ethical and societal issues when developing AI products (Weiss et al., 2023). AI governance frameworks need to be integrated into educational curricula to ensure that professionals possess the necessary skills and knowledge to adhere to ethical standards, including topics such as data privacy and bias mitigation (Akhtar et al., 2024). The stakeholder theory advocates for education to create professionals who can engage with different users and communities effectively and efficiently (Radaelli & Currie, 2024; Sharma, 2024). Ultimately, the integration of these frameworks into AI innovation processes will benefit society as a whole (Akhtar et al., 2024; Herrmann, 2023). Therefore, for various stakeholders to effectively navigate the ethical landscape of AI innovation, all these theories have been adopted in this study.

The research methods adopted in this study have been outlined in the next section of this chapter.

## 9.4 Research Methods

This chapter employs a narrative review, a qualitative research method that involves an overview and synthesis of existing knowledge on a specific topic (Theile & Beall, 2024). The research draws upon relevant literature, industry reports and policy documents to provide an overview of AI ethics (Morante et al., 2024). Documentation related to the multifaceted dimensions of responsible and ethical AI innovation was explored to allow the researchers to analyse and interpret the results to achieve the research objectives of this study. This comprehensive dataset was created from a variety of sources, including conference proceedings, academic databases, Google Scholar searches and publicly available documents. The search used a combination of keywords and Boolean operators to identify relevant literature to the study. These keywords included terms such as "ethical AI", "AI ethics", "ethical AI innovation", "ethical AI principles", "responsible AI", "AI governance", "AI best practices", "AI case studies", "incentivising ethical AI", "AI regulation", "AI education", "societal benefits of ethical AI." The literature generated from the initial search was screened for relevance through the assessment of the abstract, keywords, introduction and conclusion and was limited to literature published between 2020 and 2025, to ensure that the research is current and contributes meaningfully to the existing body of knowledge. Further, only documentation published in English was considered in this study. Literature that did not explicitly address AI ethics in relation to the research objectives was excluded from the study. The use of credible databases and websites enhanced the trustworthiness of findings.

The findings of the study begin with the analysis of publicly available company documentation of two prominent technology companies, namely, IBM and Microsoft, to provide guidance for other companies to adopt in their development of AI systems. These companies have been selected because they are among the top two companies identified to have complied with AI ethical principles and are at the forefront in developing AI products. The findings from these case studies highlight the benefits and incentives for companies to ensure that they develop and deploy ethical AI systems. However, these findings are focused on the perspective of large multinational companies and, therefore, may not be well-suited to be incorporated into the practices of small and medium-sized businesses. Lastly, various articles were analysed to discuss the role of education in AI ethics and conclude on the societal benefits of achieving ethically sound AI systems. The data extracted from these articles identified key themes and arguments relevant to the study. The findings were validated by cross-referencing the data extracted across various sources to ensure credibility. The findings are discussed in Sects. 9.5–9.8 of this chapter.

## 9.5 Case Studies for Best Practice

When designing and implementing any AI applications, consideration should be given to the above-mentioned ethical AI principles to ensure that ethical AI applications/programs are achieved. An investigation was done to assess whether any of these principles are being taken into consideration and implemented in existing AI. It was found that many prominent tech companies have already done so. As discussed earlier, it was noted that tech giants, a IBM and Microsoft, have set the tone in compliance by ensuring that they balance their innovation with transparency, fairness, accountability and regulatory compliance (King, 2025). An examination into these companies was done to identify how ethical AI principles have been integrated to ensure that any AI products developed or being developed meet the required principles that have been set, in order to achieve ethical AI and thereby serve as models of best practices, as set out in the first research objective.

### *9.5.1 IBM*

In order to achieve AI ethical practices, IBM has implemented a multidisciplinary and multidimensional approach from the bottom up (Van der Poorten, 2023). This

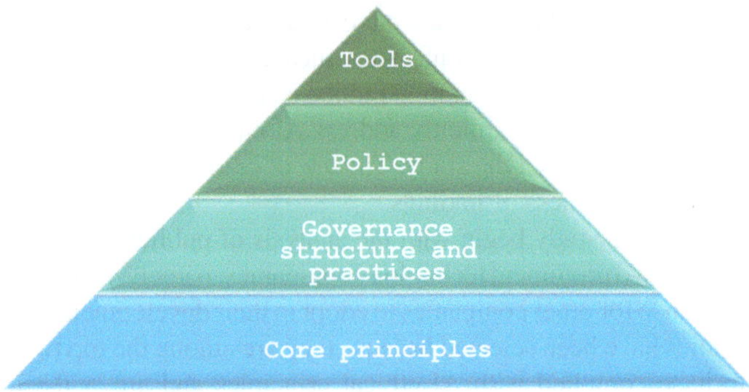


**Fig. 9.1** Summary of embedded ethical practices at IBM. *Source* Authors' own illustration

has ensured that the pillars of trust and transparency are embedded throughout their entire business (Van der Poorten, 2023). Figure 9.1 below illustrates the various levels within the IBM organisation where ethical practices have been embedded.

## Core Principles for Trust and Transparency

At the base of IBM's approach, IBM has established and continues to follow its core principles to ensure an ethical AI framework is built and to ensure the use of AI is responsible and transparent. The core principles of trust and transparency follow the following roadmap (Van der Poorten, 2023):

- The purpose of AI is to augment and enhance human intelligence and not to replace it
- Data belongs to the creator to emphasise data ownership and control
- New technology must be transparent and explainable to understand how AI makes decisions

The above-mentioned principles are further supported by ensuring compliance with the core principles suggested by UNESCO. IBM has established the following Trustworthy AI pillars (Van der Poorten, 2023):

- Ensuring that the AI system has the ability to provide human-interpretable explanations for its predictions and insights, thereby complying with the explainability principle
- Making certain that the AI system treats individuals and groups equitably, thereby complying with the fairness principle
- Sharing information on how the AI system has been designed and developed, thereby addressing the Transparency principle
- Safeguarding consumers' privacy and data rights

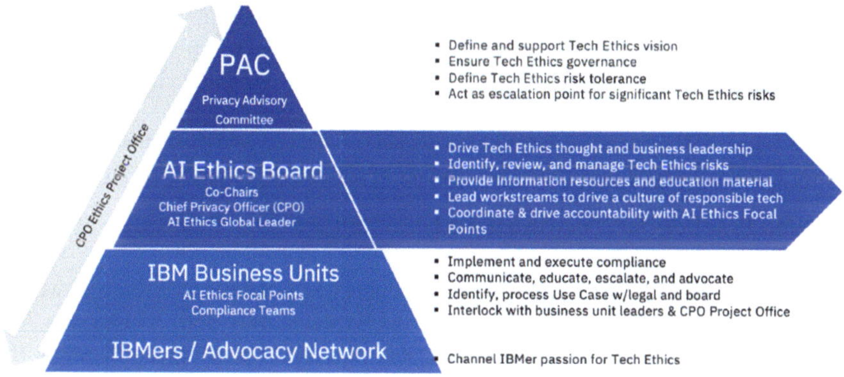


**Fig. 9.2** IBM AI ethics governance structure. *Source* Van der Poorten (2023)

## Governance Structure and Practices

To further enhance the adoption and implementation of ethical AI, IBM has established a very strong governance structure. This governance structure and its respective responsibilities are depicted and described in Fig. 9.2 below.

The AI Ethics Board is central to the ethical decision-making process for AI at IBM. Its mission is to support a centralised governance, review cases and other proposals to ensure consistency with IBM's principles and core values (Coeckelbergh, 2020), as well as the decision-making process for IBM ethics policies, practices, communications, research, products, and services (Van der Poorten, 2023). It plays a crucial role in approving and rejecting proposals and in identifying necessary conditions to proceed (Coeckelbergh, 2020). By instilling this Board, IBM can ensure that there no deviation from the ethical principles and that the core values are still being applied.

## Advocacy and Policy Initiatives

IBM actively advocates for policies that promote AI ethics, not from a company and internal perspective but from a global stance as well. IBM is involved in initiatives like the Rome Call for AI Ethics, which aims to create a shared sense of responsibility among businesses, governments, universities, and other organisations to keep humankind at the centre of technological development (Van der Poorten, 2023). IBM also participates in various organisations and initiatives such as the World Economic Forum's Global AI Action Alliance, MIT-IBM Watson AI Lab, European Commission Expert Group on AI, IEEE Global Initiative on AI Ethics, ITU AI for Good Global Summit, and Data & Trust Alliance (Van der Poorten, 2023). Through participation in these initiatives IBM as able to stay ahead of the constant changes and challenges that AI presents.

**Fig. 9.3** Flow of AI principles through Microsoft. *Source* Authors' own illustration

#### Tool and Practices for Trustworthy AI

IBM provides and utilises various tools, products and practices to build trustworthy AI (Van der Poorten, 2023). Tools such as AI Explainability 360, AI Fairness 360, Adversarial Robustness 360, AI Privacy 360, and Uncertainty Quantification 360 (Van der Poorten, 2023) assist with AI being trustworthy and product offerings such as IBM Watson Studio, IBM Watson OpenScale, and IBM Cloud Pak for Data are designed to empower responsible AI development, including features for monitoring bias, fairness, and trust. Day-to-day practices include transparency reporting, filtering undesirable data, human oversight, and team diversity. These are applied to mitigate risks (Van der Poorten, 2023).

Overall, when it comes to AI ethics, IBM ensures that from root to branch, it has a strong commitment to ensure that any design and development of AI systems have a strong ethical backbone. IBM can be seen as a role model and beacon to be followed to ensure strong ethical AI development and implementation.

### *9.5.2 Microsoft*

Microsoft's commitment to ethical AI practices is driven by the understanding that the world at large only wants to be associated with technology that they can trust (Microsoft, 2025). To achieve this, Microsoft implements a comprehensive and human-centred approach. This approach includes deeply integrating responsible AI principles into the design, development, and deployment of their AI systems (Microsoft, 2025). Figure 9.3 below depicts the various levels within the company where ethical consideration has been integrated.

#### Foundation AI Principles

Initially adopted in 2018, six principles guide Microsoft's approach to ensure responsible AI. The principles have been summarised in Table 9.2 below. These principles are continuously reviewed and refined to adapt to the ever-changing AI capabilities, risks and regulatory requirements.

In comparison with IBM, it can seem that both companies have adopted a very similar approach when it comes to ensuring that ethical AI is achieved. Both companies have considered the global principles set and incorporated these principles as a

**Table 9.2** Microsoft's foundational AI principles

| Principle | Application |
|---|---|
| Fairness | AI systems should treat all people fairly |
| Reliability and safety | AI systems should perform reliably and safely |
| Privacy and security | AI systems should be secure and respect privacy |
| Inclusiveness | AI systems should empower and engage all people, irrespective of their backgrounds |
| Transparency | AI systems should be understandable |
| Accountability | People should be accountable for AI systems |

*Source* Microsoft (2025)

base and starting point when developing AI products. They ensure ethical principles are at the foundation of everything related to AI.

## Governance Structure

Microsoft has established a comprehensive governance structure that consistently upholds all its AI principles across the entire AI development lifecycle (Microsoft, 2025). The following structures have been implemented to continuously oversee that the principles are upheld (Microsoft, 2025):

- **Office of Responsible AI:** This office is responsible for advising teams across the company on legal and regulatory requirements and managing the Responsible AI Governance Community.
- **Responsible AI Governance Community:** This community comprises a dedicated network of Responsible AI leaders and champions embedded throughout various divisions, including Corporate Vice Presidents, Division Leads, and Lead Responsible AI Champs. These CVPs are accountable executives overseeing their group's adherence to responsible AI policies.
- **AI Ethics and Effects in Engineering and Research committee:** This committee leverages scientific and engineering talent to provide expertise on emerging trends related to the enactment of Microsoft's responsible AI principles.

From an overall standpoint, it might seem that the governance structures deployed by both companies seem different but when performing a comparison between the objectives set out by these structures, various comparisons can be drawn between the two companies. In summary, both governance structures aim to address compliance with ethical standards, managing the risks embedded in AI as well as ensuring that ethical AI compliance is maintained throughout the company.

### Development and Deployment Practices

Microsoft implements a Human-Centred Design approach. By implementing this approach, Microsoft prioritises that humans are at the centre of all processes, such as development, design and deployment (Microsoft, 2025).

The Sensitive Uses and Emerging Technologies Program has also been instituted at Microsoft. This consists of a team of multidisciplinary experts who provide counselling for high-impact and high-risk uses of AI. Any system that has an impact on an individual's legal status, life opportunities or presents a risk is reported for review (Microsoft, 2025).

From a regulatory perspective, Microsoft prepares and complies with new regulatory requirements. This is achieved by reviewing existing systems, updating policies and updating contracts to prohibit customers from engaging in prohibited practices (Microsoft, 2025).

### Transparency and Collaboration

To further emphasise the implementation of AI ethics, Microsoft ensures that it is transparent regarding its AI. This transparency is achieved by publishing transparency reports (Microsoft, 2025). These reports provide insight into Microsoft's practices regarding AI. To date, Microsoft has issued its second report, called the "Responsible AI Transparency Report (Microsoft, 2025). The is a significant difference implemented by Microsoft when compared to IBM. IBM does not issue any report regarding this.

Microsoft's stance regarding building trust in AI requires collaboration, which requires contribution from all users across the supply chain, which includes model developers, app builders as well as system users (Microsoft, 2025). From a collaborative point of view, Microsoft does not stop at the end of the supply chain. The collaboration includes stakeholders on a global scale. They work with these stakeholders in order to build coherent governance approaches and advance standards for testing AI systems. They also support the development of the EU AI Act Code of Practice for GPAI models, which is a tool designed to ensure AI complies with the Act's requirement for transparency, copyright and safety (Microsoft, 2025). In aligning with IBM's approach of participating in various global efforts to ensure ethical AI, Microsoft also engages with various stakeholders to ensure that ethical AI standards are maintained.

By implementing all these policies and practices and with global collaboration, Microsoft aims to ensure that its AI technologies are developed and deployed responsibly as well as earning and maintaining the end users' trust.

In conclusion, when pitting these two global technological powerhouses against each other when it comes to addressing ethical AI compliance, it can be agreed that both of these companies have gone to significant lengths to achieve AI that is ethical and in doing so it can also be seen that the processes implemented are well aligned. They have established the required principles at the core of what they do as well as through their processes. They are transparent and collaborative in the practices they follow and hence serve as best practices as well as the leaders to be followed to achieve ethical AI.

## 9.6 Incentivising Companies to Prioritise AI

Development of AI often outpaces the establishment of robust ethical guidelines and regulatory frameworks, creating a critical gap between technological innovation and societal safeguards (Alahmed et al., 2023). This disparity underscores the urgent need to incentivise companies to prioritise ethical practices in their AI development processes, moving beyond mere compliance to foster a culture of responsible innovation (Sharma et al., 2024). Incentivising companies to prioritise ethical practices in AI development is essential for fostering a culture of responsibility and accountability within the industry, and doing so offers benefits for businesses and society (Uddin, 2023). Companies that consider and implement ethical considerations when developing AI only serve to enhance their reputation in the public eye which in turn builds trust from a consumer perspective as well as attracting top talent. This ultimately has a positive impact on the company as a result (Uddin, 2023). In conclusion when one assesses whether the cost outweighs the benefit in developing ethical AI, the conclusion reached is that the incentive for doing so, has a positive impact on the consumer by enhancing the reputation of a company unlike operational setbacks, legal penalties as well as a degrading reputation as a result of non-compliance.

## 9.7 AI Ethics in Education

The use of AI has gained significant momentum in various aspects of life. Further to understanding how established companies have integrated ethical AI principles into their systems and processes, it is also essential for future professionals to be equipped with these skills. This section addresses the third research objective, which aims to explore the impact that education can have on promoting ethical AI among current and future professionals.

The need for skilled professionals who are capable of designing, developing and implementing ethical AI systems is crucial. The content of curricula, training programmes and workshops for current and future professionals must incorporate these principles to promote the innovation of responsible AI, which mitigates risks efficiently and effectively (du Boulay, 2023; Raina et al., 2023). This involves integrating ethical considerations in conjunction with the technical aspects of AI development into course material (Dignum, 2021). Case studies, discussions of real-life scenarios and simulations that mimic ethical AI dilemmas should also be incorporated into courses across various disciplines, including computer science, engineering, humanities, business and law (Kwon, 2023).

Courses should cater for different users across industries. AI ethics should be taught in courses catered for AI developers, policymakers and other relevant stakeholders to enhance their understanding of ethical AI principles and best practices (Alghowinem et al., 2024). To achieve a curriculum that encompasses a comprehensive approach to AI ethics, it must discuss ethical complexities faced within various disciplines and across multidisciplinary collaborations (Peters et al., 2020).

The course content should cover a range of ethical AI principles. These principles include topics such as the need to prioritise data privacy, eliminate algorithmic bias, achieve transparency and accountability and ensure that AI results are validated through some form of human oversight (Chiu et al., 2024). It is important for these principles to be taught for various reasons. The results published by AI are generated based on algorithms that cannot necessarily ensure its fairness and neutrality (Lim et al., 2022). Additionally, AI has historically been biased against certain demographics such as women, people of indigenous descent and low-income individuals and communities (Williams et al., 2023), resulting in discriminatory outcomes. By incorporating specifics of generalised bias across different disciplines as part of the AI ethics curriculum, current and future developers are cognisant of areas to focus on to ensure that ethically sound AI products are developed to promote equity and fairness. Another major ethical concern is the lack of explainability and transparency exhibited by AI systems. To address this challenge, AI systems must be designed with explainability in mind (Akhtar et al., 2024).

Users of AI must also be taught to use it responsibly. In addition to being taught the technical skills of AI development, students also need to be taught how to use AI effectively while abiding by ethical principles (Borenstein & Howard, 2021; Yang et al., 2025). Educators need to explain to students how AI works and to equip them with the skills and resources to critically evaluate the output generated by AI for any potential biases or errors (Kurtz et al., 2024). This ensures that it will be used to benefit society (Chiu et al., 2024).

Ethical AI principles should be consistently updated in course material. Through the continuous collaboration between AI developers and users, feedback must be sought and provided on the performance of AI products (Altenburger, 2023) to ensure that course content is proactively updated (Akhtar et al., 2024). It is also important for current professionals to keep abreast with these developments as they arise by attending continuous professional development opportunities such as online courses, webinars, conferences and workshops (Foltynek et al., 2023). Discussions and collaboration amongst experts from different disciplines can promote a more holistic understanding and knowledge-sharing platform of AI ethics.

AI education should encompass more than just theoretical knowledge, it must also equip students with practical skills. This approach will foster the necessary awareness to ensure that students and professionals can make ethical decisions when designing and developing AI products (Zhang et al., 2023). It should also equip them with practical problem-solving skills to navigate issues as they arise. By integrating AI ethics into educational curricula, future generations of AI developers will be better prepared to address ethical challenges and responsibly mitigate potential risks associated with AI technology (Raina et al., 2023; Weichert et al., 2025).

Therefore, it is apparent that education plays a crucial role in promoting ethical AI. Incorporating the principles of ethical AI into courses ensures that skills and competencies are transferred to current and future professionals to ensure that they are able to make ethically sound decisions to identify and mitigate various ethical dilemmas as they arise (Usher & Barak, 2024). Through education, ethical AI can be achieved from as early as graduate level, in which the fundamental principles of AI can be instilled, to the development and operational level, where developers and those charged with governance are aware of the ethical requirements that need to be adhered to.

By raising awareness of ethical principles and ethical decision-making skills, education can empower the development of ethical AI products that are human-centric and promote societal well-being (Akhtar et al., 2024). The societal benefits associated with ethical AI, as set out in the fourth research objective, will be discussed in the next section.

## 9.8 Societal Benefits of Ethical AI

Ethical AI refers to the design, development, deployment and post-deployment monitoring of processes that adhere to ethical principles, best practices and societal values (Ansarullah et al., 2024). This can be achieved through the promotion of AI products that prioritise fairness, transparency and accountability to ensure that AI is used to benefit society rather than cause harm or promote bias (Van de Poel, 2020). Therefore, a fundamental characteristic of the innovation of ethical AI products is to ensure that it is beneficial to society.

The various biases exhibited by AI pose major ethical challenges to the fairness and inclusivity of AI technology. Ethically developed AI ensures that the benefits thereof are fairly distributed amongst all groups and avoids discrimination against marginalised and vulnerable populations, which promotes social justice and equal opportunities for all (Akhtar et al., 2024; Oyeniran et al., 2022).

Ethical AI products can safeguard individuals, businesses and government from risks. Applying ethical frameworks in the development of AI products can protect individuals, businesses and society against the unintended consequences of errors in AI algorithms (Akhtar et al., 2024), such as the violation of privacy or the spread of misinformation. Further, businesses and government can limit their exposure to any potential reputational or legal repercussions by utilising ethically sound AI programmes (Oyeniran et al., 2022).

Developing AI systems with an emphasis on transparency and accountability fosters trust amongst users and stakeholders (Akhtar et al., 2024). For AI products to be considered transparent and accountable, it must provide insight into how AI algorithms are configured for decision-making purposes and can be held responsible for the output generated. When AI products are developed ethically and abide by societal values, they gain greater acceptance and adoption by society (McKee et al., 2023; Verma et al., 2024).

The development of ethical AI products can positively influence societal well-being by addressing critical challenges across various sectors. In education, the use of AI systems can provide individualised learning plans, identify students or areas where students are struggling and support teachers in delivering more effective content (Akhtar et al., 2024). In healthcare, ethical AI programmes can improve the accuracy of patient diagnosis and create personalised treatment plans, resulting in improved patient outcomes and cost savings (Verma et al., 2024). Furthermore, ethical AI can address environmental challenges such as climate change by analysing large volumes of data to identify patterns to optimise energy consumption, reduce waste and suggest more sustainable practices (Akhtar et al., 2024). It can also effectively solve complex issues such as social justice, public safety and help to achieve sustainable development goals (Tomašev et al., 2020). Taking into consideration the numerous benefits that can be achieved from both a company and consumer perspective through the implementation and use of ethical AI, the importance of ethical AI cannot be underestimated.

## 9.9 Conclusion and Future Research

The rapid expansion and integration of AI across various aspects of society and industry necessitate the development of ethical AI systems. Ethical principles must be upheld in every stage of the development process, that is, from design, to development, deployment and post-deployment. This is to ensure that all parties responsible for AI and its governance can identify and mitigate ethical dilemmas as they arise.

IBM and Microsoft were identified as models of best practices in achieving ethical AI. An in-depth investigation into these companies brought to light actions and policies that can be implemented to achieve ethical AI. It was found that IBM implemented a multidisciplinary and multidimensional approach to ensure that the pillars of trust and transparency, supported by its core values, are applied throughout its business model. From Microsoft's perspective, AI processes are centred around a collaborative human-centric approach that ensures fairness, reliability and safety, privacy and security, inclusivity, transparency and accountability for all. Both companies were found to utilise various tools and products that are supported by policies that advocate for ethical AI. Further, they have both established comprehensive governance structures to ensure compliance with ethical standards throughout the development lifecycle to build lasting, trustworthy AI products.

In summary, for companies to implement AI that meets ethical standards, companies should ensure that ethical principles are adhered to from the design phase to post-deployment phase. Further, it is also necessary for policies to be implemented to support ethical AI and to be continuously supported by a strong governance structure that mitigates ethical risks as they arise.

When investigating the need to incentivise companies to achieve ethical AI, the study found that the benefits of ethical AI practices outweigh the mere requirement for compliance. Some of the benefits achieved include enhanced reputation and increased customer and stakeholder trust and by taking a proactive approach not only mitigates risks but also positions companies as leaders in responsible innovation, ensuring AI contributes to a more inclusive and equitable society.

When exploring the crucial role education plays in ensuring ethical AI. It was found that current and future professionals must be made aware of the ethical principles of AI and that these professionals be equipped with the requisite skills and competencies to efficiently and effectively address complex ethical dilemmas inherent in AI technology. To achieve this, comprehensive curricula, training programmes and workshops should extend beyond providing the technical skills to develop AI but also include ethical considerations as applicable across disciplines and be designed to cater a wide range of users. AI education should also enable users to critically evaluate the results generated by AI to ensure that it upholds all ethical principles. The content of courses should be consistently updated to combat new risks as they arise in the ever-developing field of AI. The importance of education and the impact it has on promoting ethical AI must be prioritised.

Ethical AI can be summarised as AI that complies with ethical principles, best practices and societal values throughout the entire AI development process. When AI is developed ethically, it ensures equitable results for all that lack bias, mitigates risks and addresses critical challenges. As an added incentive, it builds trust amongst users and stakeholders. Therefore, it must be given the necessary priority to benefit society at large.

Further studies can be performed to understand the capabilities of SMEs as well as companies in developing countries to gain an understanding of whether ethical AI is being achieved or can be achieved, given the limited resources available to these entities.

## References

Akhtar, M., Kumar, M., & Nayyar, A. (2024). *Towards ethical and socially responsible explainable AI*. Springer.

Alahmed, Y., Abadla, R., Ameen, N., & Shteiwi, A. (2023). Bridging the gap between ethical AI implementations. *International Journal of Membrane Science and Technology, 10*(3), 3034–3046.

Alghowinem, S., Bagiati, A., Salazar-Gómez, A. F., & Breazeal, C. (2024). Leading in the AI era: An interactive experiential hands-on learning approach for professionals and leaders. [Paper presentation]. In *ASEE annual conference and exposition, conference proceedings*. Retrieved February 23, 2025 from https://www.scopus.com/inward/record.uri?eid=2-s2.0-85202074009&partnerID=40&md5=505c775bf13bf8362024c83044fb0d24

Ali, S. J., Christin, A., Smart, A., & Katila, R. (2023). Walking the walk of AI ethics: Organizational challenges and the individualization of risk among ethics entrepreneurs. [Paper presentation]. In *ACM international conference proceeding series*. Retrieved February 25, 2025 from https://www.scopus.com/inward/record.uri?eid=2-s2.0-85163664446&doi=10.1145%2f3593013.3593990&partnerID=40&md5=4ee4db74342eb4a6c5e593e7e2d8e7e9

Altenburger, R. (2023). Artificial intelligence: Management challenges and responsibility. In R. Schmidpeter & R. Altenburger (Eds.), *Responsible artificial intelligence: Challenges for sustainable management* (pp. 1–8). Springer.

Ansarullah, S. I., Kirmani, M. M., Alshmrany, S., & Firdous, A. (2024). Ethical issues around artificial intelligence. In A. Hamadani, N. A. Ganai, H. Hamadani, & J. Bashir Elsevier (Eds.), *A biologist's guide to artificial intelligence: Building the foundations of Artificial Intelligence and Machine Learning for achieving advancements in life sciences* (pp. 301–314).

Batool, A., Zowghi, D., & Bano, M. (2025). AI governance: A systematic literature review. *AI and Ethics, 5*, 3265–3279. https://doi.org/10.1007/s43681-024-00653-w

Borenstein, J., & Howard, A. (2021). Emerging challenges in AI and the need for AI ethics education. *AI and Ethics, 1*(1), 61–65.

Brand, D. (2022). Responsible artificial intelligence in government: Development of a legal framework for South Africa. *JeDEM-eJournal of eDemocracy and Open Government, 14*(1), 130–150.

Chiu, T. K., Ahmad, Z., Ismailov, M., & Sanusi, I. T. (2024). What are artificial intelligence literacy and competency? A comprehensive framework to support them. *Computers and Education Open, 6*, 100171.

Coeckelbergh, M. (2020). *AI ethics*. MIT Press.

Dignum, V. (2021). The role and challenges of education for responsible AI. *London Review of Education, 19*(1), 1–11.

du Boulay, B. (2023). Artificial intelligence in education and ethics. In O. Zawacki-Richter & I. Jung (Eds.), *Handbook of open, distance and digital education* (pp. 93–108).

Du, J. (2025). *Toward responsible and beneficial AI: Comparing regulatory and guidance-based approaches*. Unpublished Philippines University.

ENAI Recommendations on the Ethical Use of Artificial Intelligence in Education, Foltynek, T., Bjelobaba, S., Glendinning, I., Khan, Z. R., Santos, R., Pavletic, P., & Kravjar, J. (2023) *ENAI recommendations on the ethical use of artificial intelligence in education* (pp. 1–4). Springer.

Hernández, E. G. (2024). Towards an ethical and inclusive implementation of artificial intelligence in organizations: A multidimensional framework. arXiv preprint arXiv:2405.01697

Herrmann, H. (2023). What's next for responsible artificial intelligence: A way forward through responsible innovation. *Heliyon, 9*(3), e14379. https://doi.org/10.1016/j.heliyon.2023.e14379

Huang, C., Zhang, Z., Mao, B., & Yao, X. (2022). An overview of artificial intelligence ethics. *IEEE Transactions on Artificial Intelligence, 4*(4), 799–819.

Kandasamy, U. C. (2024). Ethical leadership in the age of AI challenges, opportunities and framework for ethical leadership. arXiv preprint arXiv:2410.18095

King, C. (2025). *Top 10: Ethical AI companies*. Retrieved March 1, 2025 from https://sustainabilitymag.com/top10/top-10-ethical-ai-companies

Kurtz, G., Amzalag, M., Shaked, N., Zaguri, Y., Kohen-Vacs, D., Gal, E., Zailer, G., & Barak-Medina, E. (2024). Strategies for integrating generative AI into higher education: Navigating challenges and leveraging opportunities. *Education Sciences, 14*(5), 503.

Kwon, J. (2023). A study on ethical awareness changes and education in artificial intelligence society. *Revue D'intelligence Artificielle, 37*(2), 341–345. https://doi.org/10.18280/ria.370212

Lim, J., Seo, J., & Kwon, H. (2022). The role of higher education for the ethical AI society. [Paper presentation]. In *The international FLAIRS conference proceedings*.

McKee, K. R., Bai, X., & Fiske, S. T. (2023). Humans perceive warmth and competence in artificial intelligence. *Iscience, 26*(8), 107256.

Microsoft. (2025). Responsible AI transparency report.

Morante, G., Viloria-Nunez, C., Florez-Hamburger, J., & Capdevilla-Molinares, H. (2024). Proposal of an ethical and social responsibility framework for sustainable value generation in AI. [Paper presentation]. In *2024 IEEE technology and engineering management society, TEMSCON LATAM 2024*. Retrieved February 24, 2025 from https://www.scopus.com/inward/record.uri?eid=2-s2.0-85209354981&doi=10.1109%2fTEMSCONLATAM61834.2024.10717855&partnerID=40&md5=432ff1a0390a0f2ec6e73cd90ba1ee60

Oyeniran, C., Adewusi, A. O., Adeleke, A. G., Akwawa, L. A., & Azubuko, C. F. (2022). Ethical AI: Addressing bias in machine learning models and software applications. *Computer Science & IT Research Journal, 3*(3), 115–126.

Peters, D., Vold, K., Robinson, D., & Calvo, R. A. (2020). Responsible AI—Two frameworks for ethical design practice. *IEEE Transactions on Technology and Society, 1*(1), 34–47.

Qian, Y., Siau, K. L., & Nah, F. F. (2024). Societal impacts of artificial intelligence: Ethical, legal, and governance issues. *Societal Impacts, 3*, 100040. https://doi.org/10.1016/j.socimp.2024.100040

Radaelli, G., & Currie, G. (2024). Recognize your audience: Stakeholders' coaptation work to improve political representation in innovation programs. *Journal of Product Innovation Management, 41*(3), 677–700. https://doi.org/10.1111/jpim.12719

Raina, A., Mundra, K., Prasad, P., & Mishra, S. C. (2023). Fostering ethics in AI: perceptions from the Indian AI curriculum. [Paper presentation]. In *31st International conference on computers in education, ICCE 2023—Proceedings*. Retrieved March 2, 2025 from https://www.scopus.com/inward/record.uri?eid=2-s2.0-85181770489&partnerID=40&md5=699a575e490a9676b26985dbac1ae652

Sanderson, C., Lu, Q., Douglas, D., Xu, X., Zhu, L., & Whittle, J. (2022). Towards implementing responsible AI. [Paper presentation]. In *2022 IEEE international conference on big data (big data)*.

Santa Gonzalez, R., Piansky, R., Bae, S. M., Biddle, J., & Molzahn, D. (2024). Beyond algorithmic fairness: A guide to develop and deploy ethical AI-enabled decision-support tools. arXiv e-prints: arXiv:2409.11489

Sharma, A., Singh, G., & Bhalla, S. (2024). A roadmap of byte-sized morality in traversing with ethical landscape of artificial intelligence. [Paper presentation]. In *2024 15th International conference on computing communication and networking technologies, ICCCNT 2024*. Retrieved February 23, 2025 from https://www.scopus.com/inward/record.uri?eid=2-s2.0-85211092726&doi=10.1109%2fICCCNT61001.2024.10724618&partnerID=40&md5=237fe909916bd1037969bf1c3d4f9a0d

Sharma, S. (2024). Benefits or concerns of AI: A multistakeholder responsibility. *Futures, 157*, 103328. https://doi.org/10.1016/j.futures.2024.103328

Shukla, S. (2024). Principles governing ethical development and deployment of AI. *Journal of Artificial Intelligence Ethics, 7*(1), 45–60.

Smiee, K. C., Brophy, S., Attwood, S., Monks, P., & Webb, D. (2022). From ethical artificial intelligence principles to practice: A case study of university-industry collaboration. [Paper presentation]. In *Proceedings of the international joint conference on neural networks*. Retrieved February 23, 2025 from https://www.scopus.com/inward/record.uri?eid=2-s2.0-85140752244&doi=10.1109%2fIJCNN55064.2022.9892760&partnerID=40&md5=552e22438472008ffffebd579d6b311e

Sun, N., Miao, Y., Jiang, H., Ding, M., & Zhang, J. (2024). From principles to practice: A deep dive into AI ethics and regulations. arXiv preprint arXiv:2412.04683

Thamik, H., & Wu, J. (2022). The impact of artificial intelligence on sustainable development in electronic markets. *Sustainability (Switzerland)*. https://doi.org/10.3390/su14063568

Theile, C. M., & Beall, A. L. (2024). Narrative reviews of the literature: An overview. *Journal of Dental Hygiene, 98*(1), 78–82.

Tomašev, N., Cornebise, J., Hutter, F., Mohamed, S., Picciariello, A., Connelly, B., Belgrave, D. C., Ezer, D., Haert, F. C., & Mugisha, F. (2020). AI for social good: Unlocking the opportunity for positive impact. *Nature Communications, 11*(1), 2468.

Uddin, A. A. (2023). The era of AI: Upholding ethical leadership. *Open Journal of Leadership, 12*(4), 400–417.

UNESCO. (2022). *Recommendation on the ethics of artificial intelligence*. United Nations Educational, Scientific and Cultural Organization.

Usher, M., & Barak, M. (2024). Unpacking the role of AI ethics online education for science and engineering students. *International Journal of STEM Education, 11*(1), 35.

Van de Poel, I. (2020). Embedding values in artificial intelligence (AI) systems. *Minds and Machines, 30*(3), 385–409.

Van der Poorten, M. (2023). AI ethics at IBM. Retrieved February 10, 2025 from https://ifhp.com/wp-content/uploads/2023/12/IBM-Data-Ethics-how-to-operationalize-MLAI-while-respecting-the-ethical-aspects.pdf

Verma, S., Paliwal, N., Yadav, K., & Vashist, P. C. (2024). Ethical considerations of bias and fairness in AI models. [Paper presentation]. In *2024 2nd international conference on disruptive technologies, ICDT 2024*. Retrieved February 25, 2025 from https://www.scopus.com/inward/record.uri?eid=2-s2.0-85191260148&doi=10.1109%2fICDT61202.2024.10489577&partnerID=40&md5=cc91f37977db93319352bb07d0f17276a

Weichert, J., Dunlap, D., Farghally, M., & Eldardiry, H. (2025). The AI policy module: Developing computer science student competency in AI ethics and policy. arXiv preprint arXiv:2506.15639

Weiss, A., Vrecar, R., Zamiechowska, J., & Purgathofer, P. (2023). It's only a bot! How adversarial chatbots can be a vehicle to teach responsible AI. In R. Schmidpeter & R. Altenburger (Eds.), *Responsible artificial intelligence: Challenges for sustainable management* (pp. 235–250). Springer.

Wiesmüller, S., Fischer, N., Mehnert, W., & Ammon, S. (2023). Responsible AI adoption through private-sector governance. In R. Schmidpeter & R. Altenburger (Eds.), *Responsible artificial intelligence: Challenges for sustainable management* (pp. 111–132). Springer.

Williams, R., Ali, S., Devasia, N., DiPaola, D., Hong, J., Kaputsos, S. P., Jordan, B., & Breazeal, C. (2023). AI+ ethics curricula for middle school youth: Lessons learned from three project-based curricula. *International Journal of Artificial Intelligence in Education, 33*(2), 325–383.

Yang, Y., Zhang, Y., Sun, D., He, W., & Wei, Y. (2025). Navigating the landscape of AI literacy education: Insights from a decade of research (2014–2024). *Humanities and Social Sciences Communications, 12*(1), 1–12.

Zhang, H., Lee, I., Ali, S., DiPaola, D., Cheng, Y., & Breazeal, C. (2023). Integrating ethics and career futures with technical learning to promote AI literacy for middle school students: An exploratory study. *International Journal of Artificial Intelligence in Education, 33*(2), 290–324.

# Chapter 10
# The Future of AI Governance

**Olayinka Erin**

**Abstract** The rapid evolution of artificial intelligence (AI) has generated both unprecedented opportunities and complex governance challenges. This study examines the future of AI governance by analyzing existing regulatory frameworks, identifying governance gaps, and proposing adaptive approaches that balance innovation with ethical responsibility. Using a qualitative, comparative policy analysis, the research focuses on the European Union (EU), United States (US), and China, alongside international organizations such as the OECD and UNESCO. Data were derived from academic publications, regulatory documents, and policy reports published between 2017 and 2023, enabling a thematic evaluation of divergent governance models, ethical principles, accountability mechanisms, stakeholder inclusion, adaptive regulation, and international cooperation. The findings highlight significant divergences in governance: the EU's risk-based and rights-oriented AI Act, the US's decentralized and industry-driven model, and China's centralized, state-controlled approach. While ethical principles such as fairness, transparency, and accountability are widely endorsed, enforcement gaps persist, raising concerns of "ethics washing." Liability frameworks remain underdeveloped, and stakeholder participation is uneven, with limited inclusivity in authoritarian contexts. Adaptive mechanisms such as regulatory sandboxes and public–private partnerships show promise but require further empirical validation. Moreover, global cooperation is hampered by geopolitical competition, producing fragmented governance regimes. The study concludes that effective AI governance demands a global, multidisciplinary, and inclusive approach that integrates legal clarity, ethical safeguards, and adaptive oversight. Policy implications include the creation of interoperable global standards, enforceable liability mechanisms, binding ethical requirements, stakeholder-inclusive councils, and expanded regulatory sandboxes. By embedding fairness, accountability, and human rights into governance structures, societies can harness AI's benefits while mitigating its risks and safeguarding democratic values.

O. Erin (✉)
Department of Accountancy, College of Business and Economics, University of Johannesburg, Johannesburg, South Africa
e-mail: oerin@uj.ac.za



M. Adelowotan and H. Coovadia (eds.), *AI and Accountability*, CSR, Sustainability, Ethics & Governance, https://doi.org/10.1007/978-3-032-20091-4_10

## 10.1 Introduction

The rapid evolution of artificial intelligence (AI) technologies has redefined the dynamics of human interaction, business operations, public service delivery, and global governance (Tsamados et al., 2022). From facial recognition systems and algorithmic trading to AI-driven medical diagnostics and autonomous vehicles, AI has become a transformative force across virtually all sectors of society (Reddy et al., 2020). Governments, corporations, and civil society organizations are increasingly leveraging AI to enhance efficiency, improve decision-making, and gain competitive advantages. However, the very characteristics that make AI powerful its autonomy, scalability, and ability to learn and evolve. Orr and Davis (2020) believe that AI is a complex and potentially disruptive technology that demands robust governance. Consensus from academic literature refers to AI governance as the structures, policies, norms, and legal frameworks that regulate the development and deployment of AI technologies (Ibanez & Olmeda, 2022; Koniakou, 2023; Shneiderman, 2020). Unlike traditional technologies, AI's capacity to simulate human cognition and act autonomously raises unique ethical, legal, and societal concerns (Gasser & Almeida, 2017; Hickok, 2021). These include algorithmic bias, lack of transparency (or "black box" decision-making), accountability in AI-driven decisions, job displacement, and the misuse of AI in surveillance or warfare (Hagendorff, 2020). As AI systems increasingly make or influence decisions that affect people's lives, the need for effective governance mechanisms becomes more urgent.

Global responses to AI governance have been diverse and fragmented. The European Union has taken the lead in creating a comprehensive regulatory framework through the Artificial Intelligence Act, which classifies AI systems based on their risk levels and prescribes obligations accordingly (Berente et al., 2021). The United States, in contrast, has adopted a sector-specific and decentralized approach, relying heavily on voluntary guidelines and industry self-regulation (Carter, 2020). China has pursued a centralized strategy, emphasizing state control and alignment with national objectives (Al Zadjali, 2020). International organizations such as the OECD, UNESCO, and the United Nations have issued ethical principles and policy recommendations aimed at harmonizing AI governance on a global scale. Despite these efforts, a universally accepted and enforceable governance framework remains elusive.

While existing scholarship has increasingly acknowledged the transformative potential of AI, far less attention has been paid to the institutional, political, and governance infrastructures required to steer these technologies ethically and responsibly (Abrams et al., 2019; Hagendorff, 2020; McDuie-Ra & Gulson, 2020). Much of the current debate remains fragmented, split between technical discussions driven by computer scientists, regulatory debates focused on compliance, and ethical analyses grounded in philosophy. This fragmentation has created a significant gap in understanding how societies can build coherent, future-oriented AI governance architectures capable of managing uncertainty, mitigating systemic risks, and ensuring democratic oversight. As governments, international organizations, and private sector actors experiment with divergent governance models, a critical question emerges: *What guiding principles and design features should inform the next generation of AI governance frameworks?* Addressing this question is essential not only for ensuring accountability and transparency but also for promoting global equity, preventing regulatory capture, and safeguarding vulnerable communities. By situating AI governance within broader debates on institutional trust, global power asymmetrics, and technological justice, this paper contributes to a more holistic and forward-looking understanding of how AI can be governed in ways that align with societal values and long-term public interest.

### 10.1.1 Problem Statement

While AI offers substantial societal benefits, its unregulated or poorly regulated use poses significant risks. The existing governance models, though evolving, remain inconsistent, uncoordinated, and often insufficient to address the cross-border, interdisciplinary, and rapidly evolving nature of AI technologies. For instance, the challenge of algorithmic bias, where AI systems perpetuate or exacerbate societal inequalities, persists due to inadequate regulatory oversight. Moreover, there is a growing concern about the opacity of AI systems, especially those based on complex machine learning algorithms that operate as "black boxes," making it difficult to interpret their decision-making processes. These concerns are further amplified by geopolitical tensions and technological nationalism, which hinder global cooperation on AI governance.

There is also a gap in accountability mechanisms, particularly in determining liability for harms caused by AI systems (Buhmann & Fieseler, 2021). As AI technologies become more autonomous, the question of who should be held responsible for their actions, the developer, the deployer, or the AI itself remains unresolved. In addition, the pace of AI development often outstrips the speed at which legal and regulatory frameworks can adapt, resulting in a governance lag. This misalignment between technological innovation and policy response creates vulnerabilities that can be exploited, whether intentionally (e.g., through malicious use) or unintentionally (e.g., due to flawed system design). Furthermore, current governance frameworks often lack inclusivity and fail to incorporate the voices of marginalized groups, leading to a narrow understanding of AI's social impact. Ethical concerns such as fairness, transparency, and respect for human rights are frequently overshadowed by economic and strategic considerations (Deloitte, 2021). Without proactive and inclusive governance, AI risks entrenching existing power imbalances and undermining democratic values.

A compelling illustration of these governance gaps can be seen in the widely cited case of the AI-driven recruitment tool used by Amazon, which was discontinued after it was revealed to systematically disadvantage female applicants. The algorithm had been trained on historical hiring data dominated by male candidates, resulting in biased recommendations that effectively reproduced and amplified existing gender inequalities (Hickok, 2021). This incident demonstrates how opaque data pipelines, inadequate oversight, and the absence of robust accountability mechanisms can convert organizational biases into large-scale, automated discrimination. It also highlights the broader risk that poorly governed AI systems, whether deployed in hiring, credit scoring, policing, or public services, can entrench structural injustices under the guise of efficiency and objectivity. Such real-world failures underscore the urgency of developing governance frameworks that ensure transparency, auditability, and fairness in AI design and deployment, particularly as governments and firms increasingly rely on algorithmic decision-making in high-stakes domains.

This study aims to explore the future trajectory of AI governance by critically examining existing regulatory frameworks, identifying key governance challenges, and assessing emerging models that promise to enhance ethical, effective, and inclusive oversight of AI systems. By evaluating the strengths and limitations of current approaches in regions such as the European Union, the United States, and China, as well as contributions from international bodies like the OECD and UNESCO, this study seeks to provide a comprehensive understanding of global AI governance landscapes. The research further intends to analyze the theoretical and practical implications of adopting adaptive and dynamic governance models, including risk-based regulations, AI ethics principles, public–private partnerships, and international cooperation mechanisms. In doing so, the study contributes to the academic discourse on how AI can be governed in a manner that promotes innovation while safeguarding societal values.

Ultimately, the goal is to propose actionable insights and policy recommendations that inform the design of future AI governance frameworks. These frameworks must be agile, context-sensitive, and capable of addressing the multifaceted nature of AI risks and opportunities. The study emphasizes the importance of interdisciplinary collaboration, global harmonization of standards, and continuous regulatory adaptation in building a governance ecosystem that supports responsible AI development and deployment.

The scope of this study encompasses a comparative analysis of AI governance frameworks across major geopolitical actors (EU, US, China), with an emphasis on regulatory design, ethical standards, implementation challenges, and stakeholder involvement. It also considers the contributions of global institutions such as the OECD, UNESCO, and the United Nations in shaping international norms and facilitating policy alignment. The study adopts a multidisciplinary lens, integrating insights from law, ethics, public policy, computer science, and international relations to provide a holistic understanding of AI governance. The significance of this study lies in its potential to inform both policy and academic debates on AI governance. As governments and organizations grapple with the implications of AI deployment, there is a pressing need for evidence-based, context-aware, and future-oriented governance models. This research provides a timely contribution by synthesizing existing knowledge, identifying gaps, and proposing forward-looking strategies that align technological innovation with democratic principles and human rights. Moreover, the study highlights the importance of participatory governance, where diverse voices, including those of civil society, industry, and academia, are involved in shaping

AI policies. In doing so, it seeks to advance an inclusive vision of AI governance that prioritizes fairness, accountability, and sustainability. By fostering dialogue and collaboration among stakeholders, the study aims to support the creation of robust and equitable AI governance frameworks that can withstand the complexities of a rapidly changing technological landscape.

## 10.2 Literature Review

### *10.2.1 Theoretical Framework*

This study on the future of AI governance is underpinned by the Responsible Innovation (RI) framework, which emphasizes that technological development should align with societal needs, ethical values, and long-term sustainability. Responsible Innovation, as articulated by Stilgoe et al. (2018), is built on four dimensions: anticipation, reflexivity, inclusion, and responsiveness. These principles provide a conceptual lens to evaluate whether AI governance frameworks can adequately anticipate risks, encourage reflexive policymaking, include diverse stakeholders, and remain responsive to emerging challenges. Applying the RI framework helps explain why governance models that merely endorse ethical principles without enforceable mechanisms often fail to prevent issues such as algorithmic bias, opacity, or ethics washing. The framework underscores that AI governance must go beyond technical regulation, embedding accountability, inclusivity, and adaptability into institutional structures.

In addition, the study draws from institutional theory, which examines how organizational practices are shaped by broader cultural, political, and regulatory environments (Gasser & Almeida, 2017; Hickok, 2021). Institutional isomorphism, the tendency of organizations to adopt similar structures under coercive, normative, or mimetic pressures, provides insights into why AI governance frameworks across jurisdictions often converge around shared ethical principles such as fairness and transparency. However, institutional theory also highlights the persistence of divergence, as national political ideologies and strategic priorities influence the design and enforcement of governance models (Birkstedt et al., 2023). For example, the EU's risk-based model reflects a normative emphasis on human rights, the US approach is shaped by market liberalism and innovation culture, while China's centralized framework aligns with state control and social stability.

Combining responsible innovation with institutional theory offers a robust foundation for this study. RI highlights the ethical and societal imperatives of AI governance, while institutional theory explains the institutional dynamics and variations across geopolitical contexts. Together, they provide a holistic lens to assess whether governance structures are capable of both embedding ethical safeguards and adapting to diverse political and cultural environments. This integrated theoretical framing supports the study's comparative analysis by linking ethical imperatives with institutional realities. It enables the evaluation of governance frameworks not only in terms of their regulatory provisions but also in terms of their inclusivity, adaptability, and alignment with democratic and human rights values. Ultimately, this dual framework guides the formulation of policy implications, emphasizing the need for adaptive, participatory, and globally harmonized approaches to AI governance.

A combined application of Responsible Innovation (RI) theory and institutional theory offers a more comprehensive and analytically robust foundation for examining AI governance than relying on either framework independently or on alternative approaches. RI theory foregrounds normative principles: anticipation, reflexivity, inclusion, and responsiveness that clarify *how* AI systems ought to be governed to ensure ethical and socially aligned outcomes (Birkstedt et al., 2023). However, RI alone cannot fully explain *why* governance failures persist or *how* organizational and societal structures shape the adoption of responsible practices. Institutional theory complements RI by illuminating the regulatory pressures, cultural norms, organizational routines, and power dynamics that influence governance behaviour in real-world settings (Stilgoe et al., 2018). Together, these frameworks bridge the normative–descriptive divide: RI provides the ethical aspirations and evaluative criteria for responsible AI, while institutional theory explains the institutional constraints, incentives, and path dependencies that enable or hinder their implementation. This synergy offers deeper explanatory power than alternative theories such as stakeholder theory or technological determinism because it captures both the moral imperatives and institutional realities of AI governance, thereby providing a more holistic understanding of how responsible AI can be meaningfully achieved.

## 10.2.2 Conceptual Discussion

The field of AI governance has witnessed substantial scholarly attention in recent years, with researchers from multiple disciplines exploring its theoretical underpinnings, practical implications, and regulatory approaches. The literature reveals a consensus on the urgent need for governance mechanisms that are adaptive, inclusive, and responsive to the socio-technical complexities of AI. In this section, the review draws on interdisciplinary scholarship to provide an overview of key debates and conceptual frameworks, comparative governance models, and emerging trends that shape the global discourse on AI governance.

### Conceptualizing AI Governance

AI governance has been conceptualized in various ways across legal, ethical, policy, and technological domains. According to Stilgoe et al. (2018), AI governance encompasses both the ethical principles and the institutional frameworks required to guide the development and deployment of AI technologies. Their framework emphasizes beneficence, non-maleficence, justice, autonomy, and explicability. These principles serve as foundational elements in ethical AI design and inform regulatory considerations across jurisdictions. Another conceptual approach is offered by the Jobin et al. (2019), which identifies five value-based principles for responsible AI: inclusive growth, human-centered values, transparency, robustness, and accountability. These principles have gained widespread international acceptance and form the basis of numerous national strategies and corporate policies. Similarly, the Gasser and Almeida (2017) recommendation on the Ethics of Artificial Intelligence underscores the importance of safeguarding human rights, ensuring diversity and inclusiveness, and promoting environmental sustainability in AI governance.

## Comparative Governance Approaches

The global landscape of AI governance is marked by divergent regulatory approaches. In the European Union, the proposed Artificial Intelligence Act introduced in 2021 offers a comprehensive risk-based framework that classifies AI systems into unacceptable, high-risk, limited-risk, and minimal-risk categories. High-risk applications, such as biometric surveillance and critical infrastructure, are subject to stringent requirements regarding data quality, transparency, and human oversight. Scholars such as Birkstedt et al. (2023) argue that the EU's approach represents the most ambitious attempt to regulate AI comprehensively, balancing innovation with fundamental rights.

By contrast, the United States has adopted a more decentralized, sector-specific approach. The National Institute of Standards and Technology (NIST) has released voluntary guidelines in 2023, such as the AI Risk Management Framework, which encourage industry-led best practices without imposing legal obligations. Scholars like Mazurek and Małagocka (2019) and Larsson (2020) note that this market-driven approach may be more adaptable but lacks enforceability, potentially leading to inconsistent protection across sectors.

China, on the other hand, has integrated AI governance into its broader digital policy strategy. The Chinese government has released regulations such as the Internet Information Service Algorithm Recommendation Management Provisions in 2022, which mandate transparency in algorithmic content delivery. While these regulations prioritize social stability and ideological alignment, scholars like Minkkinen et al. (2022a) caution that they may also facilitate state surveillance and restrict civil liberties.

## Ethical and Legal Challenges

The literature identifies several persistent challenges in AI governance. Chief among them is algorithmic bias, which arises when training data reflect societal prejudices or when model design reinforces discriminatory outcomes. Studies by Mittelstadt (2019 and Perry and Uuk (2019) demonstrate how biased AI systems can disproportionately affect marginalized communities in areas such as hiring, law enforcement, and lending. Another key concern is the opacity of AI systems, particularly those based on deep learning, which operate as "black boxes" with limited explainability. Researchers like Carrillo (2020) and Seppala et al. (2021) argue that lack of transparency undermines accountability and erodes public trust. Legal scholars emphasize the need for explainable AI (XAI) as a prerequisite for regulatory compliance and ethical deployment.

The issue of accountability also features prominently in the literature. As AI systems become more autonomous, attributing legal responsibility becomes complex. Theories of distributed responsibility (Sharma et al., 2020) and strict liability (Truby, 2020) have been proposed, but consensus remains elusive. Regulatory frameworks must grapple with questions of intent, foreseeability, and causal attribution in AI-related harms.

#### Emerging Governance Models and Innovations

To address these challenges, scholars and practitioners have proposed innovative governance models. One promising approach is adaptive regulation, which emphasizes iterative policy development informed by real-time feedback and stakeholder engagement. This model is reflected in regulatory sandboxes, where experimental AI applications can be tested under regulatory supervision. Scholars such as Larsson and Heintz (2020) advocate for "agile governance" that can keep pace with technological change without stifling innovation.

Public–private partnerships (PPPs) are another emerging trend in AI governance. Initiatives such as the Partnership on AI and the AI Now Institute exemplify collaborative efforts between academia, industry, and civil society to develop ethical guidelines, promote transparency, and conduct impact assessments. According to Lu (2019), partnerships enhance legitimacy and foster multi-stakeholder trust. International standardization is also gaining traction. The International Organization for Standardization (ISO) and the Institute of Electrical and Electronics Engineers (IEEE) are developing technical standards and audit frameworks for AI systems. The ISO/IEC 42001 standard, for instance, aims to establish a management system for AI, including processes for risk management, stakeholder consultation, and continuous improvement.

### *10.2.3 Gaps and Future Research Directions*

Despite these advances, significant gaps remain in the literature. First, there is limited empirical research evaluating the effectiveness of existing AI governance frameworks. Most studies focus on normative analysis or theoretical proposals, leaving a void in real-world implementation evidence (Al Zadjali, 2020; Ibanez & Olmeda, 2022; Koniakou, 2023; Papagiannidis et al., 2023). Second, the voices of developing countries and marginalized communities are underrepresented in global AI governance discourse. Scholars such as Mokander and Floridi (2021) call for a decolonial approach that recognizes diverse epistemologies and promotes equitable participation. Third, the intersection of AI governance with other regulatory domains such as data protection, cybersecurity, and labor rights requires further exploration. Integrative frameworks that account for these interdependencies are essential for comprehensive governance. Finally, the role of education and capacity-building in fostering ethical AI practices remains underexplored. Future research should investigate how curricula, professional training, and public awareness campaigns can support responsible AI adoption.

In summary, the literature underscores the complexity and urgency of AI governance. While substantial progress has been made in articulating principles and proposing models, implementation challenges persist. A holistic, inclusive, and adaptive approach is necessary to navigate the evolving landscape of AI technologies and ensure that governance frameworks uphold human dignity, democratic values, and social justice.

## 10.3 Methodology

This study adopts a **qualitative, comparative policy analysis** approach to explore the evolving landscape of AI governance frameworks across various jurisdictions and institutions. Given the normative and conceptual nature of AI governance (Orr & Davis, 2020), a qualitative design is appropriate to examine the ethical, legal, and institutional dimensions of regulatory models. The methodology is grounded in document analysis and thematic interpretation, drawing from a wide array of academic, regulatory, and policy sources.

### *10.3.1 Research Design*

The research employs a **comparative case study method,** focusing on three major geopolitical actors, the **European Union (EU), the United States (US), and China** alongside selected international organizations such as the **OECD, UNESCO,** and the **United Nations**. These cases were selected through **purposive sampling** based on their leadership roles, distinctive governance approaches, and influence in global AI policy debates. This comparative design enables a structured analysis of both convergences and divergences in AI governance practices, and it facilitates an exploration of emerging best practices and regulatory gaps. The study also incorporates a **thematic analysis** of global ethical frameworks, with particular attention to values such as accountability, transparency, fairness, and inclusivity.

Data for this study were collected from **secondary sources,** especially from peer-reviewed journal articles published between **2017 and 2023**, ensuring the analysis captures the most recent developments in AI governance discourse. Based on the objective of this study and relevant literature reviewed, this study identified six (6) thematic areas: (i) **divergent AI governance Approaches**, (ii) **ethical principles vs. enforcement gaps in AI**, (iii) **accountability and liability challenges in AI**, (iv) **stakeholder engagement and inclusivity in AI**, (v) **adaptive governance and innovation-supportive mechanisms in AI**, and (vi) **international cooperation and fragmentation in AI**. These thematic areas were derived from an in-depth analysis of 40 studies published during the specified period.

The study is subject to few limitations. First, the absence of empirical interviews or surveys limits the depth of stakeholder perspectives included. Second, the analysis is based solely on **documented policies and public frameworks,** which may not fully reflect enforcement realities or informal governance practices. Third, given the dynamic nature of AI regulation, some findings may evolve as jurisdictions update their legislative agendas. Despite these limitations, the methodological approach allows for a robust and context-rich analysis of the current and emerging landscape of AI governance.

## 10.4 Findings and Discussion

This section presents and interprets the key findings from the comparative analysis of AI governance frameworks across the **European Union (EU), United States (US), China,** and selected international organizations such as the **OECD** and **UNESCO**. The findings are structured around key thematic areas, including regulatory design, ethical integration, enforcement mechanisms, and adaptability to emerging risks.

### *10.4.1 Divergent Governance Approaches*

A central finding of this study is the **divergence in regulatory approaches** to AI governance across jurisdictions. These differences are rooted in varying legal traditions, political ideologies, and economic priorities. The **European Union** has emerged as a global leader in AI regulation with its **Artificial Intelligence Act in 2021**. The EU employs a **risk-based classification system** (European Commission, 2020; KPMG, 2021)**,** categorizing AI systems as unacceptable, high-risk, limited-risk, or minimal-risk. High-risk systems are subject to rigorous requirements, including transparency obligations, human oversight, and conformity assessments. This approach reflects the EU's prioritization of **fundamental rights and ethical safeguards** in digital policy (Laato et al., 2022).

In contrast, the **United States** follows a **decentralized, sector-specific model**, where oversight is fragmented across various agencies (Deloitte, 2021; Schiff et al., 2020). Rather than enforcing binding legislation, the US relies on **voluntary guidelines** such as the **NIST AI Risk Management Framework** of 2023, which emphasizes flexibility and industry-led innovation. While this approach supports rapid technological development, it has been criticized for lacking accountability and consistency (Barredo-Arrieta et al., 2020; Feijoo et al., 2020).

**China's AI governance** is highly centralized and tied to national strategic objectives (Metcalf et al., 2021; Perry & Uuk, 2019). The Chinese government has implemented measures such as the **Algorithm Recommendation Provisions of 2022** and the **Generative AI Regulation of 2023** to control the deployment of algorithms in social media, e-commerce, and generative systems. These policies prioritize **state security, social stability, and ideological alignment**, which has raised concerns about state overreach and limited individual rights. This divergence illustrates the **absence of a unified global standard**, complicating efforts to harmonize AI governance and increasing the risk of regulatory arbitrage, where companies exploit differences between jurisdictions.

### *10.4.2 Ethical Principles vs. Enforcement Gaps*

Another key finding is the **wide adoption of ethical AI principles** across governance frameworks, but **limited enforceability and operationalization** of those principles. Most jurisdictions and organizations reference common ethical tenets such as fairness, transparency, accountability, and human-centeredness. For instance, the **OECD AI Principles** and the **UNESCO Recommendation on the Ethics of AI** have been widely endorsed and provide soft-law guidance to countries and corporations (Papagiannidis et al., 2023; Roski et al., 2021).

However, the translation of these principles into **enforceable obligations** remains inconsistent. In many cases, ethical frameworks serve as aspirational codes rather than binding standards. This is particularly true in the US and emerging economies, where compliance is voluntary and often driven by market incentives rather than legal mandates (De-Almeida et al., 2021; Minkkinen et al., 2022b). Even within the EU's AI Act, scholars have raised concerns that enforcement capacity particularly in smaller member states, may lag behind the complexity of AI systems, creating **compliance gaps** (Mantymaki et al., 2022). This disconnect between **principle and practice** creates an environment where companies may **"ethics-wash"** their AI systems using ethical language without implementing meaningful safeguards (Bu, 2021; Schiff et al., 2020). A credible AI governance framework must therefore include mechanisms for **monitoring, auditing, and penalizing non-compliance** (Mokander and Floridi (2021).

### *10.4.3 Accountability and Liability Challenges*

The question of **who is accountable** when AI systems cause harm is unresolved across most jurisdictions. The EU has proposed an **AI Liability Directive**, which would amend existing product liability rules to cover AI-related damages. (Schiff et al., 2020; Sharma et al., 2020). However, implementation remains in early stages, and questions persist about how to attribute fault when AI operates with autonomy or through complex machine learning processes. In the US, liability is typically handled under **existing tort law**, but these frameworks often fall short when addressing harms caused by black-box systems or distributed algorithmic decision-making (Gasser & Almeida, 2017; Hickok, 2021). China's regulatory model currently lacks a robust liability framework for individual users or developers, focusing more on **platform-level accountability** and state oversight (Ibanez & Olmeda, 2022; Koniakou, 2023; Shneiderman, 2020). Overall, there is no international consensus on how to balance ***developer, deployer, and user responsibilities***, nor how to ensure AI systems are auditable and explainable in the context of litigation.

### *10.4.4 Stakeholder Engagement and Inclusivity*

An emerging governance theme is the role of **multi-stakeholder engagement** (Ibanez & Olmeda, 2022; Koniakou, 2023; Shneiderman, 2020), which varies significantly across regions. The EU has incorporated stakeholder feedback through public consultations on the AI Act and collaborations with civil society organizations and academic institutions (Deloitte, 2021; Orr & Davis, 2020). In the US, industry-driven initiatives such as the **Partnership on AI** and **AI Now Institute** have sought to fill gaps in policy discourse, promoting transparency and social accountability (Reddy et al., 2020; Tsamados et al., 2022). In contrast, China's governance process remains largely **top-down**, with limited public participation or civil society involvement. Governance is closely aligned with state priorities, and dissenting voices may be excluded from shaping regulatory outcomes (Larsson and Heintz (2020). This finding highlights the importance of **inclusive governance**, where affected communities, especially marginalized and vulnerable groups, have a seat at the table. Without such inclusivity, AI systems risk perpetuating inequality and bias.

### *10.4.5 Adaptive Governance and Innovation-Supportive Mechanisms*

There is growing recognition that AI governance must be **adaptive and forward-looking,** especially in light of rapid technological advances like generative AI (e.g., ChatGPT, DALL·E). The EU's **regulatory sandboxes** allow innovators to test high-risk AI applications under supervisory guidance (Stilgoe et al., 2018; Schiff et al., 2020). This reflects a **proactive approach** to balancing innovation and risk management. The US supports **industry self-regulation** and iterative learning (Mokander & Floridi, 2021), emphasizing **agility and experimentation** in governance models. China has also launched **pilot zones** for AI development, allowing localized testing of new technologies under regulatory supervision. These practices suggest a shift toward **dynamic governance**, which embraces flexibility, real-time policy revision, and continuous stakeholder feedback. However, the **effectiveness of these mechanisms** in curbing harms and ensuring accountability remains under-studied and requires empirical assessment.

### *10.4.6 International Cooperation and Fragmentation*

While global bodies such as the **OECD, EU, G20, and UNESCO** have provided foundational ethical principles, their influence on binding national legislation is limited. The lack of **interoperability among national regulations** impedes cross-border data sharing, collaborative AI research, and joint risk mitigation. Geopolitical tensions particularly between the US, EU, and China further limit opportunities for unified governance models (Buhmann & Fieseler, 2021; Mokander & Floridi, 2021). As a result, a **fragmented regulatory ecosystem** is emerging, in which companies must navigate divergent compliance obligations and ethical expectations. This fragmentation presents long-term risks for **global coordination, standardization,** and **data governance.** Without deliberate efforts toward convergence, AI governance will likely remain siloed and inconsistent (Table 10.1).

**Table 10.1** Summary of key findings

| S/N | Theme | Finding | Documented literature |
|---|---|---|---|
| 1 | Regulatory models | EU leads with risk-based law; US favors decentralization; China centralizes control | Barredo-Arrieta et al. (2020), Feijoo et al. (2020) |
| 2 | Ethical integration | Principles widespread but often lack enforcement | De-Almeida et al. (2021), Minkkinen et al. (2022b), Roski et al. (2021), Papagiannidis et al. (2023) |
| 3 | Accountability and liability | Legal frameworks remain underdeveloped across jurisdictions | (Shneiderman (2020), Ibanez and Olmeda (2022), Koniakou (2023) |
| 4 | Stakeholder participation | EU and US emphasize engagement; China adopts top-down approach with state supervision | Orr and Davis (2020), Deloitte (2021), Reddy et al. (2020), Tsamados et al. (2022) |
| 5 | Adaptive governance | Regulatory sandboxes and pilot zones emerging, but empirical gaps remain | Stilgoe et al. (2018), Schiff et al. (2020) |
| 6 | Global cooperation | Fragmentation persists; harmonization efforts still weak | Buhmann and Fieseler (2021), Mokander and Floridi (2021) |

## 10.5 Conclusion and Policy Implications

The global governance of artificial intelligence (AI) is entering a pivotal phase as societies grapple with the dual imperatives of technological innovation and ethical responsibility. This study has examined the evolving landscape of AI governance, highlighting how jurisdictions such as the European Union, United States, and China have adopted divergent regulatory approaches each shaped by distinct legal cultures, political priorities, and strategic interests. The findings demonstrate that while ethical principles such as transparency, fairness, and accountability have gained widespread acceptance, their practical implementation remains uneven and often lacks enforceability.

The analysis also reveals persistent challenges, including regulatory fragmentation, algorithmic opacity, unclear liability mechanisms, and limited stakeholder inclusion particularly in non-democratic or centralized governance models. Despite these shortcomings, emerging practices such as regulatory sandboxes, public–private partnerships, and international standard-setting efforts (e.g., OECD, ISO, UNESCO) offer promising avenues for future adaptive and harmonized governance models. Crucially, the study underscores the need for a global, multidisciplinary, and inclusive approach to AI governance, one that transcends geopolitical divides and centers human rights, sustainability, and democratic values. As AI systems become more integrated into decision-making processes that affect lives, economies, and institutions, governance frameworks must evolve accordingly. The future of AI governance depends not only on technical regulation but also on fostering public trust, institutional legitimacy, and a shared global vision.

Based on the findings of this study, the following policy implications are recognized. First, it is important to encourage collaboration between major regulatory bodies, including the EU, US, China, and international organizations (e.g., OECD, UN, ISO) to create interoperable governance standards. Support the development of a **global AI governance charter** to facilitate cross-border cooperation, data sharing, and ethical alignment. Secondly, there is need to introduce clear and enforceable **liability frameworks** that attribute responsibility across the AI lifecycle from developers to deployers. Thirdly, institutions should embed binding ethical principles (fairness, transparency, explainability, non-discrimination) into AI legislation, particularly for public sector use. It should be required that all AI systems with social impact undergo **ethics reviews** and be subject to **human-in-the-loop oversight.** Fourthly, there is need to create **multi-stakeholder councils** that include civil society, industry, academia, and affected communities in AI policy design and review. This will ensure that **marginalized voices and Global South perspectives** are represented in governance deliberations and capacity-building efforts.

Fifth, there is need to expand the use of **regulatory sandboxes** and innovation testbeds to allow real-time policy experimentation and iterative learning. Also, it is important for institutions to develop a **risk-based classification systems** that prioritize oversight based on the potential for harm, not only technological novelty.

Lastly, there is need for ongoing support and training programs for regulators, policymakers, and judiciary officials to understand AI systems and governance tools. Launch public awareness campaigns to improve AI literacy and foster informed democratic participation in AI debates.

These policy implications aim to bridge the gap between principle and practice, and between national sovereignty and global coordination. By embedding ethical foresight, legal clarity, and institutional adaptability into AI governance, societies can navigate the uncertainties of AI innovation while safeguarding public interest and human dignity.

## References


Abrams, M., Abrams, J., Cullen, P., & Goldstein, L. (2019). Artificial intelligence, ethics, and enhanced data stewardship. *IEEE Security Privacy, 17*(2), 17–30.

Al Zadjali, H. (2020). Building the right AI governance model in Oman. In *Proceedings of the 13th international conference on theory and practice of electronic governance* (pp. 116–119). https://doi.org/10.1145/3428502.3428516

Barredo Arrieta, A., Dıaz-Rodrıguez, N., Del Ser, J., Bennetot, A., Tabik, S., Barbado, A., Garcia, S., Gil-Lopez, S., Molina, D., Benjamins, R., Chatila, R., & Herrera, F. (2020). Explainable artificial intelligence (XAI): Concepts, taxonomies, opportunities and challenges toward responsible AI. *Information Fusion, 58*, 82–115. https://doi.org/10.1016/j.inffus.2019.12.012

Berente, N., Gu, B., Recker, J., & Santhanam, R. (2021). Managing artificial intelligence. *MIS Quarterly, 45*(3), 1433–1450. https://doi.org/10.25300/MISQ/2021/16274

Birkstedt, T., Minkkinen, M., Tandon, A., & Mäntymäki, M. (2023). AI governance: Themes, knowledge gaps and future agendas. *Internet Research, 33*(7), 133–167. https://doi.org/10.1108/INTR-01-2022-0042

Bu, Q. (2021). The global governance on automated facial recognition (AFR): Ethical and legal opportunities and privacy challenges. *International Cybersecurity Law Review, 2*(1), 113–145. https://doi.org/10.1365/s43439-021-00022-x

Buhmann, A., & Fieseler, C. (2021). Towards a deliberative framework for responsible innovation in artificial intelligence. *Technology in Society*. https://doi.org/10.1016/j.techsoc.2020.101475

Carter, D. (2020). Regulation and ethics in artificial intelligence and machine learning technologies: Where are we now? Who is responsible? Can the information professional play a role? *Business Information Review, 37*(2), 60–68. https://doi.org/10.1177/0266382120923962

de Almeida, P. G. R., dos Santos, C. D., & Farias, J. S. (2021). Artificial intelligence regulation: A framework for governance. *Ethics and Information Technology, 23*(3), 505–525. https://doi.org/10.1007/s10676-021-09593-z

Deloitte. (2021). AI governance survey: A shift in the ways companies use and invest in AI brought about by changes in the social landscape. Retrieved June 20, 2022, from https://www2.deloitte.com/content/dam/Deloitte/global/Documents/gx-risk-ai-governance-survey.pdf

European Commission. (2020). White paper on artificial Intelligence—A European approach to excellence and trust. Retrieved June 1, 2022, from https://eur-lex.europa.eu/legal-content/EN/TXT/PDF/?uri5CELEX:52020DC0065

Feijoo, C., Kwon, Y., Bauer, J. M., Bohlin, E., Howell, B., Jain, R., Potgieter, P., Vu, K., Whalley, J., & Xia, J. (2020). Harnessing artificial intelligence (AI) to increase wellbeing for all: The case for a new technology diplomacy. *Telecommunications Policy, 44*, 6. https://doi.org/10.1016/j.telpol.2020.101988

Gasser, U., & Almeida, V. A. F. (2017). A layered model for AI governance. *IEEE Internet Computing, 21*(6), 58–62. https://doi.org/10.1109/MIC.2017.4180835

Hagendorff, T. (2020). The ethics of AI ethics—An evaluation of guidelines. *Minds and Machines, 30*(1), 99–120. https://doi.org/10.1007/s11023-020-09517-8

Hickok, M. (2021). Lessons learned from AI ethics principles for future actions. *AI and Ethics, 1*(1), 41–47. https://doi.org/10.1007/s43681-020-00008-1

Ibanez, J. C., & Olmeda, M. V. (2022). Operationalising AI ethics: How are companies bridging the gap between practice and principles? *An Exploratory Study. AI and Society, 37*, 4. https://doi.org/10.1007/s00146-021-01267-0

Jobin, A., Ienca, M., & Vayena, E. (2019). The global landscape of AI ethics guidelines. *Nature Machine Intelligence, 1*(9), 389–399. https://doi.org/10.1038/s42256-019-0088-2

Koniakou, V. (2023). From the 'rush to ethics' to the 'race for governance' in artificial intelligence. *Information Systems Frontiers, 25*(1), 71–102. https://doi.org/10.1007/s10796-022-10300-6

KPMG. (2021). The shape of AI governance to come. Retrieved 20 May 2022, from https://home.kpmg/xx/en/home/insights/2020/12/the-shape-of-ai-governance-to-come.html

Laato, S., Tiainen, M., Islam, A. K. M. N., & Mäntymäki, M. (2022). How to explain AI systems to end users: A systematic literature review and research agenda. *Internet Research, 32*(7), 1–31. https://doi.org/10.1108/INTR-08-2021-0600

Larsson, S. (2020). On the governance of artificial intelligence through ethics guidelines. *Asian Journal of Law and Society, 7*(3), 437–451. https://doi.org/10.1017/als.2020.19

Larsson, S., & Heintz, F. (2020). Transparency in artificial intelligence. *Internet Policy Review, 9*(2), 1–16. https://doi.org/10.14763/2020.2.1469

Lu, Y. (2019). Artificial intelligence: A survey on evolution, models, applications and future trends. *Journal of Management Analytics, 6*(1), 1–29. https://doi.org/10.1080/23270012.2019.1570365

Mantymaki, M., Minkkinen, M., Birkstedt, T., & Viljanen, M. (2022). Defining organizational AI governance. *AI and Ethics, 2*(4), 603–609. https://doi.org/10.1007/s43681-022-00143-x

Mazurek, G., & Małagocka, K. (2019). Perception of privacy and data protection in the context of the development of artificial intelligence. *Journal of Management Analytics, 6*(4), 344–364.

McDuie-Ra, D., & Gulson, K. (2020). The backroads of AI: The uneven geographies of artificial intelligence and development. *Area, 52*(3), 626–633.

Metcalf, J., Moss, E., Watkins, E. A., Singh, R., & Elish, M. C. (2021). Algorithmic impact assessments and accountability: The co-construction of impacts. In *Proceedings of the 2021 ACM conference on fairness, accountability, and transparency* (pp. 735–746). https://doi.org/10.1145/3442188.3445935.

Minkkinen, M., Laine, J., & Mantymaki, M. (2022a). Continuous auditing of artificial intelligence: A conceptualization and assessment of tools and frameworks. *Digital Society, 1*(3), 21. https://doi.org/10.1007/s44206-022-00022-2

Minkkinen, M., Niukkanen, A., & Mantymaki, M. (2022b). What about investors? ESG analyses as tools for ethics-based AI auditing. *AI and Society*. https://doi.org/10.1007/s00146-022-01415-0

Mittelstadt, B. (2019). Principles alone cannot guarantee ethical AI. *Nature Machine Intelligence, 1*(11), 501–507. https://doi.org/10.1038/s42256-019-0114-4

Mokander, J., & Floridi, L. (2021). Ethics-based auditing to develop trustworthy AI. *Minds and Machines, 31*(2), 323–327. https://doi.org/10.1007/s11023-021-09557-8

Orr, W., & Davis, J. L. (2020). Attributions of ethical responsibility by artificial intelligence practitioners. *Information, Communication and Society, 23*(5), 719–735. https://doi.org/10.1080/1369118X.2020.1713842

Papagiannidis, E., Enholm, I. M., Dremel, C., Mikalef, P., & Krogstie, J. (2023). Toward AI governance: Identifying best practices and potential barriers and outcomes. *Information Systems Frontiers, 25*(1), 123–141. https://doi.org/10.1007/s10796-022-10251-y

Perry, B., & Uuk, R. (2019). AI governance and the policymaking process: Key considerations for reducing AI risk. *Big Data and Cognitive Computing, 3*(2), 26. https://doi.org/10.3390/bdcc3020026

Reddy, S., Allan, S., Coghlan, S., & Cooper, P. (2020). A governance model for the application of AI in health care. *Journal of the American Medical Informatics Association, 27*(3), 491–497. https://doi.org/10.1093/jamia/ocz192

Robles Carrillo, M. (2020). Artificial intelligence: From ethics to law. *Telecommunications Policy, 44*, 6. https://doi.org/10.1016/j.telpol.2020.101937

Roski, J., Maier, E. J., Vigilante, K., Kane, E. A., & Matheny, M. E. (2021). Enhancing trust in AI through industry self-governance. *Journal of the American Medical Informatics Association, 28*(7), 1582–1590. https://doi.org/10.1093/jamia/ocab065

Schiff, D., Biddle, J., Borenstein, J., & Laas, K. (2020). What's next for AI ethics, policy, and governance? A global overview. In *Proceedings of the 2020 AAAI/ACM conference on AI, ethics, and society* (pp. 153–158). https://doi.org/10.1145/3375627.3375804

Seppala, A., Birkstedt, T., & Mantymaki, M. (2021). From ethical AI principles to governed AI. In *Proceedings of the international conference on information systems.*

Sharma, G. D., Yadav, A., & Chopra, R. (2020). Artificial intelligence and effective governance: A review, critique and research agenda. *Sustainable Futures, 2*, 100004. https://doi.org/10.1016/j.sftr.2019.100004

Shneiderman, B. (2020). Bridging the gap between ethics and practice: Guidelines for reliable, safe, and trustworthy human-centered AI systems. *ACM Transactions on Interactive Intelligent Systems, 10*(4), 31. https://doi.org/10.1145/3419764

Stilgoe, J. (2018). Machine learning, social learning and the governance of self-driving cars. *Social Studies of Science, 48*(1), 25–56. https://doi.org/10.1177/0306312717741687

Truby, J. (2020). Governing artificial intelligence to benefit the UN sustainable development goals. *Sustainable Development, 28*(4), 946–959. https://doi.org/10.1002/sd.2048

Tsamados, A., Aggarwal, N., Cowls, J., Morley, J., Roberts, H., Taddeo, M., & Floridi, L. (2022). The ethics of algorithms: Key problems and solutions. *AI and Society, 37*(1), 215–230. https://doi.org/10.1007/s00146-021-01154-8

# Conclusion: Ethical and Responsible Governance of AI

Michael Adelowotan and Hussain Coovadia

This book on Artificial Intelligence and Accountability has been written to respond to arguments by both academics and practitioners on the need to ensure responsible use of Artificial Intelligence. The question that is often asked is who is responsible when Artificial Intelligence systems make mistakes and cause damage. The main objective of this book is to ensure that ethical considerations are aligned with AI systems thus ensuring fairness and transparency.

This book delved into various issues relating to Accountability and Governance in the use of Artificial Intelligence by:

1. Identifying who should be responsible for security breaches and errors
2. Ensuring transparency in the use of AI
3. Ensuring that there are policies for oversight and governance functions
4. Aligning AI with ethical values which are usually found in humans.

The book consists of ten chapters which address various ethical concerns on Artificial Intelligence and how business organisations can overcome them through the establishment of adequate lines of responsibility, accountability and governance principles.

The first chapter dealt with the issue of **'AI Ethics and Governance'** by conceptualizing the various definitions of AI and Governance; examining different governance strategies and global frameworks developed. The chapter suggests strategies that could transform and align ethical principles to real actions. The chapter also suggests that the future of AI systems will depend on the systematic integration of

M. Adelowotan (✉)
Department of Accountancy, College of Business and Economics, University of Johannesburg, Johannesburg, South Africa
e-mail: madelowotan@uj.ac.za

H. Coovadia
Department of Commercial Accounting, College of Business and Economics, University of Johannesburg, Johannesburg, South Africa
e-mail: hcoovadia@uj.ac.za



M. Adelowotan and H. Coovadia (eds.), *AI and Accountability*, CSR, Sustainability, Ethics & Governance, https://doi.org/10.1007/978-3-032-20091-4

right based strategies and governance that will facilitate advancement of technology while ensuring human rights, justice and equality. A summary of policy implications recognized in this chapter are that there should be more collaborations between regulatory bodies in various juridictions across Europe, America, Asia and Africa thus leading to the development of global AI charter. The chapter also recommended the introduction of liability frameworks; establishment of sound ethical principles; inclusion of academia, industry experts and professional, civil society and local communities in the design and review of AI policies; development of risk-based classification systems and regular training and support for stakeholders in the AI development, deployment and usage.

The second chapter dealt with the issue of **'Machine Bias and Fairness'**. The authors explored various definitions of machine bias and explained the concept of fairness in relation to machine bias. The authors noted that bias is prevalent in many areas of operation where AI is being deployed and employed. It was recommended that in order to overcome this bias, some technical and operational approaches must be taken to ensure fairness and equity in the use of AI. Some of the suggested approaches include the integration of the principle of fairness from the onset, transparency in documentation; risk-based governance, employees' oversight; combining technical and institutional mitigation; continuous monitoring and auditing; public consultation; develop capacity and accountability measures among others.

The third chapter on **'Understanding transparency and explainability in AI governance'** explained the concepts of 'transparency and explainability with reference to AI Governance. The chapter also explored the concepts and implications of black-box AI. The chapter further examined how to overcome the challenges of black-box AI by means of Explainable AI (XAI). The chapter concluded with an explanation of how to ensure a balance between the performance of AI systems and explainability through the establishment of effective AI governance.

The fourth chapter explored the twin concepts of **'Accountability and Liability'**, In achieving the objectives of this chapter, the authors discussed the doctrinal foundations that provides guidance for AI Accountability and Liability; assessed the economic perspective economic perspective on AI Accountability and Liability; reviewed the legal and regulatory framework on AI liability and suggested strategies and practices that can lead to the promotion of responsible AI development and deployment. The authors concluded that the governance of AI system provides a lot of benefits and that this is why it has become a great concern to practitioners. To ensure responsible AI deployment, ethical accountability, human oversight and autonomy must be integrated successfully. The chapter calls for strict adherence to ethical principles such as fairness, accountability, privacy and accountability. Finally, the chapter calls for a multi-layered collaborative governance involving regulatory monitoring; technological innovation; and human centered values.

The fifth chapter on **'Data Privacy and Data Security'** explored the evolving landscape of AI deployment and employment particularly in the Sub-Saharan Africa. The chapter examined the ways in which privacy enhancing technologies when combined with relevant governance approaches can bring about the reduction of risks related to processing of data and algorithm decision making. The authors adopted an integrative approach to justify the need for a multidisciplinary strategy which combines technology, law and AI system designs that will ensure privacy and facilitate technological advancements particularly in the sub-Saharan Africa.

The sixth chapter explored the concept of **'AI Autonomy, control and human oversight'**. In view of the rising concerns that machine autonomy can lead to bias that may consequently result to reputational, legal or financial harm or loss to organisations. The chapter lends its voice to the rising campaign for safe deployment and ethical use AI systems through proper oversight, transparency and accountability. Furthermore, the chapter highlighted different types of machine autonomy and controls on AI deployment that have been proposed by the European Union, America and Africa.

The seventh chapter considered the issue of **'AI Governance in the Public and Private Sectors'**. The chapter noted that AI has emerged as a major driver of economic transformation in both the public and private sectors because of its applications in education, business, finance, banking, health, justice and health sectors to mention a few. However, the authors noted that there exists a big gap between AI deployment and its governance particularly among the developed and the developing economies. The chapter concluded that effective AI governance in both public and private sectors is essential if the benefits of AI will be harnessed for socio-economic development.

The eight chapter on **'Global Perspectives on AI Governance'** employed thematic analysis and PRISMA framework in presenting a systematic literature review on AI governance practices in financial, auditing, healthcare and legal sectors across various jurisdictions. The chapter also highlighted the broader balance between self-regulation and the oversight function by the government. The chapter also highlighted the main themes as well as the challenges in AI governance from the perspectives of key sectors and jurisdictions. The chapter recommended that an important area for future research is the development of sector-sensitive and sector specific AI governance models and how international standards on AI governance could be localised across other jurisdictions particularly the global South.

The ninth chapter on **'AI and Ethical Innovation'** examined AI ethical practices of two main IT companies, namely IBM and Microsoft with the aim of understanding how they practice ethical AI systems in their organisations with a view to establishing models for best practices in AI ethical practice for other organisations. The chapter also highlighted the need to provide incentives to business organisations who adopted ethical AI as a key business strategy. The chapter recommended that there is a need to provide necessary training and support to key employees in business organisations to enable them to identify ethical dilemmas and mitigate ethical risks occasioned by the AI deployment.

The last chapter on **'The future of AI Governance'** examined the future of AI governance using existing regulatory frameworks developed by the European Union, United States of America, China as well as those developed by international organisations such as the OECD and the UNESCO. The main objective was to facilitate an evaluation of diverse ethical principles, accountability mechanisms and governance models among other factors. The chapter provided policy implications, which include expanded regulatory sandboxes, binding ethical fairness, and the creation of global standards, among others.

In general, the book recognised the increasing awareness of the need for the employment and deployment of AI in the operations of various sectors as well as the increasing demand for ethical use of AI. Therefore, organisations can harness the benefits of AI and mitigate its risks if the values of fairness, accountability, equality, and human rights are embedded in AI governance structures.

MIX
Papier aus verantwortungsvollen Quellen
Paper from responsible sources
FSC® C105338

If you have any concerns about our products,
you can contact us on
**ProductSafety@springernature.com**

In case Publisher is established outside the EU,
the EU authorized representative is:
**Springer Nature Customer Service Center GmbH**
**Europaplatz 3, 69115 Heidelberg, Germany**

Printed by Libri Plureos GmbH
in Hamburg, Germany